Postdigital Science and Education

Series Editor
Petar Jandrić
Zagreb University of Applied Sciences, Zagreb, Croatia

Editorial Board
Carlos Escaño González, University of Sevilla, Sevilla, Spain
Derek R. Ford, DePauw University, Greencastle, IN, USA
Sarah Hayes, University of Wolverhampton, Wolverhampton, UK
Michael Kerres, University of Duisburg-Essen, Essen, Germany
Jeremy Knox, University of Edinburgh, Edinburgh, UK
Michael A. Peters, Beijing Normal University, Beijing, China
Marek Tesar, University of Auckland, Auckland, New Zealand

This series is a new, international book series dedicated to postdigital science and education. It brings together a rapidly growing community of authors and the currently highly scattered body of research. The series complements the *Postdigital Science and Education* Journal and together they provide a complete, whole-rounded service to researchers working in the field. The book series covers a wide range of topics within postdigital science and education, including learning and data analytics, digital humanities, (digital) learning, teaching and assessment, educational technology and philosophy of education.

We no longer live in a world where digital technology and media are separate, virtual, 'other' to a 'natural' human and social life. Book series engaged with technology and education tend to view the research field as concerned with the 'effects' of digital media and other technologies on the existing activities of teaching and learning in education. This still assumes a clear division between an authentic educational practice and the imposition of an external, and novel, technology. The rapid growth of research and books and articles dealing with education and research in and for the postdigital age calls for a different approach that is no longer based on a division but rather on an integration of education and technology. This book series meets that need.

This book series

- Fills the gap in the scholarly community as the first academic book series in postdigital science and education
- Explicitly focuses on postdigital themes and research approaches
- Forms a hub for a growing body of scholarship in the field
- Enables communication, dissemination, and community building for researchers, authors, and students.

More information about this series at http://www.springer.com/series/16439.

Maggi Savin-Baden
Editor

Postdigital Humans

Transitions, Transformations
and Transcendence

Editor
Maggi Savin-Baden ⓘ
School of Education
University of Worcester
Worcester, UK

ISSN 2662-5326　　　　　　ISSN 2662-5334　(electronic)
Postdigital Science and Education
ISBN 978-3-030-65591-4　　ISBN 978-3-030-65592-1　(eBook)
https://doi.org/10.1007/978-3-030-65592-1

© The Editor(s) (if applicable) and The Author(s), under exclusive license to Springer Nature Switzerland AG 2021

This work is subject to copyright. All rights are solely and exclusively licensed by the Publisher, whether the whole or part of the material is concerned, specifically the rights of translation, reprinting, reuse of illustrations, recitation, broadcasting, reproduction on microfilms or in any other physical way, and transmission or information storage and retrieval, electronic adaptation, computer software, or by similar or dissimilar methodology now known or hereafter developed.

The use of general descriptive names, registered names, trademarks, service marks, etc. in this publication does not imply, even in the absence of a specific statement, that such names are exempt from the relevant protective laws and regulations and therefore free for general use.

The publisher, the authors, and the editors are safe to assume that the advice and information in this book are believed to be true and accurate at the date of publication. Neither the publisher nor the authors or the editors give a warranty, expressed or implied, with respect to the material contained herein or for any errors or omissions that may have been made. The publisher remains neutral with regard to jurisdictional claims in published maps and institutional affiliations.

This Springer imprint is published by the registered company Springer Nature Switzerland AG
The registered company address is: Gewerbestrasse 11, 6330 Cham, Switzerland

This book is dedicated to my colleague, friend, and mentor Ron Barnett for the years of encouragement and support he has provided. Thank you.

Series Editor's Preface

A few years ago, I was in the place that many academics dream of. I spent most of my time writing books and articles, developing this or that aspect of my theories with each new publication. I had not received too many rejections, my citation count was on the rise, and I was set out for a smooth sail towards a reasonably solid academic career. Yet, something has started to feel wrong, and this feeling has exacerbated with time. My papers have been read, and cited, by a community of people with similar interest, and whose work I read, and cited—not because we deliberately created some sinister quotation cartel, but simply because our works interacted with each other. Slowly and seemingly inevitably I ended up in an obscure, self-referential, albeit very warm and cosy global community. Arguably, our mutual sharing and caring was a natural consequence of a very simple (and sad) fact: no one else seemed to care about what we were doing.

However, I refused to take this enclosure at a face value. I have a wide range of interests, my friends and family come from different circles, and I just knew that many of them are interested in issues I was writing about. However, these people were totally excluded from our academic discussions: they did not have the time, opportunity, and language to participate. After all, it took me decades to arrive to the position of a reasonably comfortable academic writer. How could they possibly catch up all these years of labour while working in arts, insurance, or whatever? This is when I started to feel the real meaning of the phrase 'ivory tower'. While my work is focused to matters of general interest to all people, its structure, language, and position within neoliberal structures of academic knowledge production and dissemination make it elitist (see Fuller 2019). And even within the academia, my work is just a small niche, situated within some larger (but nevertheless very small) niches, with little or no impact to the rest of the world. In order to achieve only modest academic success, one is expected to own their own little research hole and dig it deeper and deeper. This hedgehog approach to knowledge work, which is so prevalent in academic theory and practice, has felt tighter and tighter, until I started to feel it as a full-blown straight-jacket (see Jandrić 2017: xi–xii). I can't breathe! Not here, not like this, not anymore.

To develop a more whole-rounded, wiser, fox approach to my work, I started to look for concordances. What is it that connects my thinking, my narrow community's thinking, then wider academic circles of people working in similar fields, and my mother, son, and neighbour? What is it that bothers my fellow non-academic family and friends, trying to make a living in our more than challenging times? These questions quickly led to some very deep philosophical questions. What is the nature of today's human condition? How can we improve ways in which we approach it? Following my (then) recent works on dialogue and collectivity (Jandrić 2017), I figured out that I cannot approach this problem alone, so I decided to try my luck in academic publishing.

I immediately understood that my general ideas need a clear, deep, yet easily understandable and widely accessible gathering concept. With a group of closest academic friends, I founded *Postdigital Science and Education* journal and book series. While full story about our reasons behind and around this decision has never been written, some thinking behind it is scattered in a range of publications (Jandrić et al. 2018). I feel that things are better this way: definitions are restrictive by their nature, histories always reflect attitudes of those who write them, and an academic community will do much better with questioning unrestricted by canons.

Our work on the postdigital condition is still in its infancy. While our budding community of postdigital researchers has spent considerable time and effort into defining the concept of the postdigital and our postdigital age (see Peters and Besley 2019; Fawns 2019; Sinclair and Hayes 2019; Knox 2019, amongst others), less attention has been given to their main protagonist—the postdigital human. I am truly thankful to Maggi Savin-Baden, and to all authors in this book, who took up the challenging task to explore this important topic. So who are we, postdigital humans? How do we differ from our ancestors? What heritage, and opportunities for development, are we leaving to generations coming after us?

Tackling these essential questions, *Postdigital Humans* is the perfect inaugural book for the Postdigital Science and Education series. Edited, written, and produced as a labour of love, this book presents a powerful reminder of human costs, and opportunities, associated with techno-social development. Presenting latest results of our community's sustained research of the postdigital condition, *Postdigital Humans* is a snapshot of our current work and a hugely important stepping stone for postdigital research to come.

Zagreb, Croatia   Petar Jandrić

References

Fawns, T. (2019). Postdigital education in design and practice. *Postdigital Science and Education, 1*(1), 132–145. https://doi.org/10.1007/s42438-018-0021-8.

Fuller, S. (2019). Against academic rentiership: A radical critique of the knowledge economy. *Postdigital Science and Education, 1*(2), 335–356. https://doi.org/10.1007/s42438-019-00035-0.

Jandrić, P. (2017). *Learning in the age of digital reason*. Rotterdam: Sense.

Jandrić, P., Knox, J., Besley, T., Ryberg, T., Suoranta, J., & Hayes, S. (2018). Postdigital science and education. *Educational Philosophy and Theory, 50*(10), 893–899. https://doi.org/10.1080/00131857.2018.1454000.

Knox, J. (2019). What does the 'postdigital' mean for education? Three critical perspectives on the digital, with implications for educational research and practice. *Postdigital Science and Education, 1*(2), 357–370. https://doi.org/10.1007/s42438-019-00045-y.

Peters, M. A., & Besley, T. (2019). Critical philosophy of the postdigital. *Postdigital Science and Education, 1*(1), 29–42. https://doi.org/10.1007/s42438-018-0004-9.

Sinclair, C., & Hayes, S. (2019). Between the post and the com-post: Examining the postdigital "work" of a prefix. *Postdigital Science and Education, 1*(1), 119–131. https://doi.org/10.1007/s42438-018-0017-4.

Our revels now are ended. These our actors,
As I foretold you, were all spirits, and
Are melted into air, into thin air:
And like the baseless fabric of this vision,
The cloud-capp'd tow'rs, the gorgeous palaces,
The solemn temples, the great globe itself,
Yea, all which it inherit, shall dissolve,
And, like this insubstantial pageant faded,
Leave not a rack behind. *We are such stuff*
As dreams are made on; and our little life
Is rounded with a sleep.

(Shakespeare 1611)

Acknowledgements

This book has been a challenge to create in these liquid times of moving technologies. I am grateful to the authors in this volume, who have not only provided fabulous chapter but have been patient and diligent during the editing process. Petar Jandrić, the series editor, has been a power of strength and critique, for which I am grateful. I am also deeply thankful to my husband John who has supported the editing process and in a home of fun, busyness, and chaos is always there to steady the buffs. Any mistakes and errors are mine, a mere postdigital human.

Introduction

Maggi Savin-Baden (Ed)

When Petar Jandrić asked me to bring together a group of authors to create a text on *Postdigital Humans*, I explained that I was not the person for the job. Most of my work to date has been in researching and designing innovative pedagogy to improve student learning. My foray into digital afterlife and the postdigital arena has been relatively recent and so I felt ill equipped to undertake this task. What I realized as I was persuaded to undertake this edited collection was that the area of postdigital humans is, and remains, a complex and under-researched area that transcends a wide range of disciplines—from sociology, computer science, music, and theology to ethics and politics. The collection of chapters here is provided by a group of innovative authors sharing their ideas and reflections. What is common across all chapters is the concern about how we manage the postdigital future and in particular deal with and indeed take on surveillance capitalism and seek to avert the possibly, or even inevitability of the marketized diminishment of the human.

What this text illustrates is that the development and use of postdigital humans is occurring rapidly, but often in unexpected ways and spaces. The chapters explore approaches to developing and using postdigital humans and the impact they are having on a postdigital world. Posthumanism seeks to break down binary distinctions between 'human', 'machine', and 'text' and between 'nature' and 'culture'; it also rejects dualisms that are used to define being such as subject/object (Hayles 1999, 2012). Thus, posthumanist theory is used to question the foundational role of 'humanity'. It prompts consideration of what it means to be a human subject, and the extent to which the idea of the human subject is still useful. This overlaps with Actor Network Theory, where the arguments centre on the idea that actors may be both human and non-human, thus for example supermarket products and digital devices are seen as actors that have influence, but it not clear how all this relates to the understandings of postdigital humans. Yet at the same time digital media are currently being used to expand the possibilities of what postdigital humans might be. For example, whilst the term AI is in very common usage (even if poorly defined), the term 'postdigital humans' is less commonly used. Related terms include 'digital humans', 'autonomous agents', and avatars. However, it is often the perceptions of the user, and the human inclination to anthropomorphise, that determine whether something is 'just a programme' or a postdigital human.

This book presents current research and practices at a time when education is changing rapidly with digital, technological advances. In particular, it outlines the major challenges faced by today's employers, developers, teachers, researchers, priests, and philosophers such as the possibility for using postdigital humans for teaching, training, and practice. Broad areas include:

- Conceptions of Postdigital Humans
- Postdigital Humans and Education
- Philosophy, Ethics, and Religion

The first section of the book begins in Chapters 'What Are Postdigital Humans?' and 'Postdigital Humans: Taking Evolution in Own Hands' with an exploration of the ideas and concepts associated with postdigital humans. Chapter 'What Are Postdigital Humans?' suggests that the challenge of the postdigital human is to recognize the ways in which balance must be brought to bear and to realize the ways in which technologies such as algorithms, machine learning, and facial recognition and facial verification can foster social injustice. It begins by exploring conceptions of the postdigital and what it means to be human, then examines the idea of postdigital humans and the relationship between humans and machines. The ethical issues relating to postdigital humans are also discussed in relation to human labour, machine learning, intimacy ethics, and surveillance. In Chapter 'Postdigital Humans: Taking Evolution in Own Hands' Jandrić examines postdigital humans from an evolutionary perspective by presenting the implicit and explicit references to human beings in postdigital literature and identifying a range of viewpoints, approaches, and fields of inquiry which have shaped postdigital thinking over the past 20 years. Building on the understanding of humanity as a normative category, the chapter moves on to explore three 'performance standards' for inclusion into humanity: life, consciousness, and behaviour. The concluding part synthesizes philosophical approaches and postdigital theories and builds a postdisciplinary understanding of the postdigital human.

The second section of the book provides both a practical and philosophical stance towards the use of postdigital humans in education. It begins in Chapter 'Experience of Using a Virtual Life Coach: A Case Study of Novice Users' with an exploration of the experience of Using a Virtual Life Coach (VLC) by Victoria Mason-Robbie. This chapter explores a group of novice users' experiences of using a VLC in order to ascertain whether the technical, pedagogical, and valuable features of the VLC, and its personalisation, were able to support the well-being of users. The results of the study to evaluate the VLC are presented along with a discussion of the moral and philosophical conundrums associated with adopting the VLC to support personal and work-related challenges within the context of postdigital humans. Richard Hall in Chapter 'Venturing Beyond the Imposition of a Postdigital, Anti-human Higher Education' then examines the notion of Venturing Beyond the Imposition of a Postdigital, Anti-Human Higher Education. He argues that analysis of technology enables us to reveal the dialectical construction of our dominant mode of reproducing everyday life, which, in terms of higher education, illustrates the relationship between humans and technologies, in order to maintain the reproduction of capitalism. This chapter argues that such a relationship is morbid and lengthens the shadow of value over what it means to be human. The chapter utilizes the metaphor of composting as a way that individuals in their environments process anger, grief, and trauma and find new ways of living. It pivots around the potential for a reimagining of the integration of the digital and the human through mass intellectuality, as a new form of sociability.

In Chapter 'The Value of Postdigital Humans as Objects, or Subjects, in McDonaldised Society' the value of postdigital humans as objects, or subjects, in McDonaldised Society is explored by Sarah Hayes, where she speculates on whether new postdigital positionalities are emerging that might finally challenge more dominant, rational interpretations of what computing means in individual lives. If so, perhaps a more subjective analysis of these new forms of postdigital participation will bring the humanities into computing, instead of vice versa. This may help to reveal the unique positionality in each individual postdigital human encounter, where subjective self-description may now be seen to be more appropriate than objective rationality. The last chapter of this section on postdigital humans and education, written by Michael Fasching and Kathrin Otrel-Cass, explores educational reflections on fake news and digital identities by examining how young people manage the information they receive from different sources. They present vignettes from two projects where young people reflected on their encounters with fake news and analysed how they manage information they receive online in general.

The final section of the book explores the overlapping constructs of philosophy, ethics, and religion. It begins in Chapter 'Listening Like a Postdigital Human: The Politics and Knowledge of Noise' with an exploration of the politics and knowledge of noise by Derek Ford and Masaya Sasaki who consider how the postdigital era has or might change listening practices. It begins with a brief review of postdigital literature that emphasizes the old and the new characteristics of such an era. It then considers the aesthetic and political questions about postdigital human senses, examines key works in sound studies, and briefly revisits the history of the production and reception of music in the twentieth century. The authors suggest that digital music production eliminates noise by turning analogue signals into ones and zeros so that it becomes impossible to tell where the human ends and the digital begins. Chapter 'Ethics, Character, and Community: Moral Formation and Modelling the Human' then considers the ethical conundrums in the area of postdigital humans. Malcolm Brown draws on the work of Alasdair MacIntyre to reconstruct an account of how we become moral persons through participation in communities and create narratives which help construct the self and address both human dependency and autonomy. He, like Richard Hall in Chapter 'Venturing Beyond the Imposition of a Postdigital, Anti-human Higher Education', argues that the limitations of the dominant market model of human interaction need to be examined. He suggests that there is only a slim possibility of the chance of establishing that moral shift before it is too late to prevent the marketized diminishment of the human. Steve Fuller, in Chapter 'The Computer's Hidden Theology and Its Prospects for a Postdigital

Humanity', then explores theological unconscious of artificial intelligence, which he suggests turns on two contrasting interpretations of the *logos*, the divine word that provides the 'code' underwriting the structure of reality. The historically earlier interpretation is 'Computational Theism', which is based on the contiguity of the divine creator and the created artefact. Fuller explains that many of the early computer pioneers were nonconformist Christians who saw themselves, more or less explicitly, as engaged in a 'second creation', the consequences of which were seen as morally ambivalent. In the final section of the chapter he explores the implications of the transition from this increasingly dominant interpretation that detaches the *logos* from any personal creator to one very much in a Platonic spirit and examines implications for the emerging 'post-digital' world in which humans and advanced machines share a common ecology.

Chapters 'Postdigital Humans: Algorithmic Imagination?' and 'Transcendent Conformity: The Question of Agency for Postdigital Humans' both deal with issues of agency, but in different ways. John Reader in Chapter 'Postdigital Humans: Algorithmic Imagination?' explores the complexity of algorithms on the postdigital human condition. He suggests that if we were to assume there are two main possibilities of postdigital humans, either enhancements of existing humans employing the digital or entirely new forms of human emerging from a hybrid version of some sort, then the question is whether it is possible to incorporate into either of these the imagination which helps us to place ourselves in the position of another and to be able to show empathy which does not rest on calculation. In Chapter 'Transcendent Conformity: The Question of Agency for Postdigital Humans' Alex Thomas argues that the disintegration of ontological boundaries brought about by digital, genetic, and cybernetic developments requires an ongoing normative investigation into the structures, interests, and consequences of this process of technogenesis. He suggests that what is required is an exploration of morphological freedom in order to undermine it as a concept and thereby introduce a complexity-based posthumanist notion of agency. This final chapter in many ways brings together issues raised in other parts of the book that relate to concerns over agency, the wider complex ecology of techno-capitalist relations, notions of individual self-determination, and ways in which humanity needs to come to understand and act in the postdigital world.

References

Hayles, K. (1999). *How We Became Posthuman: Virtual Bodies in Cybernetics, Literature and Informatics*. Chicago, IL: University of Chicago Press.

Hayles, K. (2012). *How We Think: Digital Media and Contemporary Technogenesis*. Chicago, IL: University of Chicago Press.

Contents

Introduction.. xv
Maggi Savin-Baden (Ed)

Part I Conceptions of Postdigital Humans

What Are Postdigital Humans?.. 3
Maggi Savin-Baden

Postdigital Humans: Taking Evolution in Own Hands................ 17
Petar Jandrić

Part II Postdigital Humans and Education

**Experience of Using a Virtual Life Coach: A Case Study
of Novice Users**... 35
Victoria Mason-Robbie

**Venturing Beyond the Imposition of a Postdigital,
Anti-human Higher Education**.. 53
Richard Hall

**The Value of Postdigital Humans as Objects, or Subjects,
in McDonaldised Society**.. 71
Sarah Hayes

**Postdigital Truths: Educational Reflections on Fake News
and Digital Identities**... 89
Kathrin Otrel-Cass and Michael Fasching

Part III Philosophy, Ethics and Religion

**Listening Like a Postdigital Human: The Politics
and Knowledge of Noise**... 111
Derek R. Ford and Masaya Sasaki

Ethics, Character, and Community: Moral Formation and Modelling the Human 125
Malcolm Brown

The Computer's Hidden Theology and Its Prospects for a Postdigital Humanity 141
Steve Fuller

Postdigital Humans: Algorithmic Imagination? 155
John Reader

Transcendent Conformity: The Question of Agency for Postdigital Humans 169
Alexander Thomas

Index 187

About the Editor

Maggi Savin-Baden is Professor of Education at the University of Worcester and has researched and evaluated staff and student experience of learning for over 20 years and gained funding in this area (Leverhulme Trust, JISC, Higher Education Academy, MoD). She has a strong publication record of over 50 research publications and 18 books which reflect her research interests on the impact of innovative learning, digital fluency, cyber-influence, pedagogical agents, qualitative research methods, and problem-based learning. In her spare time, she runs, bakes, climbs, and attempts triathlons.

About the Authors

Malcolm Brown has been Director of Mission and Public Affairs for the Church of England since 2007. He has been a parish priest, an industrial chaplain, Principal of a Theological Training course, and led the William Temple Foundation, a think tank on theology, the economy, and urban communities, through the 1990s. He has taught Christian Ethics and Practical Theology in a number of universities. He is currently Visiting Professor in Theology at the University of Winchester and an Hon. Lecturer in the Department of Computer Science at the University of Bath where he teaches ethics in the Centre for Doctoral Training in Accountable, Responsible and Transparent AI. His books include: *After the Market* (2004), *Tensions in Christian Ethics* (2010), and *Anglican Social Theology* (ed.) (2014).

Michael Fasching, Mag is a research assistant and doctoral candidate at the University of Graz at the Institute for Educational Research and Pedagogy in the area of education and digital transformation. His research interests are fake news, digital competences, diversity, and migration. After the studies of Communication Science and Musicology at the University of Vienna, he worked as a course director at the Danube-University Krems and as a member in the research project 'Integration of Refugees in Styrian Companies' in the Department of Human Resource Management at the University of Graz.

Derek R. Ford is assistant professor of education studies at DePauw University (USA), where he teaches classes in philosophy and history of education. His work searches for the pedagogical processes latent in both oppressive systems and liberatory struggles to better inform political movements today. He has published in a variety of journals and written a few books, the latest of which is *Inhuman Educations: Jean-François Lyotard, Pedagogy, and Thought* (2021). He is chair of the education department at the Hampton Institute (a working-class think tank), an organizer with the ANSWER Coalition, and editor of LiberationSchool.org.

Steve Fuller is Auguste Comte Professor of Social Epistemology in the Department of Sociology at the University of Warwick. Originally trained in history, philosophy, and sociology of science, Fuller is the author of 25 books, which most recently have covered visions of a trans- and post-human future (or 'Humanity 2.0') and the current post-truth condition. His latest books are *Post-Truth: Knowledge as a Power Game* (Anthem 2018), *Nietzschean Meditations: Untimely Thoughts at the Dawn of the Transhuman Era* (Schwabe 2019), and *A Player's Guide to the Post-Truth Condition: The Name of the Game* (Anthem 2020).

Richard Hall is Professor of Education and Technology at De Montfort University, Leicester, UK, and a UK National Teaching Fellow. He is a Trustee of the Open Library of Humanities and sits on the Management Committee for the Leicester Primary Pupil Referral Unit. His is the author of *The Alienated Academic: The Struggle for Autonomy Inside the University* and writes about life in higher education at http://richard-hall.org.

Sarah Hayes is Professor of Higher Education Policy in the Education Observatory at the University of Wolverhampton, UK. Previously Sarah worked at Aston University, where she led programmes in Education and Sociology and is now an Honorary Professor. Sarah has also taught at the University of Worcester, at international partner institutions, and has led a range of research projects. Sarah's research spans sociology, education and policy, technological and social change and she has published in a variety of related journals. Her recent book, *The Labour of Words in Higher Education: Is it Time to Reoccupy Policy?*, was published through Brill in 2019. Her new book, *Postdigital Positionality*, is forthcoming. Sarah is an Associate Editor for *Postdigital Science and Education* (Springer). Personal website: https://researchers.wlv.ac.uk/sarah.hayes.

Petar Jandrić is Professor at the Zagreb University of Applied Sciences, Croatia, and Visiting Professor at the University of Wolverhampton, UK. His previous academic affiliations include Croatian Academic and Research Network, National e-Science Centre at the University of Edinburgh, Glasgow School of Art, and Cass School of Education at the University of East London. Petar's research interests are situated at the postdisciplinary intersections between technologies, pedagogies, and the society, and research methodologies of his choice are inter-, trans-, and anti-disciplinarity. He is Editor-in-Chief of *Postdigital Science and Education* journal https://www.springer.com/journal/42438 and book series https://www.springer.com/series/16439. Personal website: http://petarjandric.com/.

Victoria Mason-Robbie, PhD, CPsychol is a Chartered Psychologist with a range of interests within the fields of Health Psychology and Education. Victoria has published widely in psychology, medical, and teaching journals and has contributed to a number of books including co-editing *Digital Afterlife: Death Matters in a Digital Age* (2020) with Professor Maggi Savin-Baden. She is an experienced lecturer having worked in the Higher Education sector for over 15 years. Her recent focus has been on evaluating web-based avatars, pedagogical agents, and virtual humans.

About the Authors

Kathrin Otrel-Cass, PhD is a professor in educational research and digital transformation at the University of Graz, Austria. Much of her work is focused on interactions with digital materials and the consequences thereof. Her interests are in science technology practices and education, video-based research methodologies, new media in teaching, digital transformation, culturally responsive pedagogy, digital disruption, human development and science culture, techno-anthropology, and classroom-based research.

John Reader is a Senior Research Fellow with the William Temple Foundation and Honorary Senior Lecturer with the School of Education at the University of Worcester. Recent publications include *A Philosophy of Christian Materialism* cowritten with Baker and James (Routledge 2015) and *Theology and New Materialism* (Palgrave Macmillan 2017). He has also cowritten 'Technology Transforming Theology' with Maggi Savin-Baden for the William Temple Ethical Dialogue series.

Masaya Sasaki is an undergraduate student at DePauw University double majoring in Education Studies and Cognitive Science. He has previously published in *Educational Philosophy and Theory* and is interested in questions of subjectivity and intelligence in the biopolitical era.

Alexander Thomas is a PhD candidate at the University of East London whose research focuses on the ethics of transhumanism in the era of advanced capitalism. He is also a multi-award winning film director and screenwriter and was longlisted for the Academy Award for Best Live Action Short in 2016. He currently works as a Senior Lecturer in Media Production at the University of East London.

Part I
Conceptions of Postdigital Humans

What Are Postdigital Humans?

Maggi Savin-Baden

1 Introduction

This chapter begins by exploring conceptions of the postdigital, and what it means to be human. The second section examines the idea of postdigital humans and the relationship between humans and machines in the context of whole brain emulation and digital afterlife. Finally, the ethical issues relating to postdigital humans are discussed in relation to human labour, machine learning, intimacy ethics, and surveillance. In the context of a book on postdigital humans, it is first important to understand what is meant by the postdigital, the chapter being with an exploration of this. However, what is also central to the debate on postdigital humans is the issues of artificial intelligence which is currently used as singular term, as if it were one thing, when in fact it is a complex array of innovations, practices, and creations. The range of artificial intelligences also link to the new and emerging develops of digital afterlife which are discussed in the later section of the chapter. The issues raised in this chapter are designed to set the scene for the book as a whole, touching on areas that are discussed in more depth in other chapters.

2 The Postdigital

As will be seen across this text, there are many diverse understandings, definitions, and stances about the term postdigital. For many authors 'postdigital' is not temporal, it is not 'after' digital, rather it is a critical inquiry into the state of the digital world. Cramer (2015) provides a complex list of characteristics of the postdigital

---

M. Savin-Baden (✉)
School of Education, University of Worcester, Worcester, UK
e-mail: m.savinbaden@worc.ac.uk

© The Author(s), under exclusive license to Springer Nature Switzerland AG 2021
M. Savin-Baden (ed.), *Postdigital Humans*, Postdigital Science and Education,
https://doi.org/10.1007/978-3-030-65592-1_1

which are summarized in part below, along with the work of Jandrić (2019) and Andersen et al. (2014). The postdigital is seen as a stance which merges the old and the new, it is not seen as an event or temporal position, rather it is a critical perspective, a philosophy, that can be summarized as a collection of stances in the following intersecting positions:

- A disenchantment with current information systems and media and a period in which our fascination with these systems has become historical (Cramer 2015).
- The merging of the old and new by reusing and re-investigating analog technology with a tendency to focus on the experiential rather than the conceptual (Andersen et al. 2014).
- A continuation of digital cultures that is both still digital and beyond digital.
- A mutation into new and different power structures that are pervasive, covert, and therefore less obvious than other power structures.
- A blurred and messy relationship between humanism and posthumanism, physics and biology (Jandrić et al. 2018).
- The condition of the world after computerization, global networking, and the development and expansion of the digital market.
- The emergence of technoscience systems, which are transforming and transformed by global quantum computing, deep learning complexity science, artificial intelligence, and big data (Jandrić 2019).

The postdigital then is not just about positions or spaces inhabited just for a time, it is essentially ungraspable. This ungraspability relates to the way in which structures, political systems, cultures, languages, and technologies differ and change. There is no sense of the linear here, the postdigital interrupts linear trajectories and should be seen instead as a vector, that is a line of fixed length and direction but no fixed position. The vector is power, a power beyond metaphors of structure (Virilio and Lotringer 1983). Such a perspective might also be seen as a sense of living with the oblique, the idea that the postdigital should be the fusion of movement and dwelling (Virilio 1997). Thus, postdigital humans are locating in liquid spaces; people are both central to the postdigital and key players in its formulation, interruptions, and (re)creation.

3 What Does It Mean to Be Human?

Posthumanism seeks to break down binary distinctions between 'human', 'machine', and 'text' and between 'nature' and 'culture'; it also rejects dualisms that are used to define being such as subject/object (Hayles 1999, 2012). Thus, posthumanist theory is used to question the foundational role of 'humanity'. It prompts consideration of what it means to be a human subject and the extent to which the idea of the human subject is still useful. This overlaps with Actor Network Theory where the arguments centre on the idea that actors may be both human and non-human, thus, for example supermarket products and digital devices are seen as actors that have influence, but it is not clear how all this relates to the understandings of postdigital humans.

Harari, in *Homo Deus* (2017), explores the projects that will shape the twenty-first century. Much of what he argues is disturbing, such as the idea that human nature will be transformed in the twenty-first century, as intelligence becomes uncoupled from consciousness. Google and Amazon, among others, can process our behaviour to know what we want before we know it ourselves, and as Harari points out, somewhat worryingly, governments find it almost impossible to keep up with the pace of technological change. Harari challenges us to consider whether indeed there is a next stage of evolution and asks fundamental questions such as: where do we go from here? Perhaps what it means to be human is bound up with understanding of consciousness or the idea of having a soul. This is something Harari explores but he seems to mix up religion and values by using the label 'religion' for any system that organizes people, such as humanism, liberalism, and communism. He argues that 'it may not be wrong to call the belief in economic growth a religion, because it now purports to solve many if not most of our ethical dilemmas' (Harari 2017).

However, Floridi (2016) argues that information and humanity are intertwined, so that information should be considered in the sense of constitutive belonging rather than as a matter of external ownership. In this sense, 'your information' is the same as your feelings, or your body; such an intrinsic part of you that is more fundamental than any external possession over which you have a legal right. Floridi from within Communication studies talks about the differences between a first-order technology where the links are between humanity, technology, and nature; a second-order technology where the links are between humanity, technology, and humanity; and what is now a third-order technology where the links are technology to technology to technology with no human involvement at all. The Internet of Things is a prime example of the latter. Once humans are no longer in the loop, we have entered a different world which requires new concepts and even perhaps a new ethics. This in turn prompts us to question the extent to which technology is shaping our behaviour and our relationships. Reader asks:

> What exactly is the relationship between humans and technology, and could it be the case that any distance between has been so eroded that any sort of critical perspective is lost in the process? How, if at all, can we absent ourselves when the impacts of digital technology are so pervasive and invasive? (Savin-Baden and Reader 2018).

4 Artificial Intelligence

Artificial intelligence (AI) is often thought of as robots or thinking machines. In marketing, it is seen as a programme or algorithm often based on machine learning principles, yet the complexity and diversity of AI is much broader than this. Consequently, AI can be grouped broadly into three mains types. First, deep AI which involves creating virtual humans and digital immortals with sentience; the ability to feel, perceive, or experience. Second, pragmatic AI where machines are used for tasks such as mining large data sets or automating complex or risky tasks. Third, marketing AI where companies use algorithms to anticipate the customer's next move and improve the customer journey. Often when AI is spoken about in the twenty-first century, the perspectives that many people have gained is from information presented by media and film. The early days of research into AI focused on creating computer programmes that could 'understand' and manipulate symbols in order to reason, this was termed symbolic AI. Other forms are embodied AI and enactive AI. Embodied AI is where software is imported into a physical (robotic) body and exploring how that body fits into real-world environments and is based on the idea of embodied cognition—the view that intelligence is as much a part of the body as the brain. Enactive AI is seen as a form of AI that refines and complements embodied AI because it has a focus on the self-identity of the robot or virtual human, so that meaning is created by the interaction of the robot with the environment (Froese and Ziemke 2009). There is also often confusion between AI and augmented intelligence. Augmented intelligence describes either using a computer that is external to the human to help the human with mental tasks or inking computing capability directly into the brain in order to enhance the brain's processing power or memory. The focus here is broadly on the use of AI to help humans with a task, but it also extends to areas such as embodiment and postdigital humans, as these areas have direct impact on the relationship between AI and death and dying. However, whilst AI can be identified through terms such as deep, pragmatic, marketing, embodied, or enactive AI, it can also be categorized in terms of its impact and effect. Artificial intelligence is already shaping and reshaping our lives, environment, and relationship with other people. The result is that AI can be referred to as anything from a simple algorithm to a complex virtual persona who has the possibility for future sentience. The challenges of AI largely relate to the fact that many definitions are broad and unclear. Current perspectives tend to focus on the wide parameters between fear and hope, such as AI resulting in loss of work, enslaving humans and making them obsolete, to the hope of AI providing virtual human support to elderly and disabled people, and providing entertainment as well supporting security and defence systems, yet the research and understandings of between AI and postdigital humans remain inchoate.

5 Postdigital Humans

In the late 1990s and early 2000s, ideas about postdigital humans related to the enhancement of humans. For example in 1998, a set of experiments undertaken by Kevin Warwick, known as Project Cyborg, began with an implant into his arm used to control doors, lights, and heaters. Later this was developed into an implant inserted into his median nerve meaning his nervous system could be connected to the Internet. In 2007, the performance artist Stelarc had a cell-cultivated ear surgically attached to his left arm and in a number of performances he allowed his body to be controlled remotely by electronic muscle stimulators connected to the Internet. In the 2020s, postdigital humans now refer more often to the ways in which humans are seen in relationship, mutually shaping one another, whilst recognizing both what is new as well as what is already embedded in our cultures, institutions, political systems, and relationships.

The development and use of postdigital humans is occurring rapidly, but often in unexpected ways and spaces. The idea of a postdigital human in the 2020s suggests a different understanding of what it means to be human but also reflects the idea of 'post' as a critical stance towards the whole idea of being human in a digital age. We are in a world in which we are, as Virilio (1997) predicted, universally telepresent without moving our physical bodies. Thus, there is often a sense that we arrive and depart from spaces and encounters without actually doing so.

Yet digital media are currently being used to expand the possibilities of what postdigital humans might be; not ultimately about digitizing biology but perhaps more akin to Peters' (2012) notion of bio-informational capitalism, discussed later in the chapter. Postdigital human creation might also include whole brain emulation whereby brain scan data is translated into a software based on the neurons and other key parts of the brain, and the singularity, the view that there will be a time in the future when *technological* growth becomes uncontrollable and irreversible. It is suggested that 2050–2100 might be the time period in which the development of really complex postdigital humans capable of being called virtual sapiens will occur (Burden and Savin-Baden 2019) but whether active ones will emerge before then is questionable.

6 Humans and Machines

In the world of education where online learning, machines, and people coalesce, there is often a sense that there is symmetry in the relationship between computers and people. Jones argued:

> Experience can be thought of as either the essential distinguishing component of the individual human subject, or experience can be understood as the subjective component of one kind of element in a wider assemblage of humans and machines. In the later understanding of experience in assemblages human experience does not separate the human actor from other actors in a network and they are understood symmetrically. (Jones 2018: 39)

Indeed, during the Covid-19 pandemic, people were constantly tethered to machines and reliant on them for communication with loved ones, shopping, and sustaining their mental health. Yet in the debate between Fuller and Latour about whether a distinction between humans and non-humans was required for research purposes, Latour argued that 'all phenomena should be treated equally, whether it comes from something human, natural or artificial' but this clearly results into what Fuller calls the 'abdication of responsibility' (Barron 2003; Fuller and Jandrić 2019). However, within this debate it is clear that the conversation was designed to provoke discussion and therfore what was said here might not be entirely what either of them would defend fully in other contexts.

What is evident from this discussion is that central to questions about whether there can be any kind of real symmetry between people and machines should have a focus on ethical concerns, which is clearly evident in debates about face recognition and face verification.

Big Brother Watch, the independent research and campaigning group, exposes and challenges threats to privacy, freedoms, and civil liberties amid technological change in the UK. One of its main campaigns is FaceOff, which challenges the use of automated facial recognition in policing (Big Brother Watch 2019). It is clear that much of the discussions about humans and machines in the 2020s should be focusing on automated decision-making (ADM), rather than artificial intelligence. A different but related organization is AlgorithmWatch, which is a non-profit research and advocacy organization who evaluates algorithmic decision-making processes that have a social relevance. AlgorithmWatch (2019) compiled findings from 12 European countries to examine regulation and systems that have already been implemented. The company recommends that there is a need to see ADM as more than just the use of technology. Instead, they argue that the focus should be on the way technology is developed, by whom, and the ways in which it is deployed. Section 49 of General Data Protection Regulation (GDPR) states the:

Right not to be subject to automated decision-making

1. A controller may not take a significant decision based solely on automated processing unless that decision is required or authorised by law.
2. A decision is a 'significant decision' for the purpose of this section if, in relation to a data subject, it:
   (a) produces an adverse legal effect concerning the data subject, or
   (b) significantly affects the data subject. (Data Protection Act 2018)

AlgorithmWatch argues that this section of the Act is limited, as some ADM systems cannot be regulated just by data protection, such as predictive policing. This is the use of software that applies statistical data to guide decision-making. In practice, this means analyzing statistical historic data to predict increased risk of criminal activity in given geographic areas. Thus, AlgorithmWatch suggests that it is vital to ensure that stakeholders are involved in the design of criteria and that decision and evaluations about ADM include organizations—such as Big Brother Watch.

What is evident within the debates is that many of the difficulties that relate to humans *with* machines, even humans *in* the machines, is that in struggling to manage the panopticon we are both the watchers and the watched. We live, learn, and work within an invisible frame; it is not always clear what is a bot and what is not, but what is clear is that it is not clear what the algorithms are doing and who is really in control. Perhaps we are facing bio-informational capitalism writ large. Peters describes the political relationship between biology and information as bio-informational capitalism:

> the emergent form of fourth or fifth generational capitalism based on investments and returns in these new bio-industries: after mercantile, industrial, and knowledge capitalisms. .. based on a self-organizing and self-replicating code that harnesses both the results of the information and new biology revolutions and brings them together in a powerful alliance that enhances and strengthens or reinforces each other. (Peters 2012: 105)

This is not ultimately about digitizing biology but is about the application of biology to information. Peters suggests that the future will be based on the 'biologization' of the computer and its self-replicating memory.

The idea of 'uploading' a human brain to a computer is to many a very attractive one. Whole brain emulation (Hanson 2018) consists of a detailed brain scan and the scan data being translated into a software model based on the behaviour of the neurons and other key parts of the brain. The underlying software provides the generic brain biology/biochemistry/electrical models of neuron and synapse behaviour, and the scan data then details the unique connectivity of the individual brain. Closely linked to the idea of brain uploads is the concept of the technological singularity. Borrowing from the cosmological idea of a point where existing conceptions of space and time breakdown (such as in a Black Hole), a technological singularity is a point in our history where technological development has been so radical that we cannot see beyond it. Shanahan states that:

> a singularity in human history would occur if exponential technological progress brought about such dramatic change that human affairs as we understand them today came to an end…Our very understanding of what it means to be human, to be an individual, to be alive, to be conscious, to be part of the social order, all this would be thrown into question, not by detached philosophical reflection, but through force of circumstances, real and present. (Shanahan 2015: xv)

The technological singularity was popularized by Ray Kurzweil in books such as *The Singularity is Near* (Kurzweil 2005). By around 2050–2060, Kurzweil expects exponential growth to deliver enough processing power to model every human brain on the planet. For Kurzweil, though humans are still in control, so that these developments are augmentations to our abilities, not the rise of a single, possibly malevolent, super-intelligence.

There are differing opinions about whether 'the singularity' from science fiction is likely to be a myth or possibility. Snooks (2019) suggests that it is a myth, even fanciful. He suggests that the idea has no scientific basis and that predetermined mathematical data have been imposed on historical data. Snooks' argument indicates how easily (misplaced?) ideas or theories can be believed to become future realities. Yet hidden beneath discussions about such fabrications are also questions about values and morals. For example it is not clear how the question of ownership will be managed, whether open source of the future really will be open—it is already clear that the large EdTech giants are really using the data and algorithms for their own ends rather than to support and enable student learning.

Further as Burden and Savin-Baden (2019) point out, free smart digital assistants such as Amazon Echo/Alexa and Google Home have begun their invasion of our homes and as Siri and Cortana continue to develop on mobile phones, most of us will constantly be within reach of a virtual human performing the role of a personal assistant. Meanwhile the UK's National Health Service is testing an AI chatbot developed by Babylon Health,[1] and Woebot[2] is a virtual counsellor employing cognitive behavioural techniques to help address negative thinking. Peters (2012) has pointed out that it will be perilous to ignore the political implications of bio-informational capitalism. With developments in digital afterlife creation, there is an increasing interest in the management of death online despite much of the current software being an embellishment of the true possibilities. For example the use of virtual assistants, such as Siri, that provide voice and conversational interfaces, the growth of machine learning techniques to mine large data sets, and the rise in the level of autonomy being given to computer-controlled systems, all represent shifts in technology that enhance the creation of digital afterlife. Although not yet seen in this way (despite the growth of the DeathTech industry; sites and services that support the creation of digital legacies and post death digital immortals), digital afterlife creation is inherently a political and bio-informational problem.

7 Digital Afterlife and Life Unlimited

The concept of digital afterlife is defined here as the continuation of an active or passive digital presence after death (Savin-Baden et al. 2017). Other terms have been used to describe digital afterlife, including digital immortality. 'Afterlife' assumes a digital presence that may or may not continue to exist, whereas 'immortality' implies a presence for evermore. Whilst these terms may be used interchangeably, afterlife is a broader and more flexible construct as it does not contain assumptions about the duration or persistence of the digital presence. New practices suggest that the possibilities of 'living on' through such technological innovations has the potential to change the religious landscape radically. Recent developments suggest that there will be a sociopolitical and psychological impact that will affect understandings about embodiment, death, and the social life of the dead and create new forms of post-mortem veneration. Some postdigital authors suggest/imply that digital immortality, because of its digital-ness is not separable from biological/human existence (for example Jandrić et al. 2018). However, it is argued here that digital afterlife may have some continuous/contiguous components that are post-digital, but digital immortals do not. This is because to date digital immortals are passive, do not have sentience, and are unlikely to achieve it within at least the next 40 years.

---

[1] See https://www.propelics.com/healthcare-chatbots. Accessed 15 October 2020.
[2] See https://woebot.io/. Accessed 15 October 2020.

Digital afterlife may in the future be able to create the kind of symmetry between humans and machines that Jones (2018) suggests. In practice, this will mean that digital remains feed into digital afterlife creation which may result in a sentient digital immortal. However, digital afterlife now (and in the future) is not ultimately about digitizing biology. Instead it is akin to Peters' (2012) notion of bio-informational capitalism, since the focus is on collating and creating post-mortal artefacts in ways that reflect knowledge capitalisms and is 'based on a self-organizing and self-replicating code that harnesses both the results of the information and new biology revolutions and brings them together in a powerful alliance that enhances and strengthens or reinforces each other' (Peters 2012: 105).

However, in this area, authors such as Kasket (2019) also introduce questions about the unintended consequences of the digital on death, suggesting that the dead continue to 'speak' themselves. Further she asks pertinent questions about how we manage our own data and what might occur when corporations compete with us for control of these data? It is possible that the intentions of the person pre-death become distorted and re-shaped such that they no longer resemble the thoughts and wishes of that person. Hence, agency is called into question as the deceased is no longer able to act according to their will, and agency is taken over by the corporation/s that control the data. This in turn raises concerns about to what ends the data might be used. It is already clear that commercial companies are using digital mourning labour (the commodification of death for profit) to sell their products by capitalizing on the grief and mass mourning following the death of celebrities. For example after the death of David Bowie in 2016, the music and fashion industries both shared their grief on social media using images such as the thunderbolt, the signature sign of Bowie. This cyber capitalism therefore raises questions about the ethics and values of this postdigital world, which is discussed by Richard Hall in Chapter 'Venturing Beyond the Imposition of a Postdigital, Anti-human Higher Education', Malcolm Brown in Chapter 'Ethics, Character, and Community: Moral Formation and Modelling the Human', and John Reader in Chapter 'Postdigital Humans: Algorithmic Imagination?'.

8 Concerns About Postdigital Humans

Since the term postdigital human is used in wide ranging ways to cover anything from virtual humans to surveillance practices, it is important to explore a range of related concerns. These include human labour, big data, data mining and selling, machine learning, intimacy ethics, and surveillance.

From an ethical point of view, postdigital humans introduce questions about human labour and the questionable manufacturing conditions in China (Qiu 2016), Kenya (Lee 2018), and elsewhere. The hours are long, the activities repetitive and routine, and the wages are low. Qiu (2016) compares the seventeenth-century transatlantic slave trade with the iSlaves of the twenty-first century. The iSlaves Qiu defines are the Chines workers at Foxconn, an electronics company whose largest buyer is Apple. Qiu notes that student interns are paid below the minimum wage, legally supported by the Chinese Government. The challenge from Qiu is that there is a need to rethink our relationship with digital technologies and for example begin to adopt the use of Fairphone and fair trade goods across our lives. Further, as Lee (2018) points out, 'the information prepared here forms a crucial part of some of Silicon Valley's biggest and most famous efforts in AI'. Unseen labour also involves working with data, as Andrejevic et al. note:

> If one of the casualties of a fascination with the 'virtual' character of software, applications, code, and data has been a shift away from political-economic approaches to the media, the reliance of data mining on capital-intensive infrastructure reminds us of the ongoing salience of political-economic concerns. (Andrejevic et al. 2015: 385)

Our sites of production may not be ethical but as Jandrić (2019) points out, biases are not carried through cultures and people creating technology, biases are built into technology in ways that are unpredictable. This in turn raises further questions about the use of machine learning which is essentially designed to enable computers to act without being programmed.

In the field of machine learning, there has been increasing realization that there needs to be a delineation between different types of ethics: robotics ethics, machine morality, and intimacy ethics are all new areas that are being examined. For example Malle (2016) argues that robotic ethics needs to examine ethical questions about how humans should design, deploy, and treat robots. Machine morality explores issues about what moral capacities a robot or virtual human should have and how these might be implemented. It also includes issues such as moral agency, justification for lethal military robots, the use of mathematical proofs for moral reasoning and intimacy ethics. Intimacy ethics relates to the ways in which engaging with virtual humans can offer people opportunities to connect with something emotionally and feel supported, even loved, without the need to reciprocate. Borenstein and Arkin (2019) argue that the main issues that need to be considered are affective attachment, responsiveness, and the extent and duration of the proximity between the human and the robot.

Virtual humans are designed using human decision criteria and therefore ethical behaviour needs to be 'designed-in' to virtual humans. However, in the context of the range of virtual humans that are being developed or considered, designing appropriate and effective ethics standards are complex and far reaching. For example if autonomous combat robots or AIs are deployed by the military, whose fault is it if they mistakenly attack or fail to distinguish correct targets? What is most important here is that the legal context is ever-changing, and thus research for a digital age, in some respects, requires researchers to be aware of current debates and so plan research projects and data management accordingly, as well as being aware of issues of surveillance.

Surveillance is defined here as the monitoring of activities and behaviour in order to influence, manipulate, and manage people's lives. Zimmer (2008) coined the term Search 2.0 as the loss of privacy which occurs through the aggregation of users' online activities. In practice, Search 2.0 enables companies to track and aggregate people's data in ways previously impossible, since in the past people's data were separated across diverse sites. Now, as a result of social networking sites, personal data can be mined and cross referenced, sold, and reused, so that people are being classified by others through sharing their own data. Perhaps more accurately what we are dealing with is Andrejevic's *lateral surveillance:*

> Lateral surveillance, or peer–to–peer monitoring, understood as the use of surveillance tools by individuals, rather than by agents of institutions public or private, to keep track of one another, covers (but is not limited to) three main categories: romantic interests, family, and friends or acquaintances. (Andrejevic 2005: 488)

Lateral surveillance appears more sinister than the extensive government tracking that occurs, perhaps because many of us believe that this top-down surveillance has always existed. Yet lateral surveillance, whereby a person tracks their childrens' communications, monitors their lover's phone call and uses a webcam to spy on their neighbours, seems more sinister, as it has become a type of informal law enforcement and micro inquiry into others' lives. Thus, we market research, verify, and check friends and colleagues, so that '[i]n an era in which everyone is to be considered potentially suspect, we are invited to become spies—for our own good' (Andrejevic 2005: 494).

9 Conclusion: Postdigital Intervals?

Exploring the idea of the postdigital and postdigital humans may already be a project that is too late in a world of algorithms that move at a speed beyond what most of us can imagine. Yet perhaps there is a need for a pause, a postdigital interval that enables us to stand inside and outside our worlds at the same time, in the postdigital liminal. In the past, the time at university was seen as 'the gift of the interval', the central idea of which was that it was only possible to become critical of oneself and the world by being outside it. Today many students study and work at the same time. Being tethered to technology, being supported and directed by Amazon, Siri, and the personal trainer on our phone can prevent the possibility for intervals. Yet such spaces are vital in order to take a critical stance towards being the postdigital humans and to enable us to recognize the ways in which we are becoming enmeshed in our postdigital world. Most of the time being untethered means leaving the tech behind, yet it is suggested here that somehow a postdigital human needs to be able to take intervals with/in the digital.

The idea of the interval came from Elizabethan Playhouses where performances were lit by candles, and intervals were introduced so that burnt-down candles could be replaced. The idea of the postdigital interval needs to be examined so that we take a critical view, do not become dupes of cognitive capitalism and bio-informational capitalism, and global corporate EdTech interests do not remove the central pedagogical values of what it really means to be (at) a university. Postdigital humans should not be just connected to their own self-interested, self-serving networks. Instead they need to be located globally, with values that support the development of humankind, being aware of the impact that iSlavery, corporate domination, and the misplaced use of automated decision-making can have, as well as the fact that our laws do not legislate effectively in most of these domains. The challenge of the postdigital human then is to recognize the ways in which balances must be brought to bear and to realize the ways in which social injustices such as algorithms, machine learning, facial recognition, and facial verification can foster further injustices. As Peters and Jandrić note:

> While we speculate what kind of future world we will inhabit in coexistence with new forms of intelligent life, we should firmly focus on the questions what forms of intelligent life should be included in our collective decisions about the future and how we might raise them. (Peters and Jandrić 2019: 205)

Being a postdigital human requires then that we are attuned to covert political manipulation and control, really understand what counts as justice and identify the new forms of intelligence we would like to live with in the future.

References

AlgorithmWatch (2019). Automating Society – Taking Stock of Automated Decision-Making in the EU. www.algorithmwatch.org/automating-society/. Accessed 15 October 2020.

Andersen, C. U., Cox, G., & Papadopoulos, G. (2014). Postdigital research editorial. *A Peer-Reviewed Journal About, 3*(1).

Andrejevic, M., Hearn, A., & Kennedy, H. (2015). Cultural studies of data mining: introduction. *European Journal of Cultural Studies, 18*(4–5), 379–394. https://doi.org/10.1177/1367549415577395.

Andrejevic, M. (2005). The work of watching one another: Lateral surveillance, risk, and governance. *Surveillance and Society, 2*(4), 479–497. https://doi.org/10.24908/ss.v2i4.3359.

Barron, C. (2003). A strong distinction between humans and non-humans is no longer required for research purposes: A debate between Bruno Latour and Steve Fuller. *History of the Human Sciences, 16*(2), 77–99.

Big Brother Watch (2019). FaceOff, https://bigbrotherwatch.org.uk/campaigns/stop-facial-recognition/. Accessed 15 October 2020.

Borenstein, J., & Arkin, R. C. (2019). Robots, ethics, and intimacy: the need for scientific research. In D. Berkich & M. D'Alfonso M. (Eds.), *On the Cognitive, Ethical, and Scientific Dimensions of Artificial Intelligence* (pp. 299–309). Cham: Springer. https://doi.org/10.1007/978-3-030-01800-9_16.

Burden, D., & Savin-Baden, M. (2019). *Virtual Humans: Today and Tomorrow*. Florida: CRC Press.

Cramer, F. (2015). What is 'post-digital'? In D. M. Berry, & M. Dieter (Eds.), *Postdigital aesthetics: Art, computation and design* (pp. 12–26). New York: Palgrave Macmillan. https://doi.org/10.1057/9781137437204.

Data Protection Act (2018). c. 12. http://www.legislation.gov.uk/ukpga/2018/12/contents/enacted. Accessed 15 October 2020.

Floridi, L. (2016). *The 4th Revolution: How the Infosphere is Reshaping Reality*. Oxford: Oxford University Press.

Froese, T., & Ziemke, T. (2009). Enactive artificial intelligence: Investigating the systemic organization of life and mind. *Artificial Intelligence, 173*(3–4), 466–500. https://doi.org/10.1016/j.artint.2008.12.001.

Fuller, S., & Jandrić, P. (2019). The postdigital human: Making the history of the future. *Postdigital Science and Education, 1*(1), 190–217. https://doi.org/10.1007/s42438-018-0003-x.

Hanson. R. (2018). *The Age of EM: Work, Love, and Life when Robots rule the Earth*. Oxford: Oxford University Press.

Hayles, K. (1999). *How We Became Posthuman: Virtual Bodies in Cybernetics, Literature and Informatics*. Chicago, IL: University of Chicago Press.

Hayles, K. (2012). *How We Think: Digital Media and Contemporary Technogenesis*. Chicago, IL: University of Chicago Press.

Harari, Y. N. (2017). *Homo Deus: A Brief History of Tomorrow*. London: Harper.

Jandrić, P., Knox, J., Besley, T., Ryberg, T., Suoranta, J., & Hayes, S. (2018). Postdigital science and education. *Educational Philosophy and Theory, 50*(10), 893–899. https://doi.org/10.1080/00131857.2018.1454000.

Jandrić, P. (2019). The postdigital challenge of critical media literacy. *The International Journal of Critical Media Literacy, 1*(1), 26–37. https://doi.org/10.1163/25900110-00101002.

Jones, C. (2018). Experience and networked learning. In N. Bonderup Dohn, S. Cranmer, J. A. Sime, M. de Laat, & T. Ryberg (Eds.), *Networked learning: Reflections and challenges* (pp. 39–55). Springer International. https://doi.org/10.1007/978-3-319-74857-3_3.

Kasket, E. (2019). *All the Ghosts in the Machine: Illusions of Immortality in the Digital Age*. London, UK: Robinson.

Kurzweil, R. (2005). *The Singularity Is Near: When Humans Transcend Biology*. London: Penguin.

Lee, D. (2018). Why big tech pays poor Kenyans to teach self-driving cars. BBC Technology, 3 November. https://www.bbc.com/news/technology-46055595. Accessed 15 October 2020.

Malle, B. F. (2016). Integrating robot ethics and machine morality: the study and design of moral competence in robots. *Ethics Information Technology, 18*, 243–256. https://doi.org/10.1007/s10676-015-9367-8.

Peters, M. A. (2012). Bio-informational capitalism. *Thesis Eleven, 110*(1), 98–111. https://doi.org/10.1177/0725513612444562.

Peters, M. A., & Jandrić, P. (2019). AI, Human Evolution, and the Speed of Learning. In J. Knox, Y. Wang, & M. Gallagher (Eds.), *Artificial Intelligence and Inclusive Education: speculative futures and emerging practices* (pp. 195–206). Singapore: Springer Nature. https://doi.org/10.1007/978-981-13-8161-4_12.

Savin-Baden, M., Burden, D., & Taylor, H. (2017). The ethics and impact of digital immortality. *Knowledge Cultures, 5*(2). 11–19. 10.22381/KC52201711.

Savin-Baden, M., & Reader, J. (2018). Technology Transforming Theology: Digital Impacts. Rochdale: William Temple Foundation. http://williamtemplefoundation.org.uk/our-work/temple-tracts/. Accessed 15 October 2020.

Shanahan, M. (2015). *The technological singularity*. Campridge, MA: MIT Press.

Snooks, G.D. (2019). Exploding the Great Singularity Myth. IGDS Working Papers # 16. Canberra: Institute of Global Dynamic Systems. https://www.researchgate.net/publication/330993743_Exploding_the_Great_Singularity_Myth. Accessed 15 October 2020.

Virilio, P. (1997). *Open Sky*. London: Verso.

Virilio, P., & Lotringer, S. (1983). *Pure War*. New York: Semiotext(e).

Qiu, J. L. (2016). *Goodbye iSlave: a manifesto for digital abolition*. Urbana: University of Illinois Press.

Zimmer, M. (2008). The externalities of Search 2.0: The emerging privacy threats when the drive for the perfect search engine meets Web 2.0. *First Monday, 13*(3). https://firstmonday.org/article/view/2136/1944. Accessed 15 October 2020.

Postdigital Humans: Taking Evolution in Own Hands

Petar Jandrić

1 Introduction

Since the inception of the *Postdigital Science and Education* journal and book series in 2018, our community of postdigital researchers has spent considerable time and effort in defining the concept of the postdigital. While it is natural for a community to leave definitional matters in the background and focus on other topics of interest, foundational concepts are permanently in flux and definitions require periodical revisiting. As I began to examine the current work in the field with the theme of this book, I realized that much postdigital research makes only sporadic reference to (postdigital) human beings. Critical posthumanism is a foundational concept underpinning the postdigital idea (Jandrić et al. 2018), yet its influence has become increasingly covert. To bring this influence to the fore and develop theoretical background for further inquiry, the first part of this chapter examines references to postdigital humans in postdigital literature.

Building on postdigital literature, the second part of the chapter considers: Who is the postdigital human? This question immediately moves the discussion towards philosophical analyses, which, based on my recent works, can be classified into three 'performance standards' for inclusion into humanity: life, consciousness, and behaviour (Fuller and Jandrić 2019; Peters and Jandrić 2019). Not unlike critical posthumanism, much of this philosophy is implied but rarely openly explored in postdigital thinking; by examining this openly, it is possible to point up some theoretical dark spots and research opportunities. The third part of the chapter synthesizes

---

P. Jandrić (✉)
Zagreb University of Applied Sciences, Zagreb, Croatia

University of Wolverhampton, Wolverhampton, UK
e-mail: pjandric@tvz.hr

© The Author(s), under exclusive license to Springer Nature Switzerland AG 2021
M. Savin-Baden (ed.), *Postdigital Humans*, Postdigital Science and Education, https://doi.org/10.1007/978-3-030-65592-1_2

philosophical approaches and postdigital theories and builds a postdisciplinary understanding of the postdigital human.

2 The *Postdigital* Human

Early Works (1998–2018)

Early theorists of the postdigital condition almost unanimously agree that one of the key inspirations for their work has arrived from Nicholas Negroponte's Wired article 'Beyond Digital' (1998). In his article, Negroponte refers to the famous scene from the 1967 film *The Graduate* (Nichols 1967) in which young Benjamin Braddock (played by Dustin Hoffman) observes career advice given by his teacher Mr. McGuire (played by Walter Brooke) who is convinced that the future of business is in plastics. Thirty-odd years later, Negroponte observes:

> Now that we're in that future, of course, plastics are no big deal. Is *digital* destined for the same banality? Certainly. Its literal form, the technology, is already beginning to be taken for granted, and its connotation will become tomorrow's commercial and cultural compost for new ideas. Like air and drinking water, being digital will be noticed only by its absence, not its presence. (Negroponte 1998) (emphasis from the original)

In character with Wired's 1990s spirit, Negroponte's focus in this passage is firmly on technology (plastics, digital).

It is unsurprising that those inspired by Negroponte's work have taken similar approaches. Thus, the first scholarly paper that refers explicitly to the concept of the postdigital—Kim Cascone's 'The Aesthetics of Failure: "Post-Digital" Tendencies in Contemporary Computer Music'—makes only implicit reference to humans. Describing the aesthetic of the glitch, Cascone (2000: 13) writes: 'Indeed, "failure" has become a prominent aesthetic in many of the arts in the late 20th century, reminding us that our control of technology is an illusion, and revealing digital tools to be only as perfect, precise, and efficient as the humans who build them.' Notions such as 'controlling' and 'building' technologies may be interpreted as signs of technological instrumentalism and dualism between humans and technologies, yet Cascone attributes them with the first seeds of postdigital thinking. The glitch is a point of intersection between the digital machine and its human user; a fringe at which technologies become more human and humans become more technological. Cascone's aesthetic of the glitch is neither fully human nor fully technological, and it is thus postdigital.

The next definition, by Melvin L. Alexenberg in late 2000s, gives more prominence to posthumanist aspects of the postdigital condition.

> Postdigital (adjective), of or pertaining to art forms that address the humanization of digital technologies through interplay between digital, biological, cultural, and spiritual systems, between cyberspace and real space, between embodied media and mixed reality in social and physical communication, between high tech and high touch experiences, between visual, haptic, auditory, and kinesthetic media experiences, between virtual and augmented

reality, between roots and globalization, between autoethnography and community narrative, and between web-enabled peer-produced wikiart and artworks created with alternative media through participation, interaction, and collaboration in which the role of the artist is redefined. (Alexemberg 2011: 10)

Alexemberg's understanding of 'the humanization of digital technologies' avoids exploration of the dichotomy between human beings and technologies which has affected much early postdigital thinking and instead replaces it with a more dialectic notion of 'interplay between digital, biological, cultural, and spiritual systems'. Alexemberg does not reach too deeply into posthumanist thinking and literature, yet his definition opens up opportunities for further work in the field.

The next influential definition, published at Wikipedia and mirrored all over the web, suggests:

Postdigital, in artistic practice, is an attitude that is more concerned with being human, than with being digital. Postdigital is concerned with our rapidly changed and changing relationships with digital technologies and art forms. If one examines the textual paradigm of consensus, one is faced with a choice: either the 'postdigital' society has intrinsic meaning, or it is contextualised into a paradigm of consensus that includes art as a totality. (Wikipedia 2020)

Drawing on Alexemberg's definition from *The Future of Art in a Postdigital Age* (2011),[1] the Wikipedia definition is now clearly, albeit covertly, situated in posthumanism. However, the understanding of the postdigital project as being more interested in human beings than technologies is problematic in the light of sociomaterial reconfigurations of relationships between human beings and technologies which 'conceptualise knowledge and capacities as being *emergent* from the webs of interconnections between heterogeneous entities, both human and nonhuman' (Jones 2018: 47).

The next definition illustrates one example of postdigital thinking in the humanities and social sciences. In seeking to explore origins, *Postdigital Science and Education* recently published an article about a group of scholars under the pseudonym 52group and the development of their ideas about the postdigital between 2009 and 2019. In their 2009 manifesto, the 52group write:

We hold out hope for the postdigital era. We hope that it provides the framework for an environment that is good enough, firstly, to hold an individual as they identify and develop authentic personal experiences, and secondly, to stimulate that individual to extend her/his questioning and actions in the world. In this way, as their social experiences stray into what are now called digital spaces, the digital is secondary to the relationships that form and develop, and the activity that takes place, in an environment. A central actor in the postdigital era is, therefore, a significant, more experienced other against whom the individual can securely test their authentic experiences. Within the postdigital era, the personal and emotional comes to the fore and anchors cognitive development. (Cormier et al. 2019: 478)

The manifesto reveals complex and nuanced postdigital understandings of relationships between human beings and technologies. Responses to the manifesto, written by the same authors in 2015 and then again in 2019, refined these insights further.

---

[1] Alexemberg (2011: 9) freely admits his active contribution to Wiktionary and similar websites.

A good example is Mark Childs' 2015 response: 'Evolutionarily, technology created the species *Homo sapiens* as much as the other way around' (Cormier et al. 2019: 479). Referring to William Gibson's *Neuromancer* (1984) and cyberpunk literature, Childs' response is deeply situated in posthumanism. Childs' 2015 response also seems to mark the first public usage of the phrase 'postdigital humans'.

This brief overview presents a selection of some key moments in the development of postdigital thinking about human beings from Negroponte's (1998) Wired article 'Beyond Digital', through to early work done in artistic contexts, and towards the humanities and social sciences. It shows development of postdigital understanding of human relationships to technologies from early dualisms to increasingly refined posthumanist and sociomaterialist perspectives. The next section provides a selection of most recent developments in postdigital thinking.

Recent Works (2018–)

Post-2018 work builds upon early postdigital thinking using insights from a diverse body of work including critical philosophy of technology, science and technology studies, critical posthumanism, critical pedagogy, and others. 'The postdigital is hard to define; messy; unpredictable; digital and analog; technological and non-technological; biological and informational. The postdigital is both a rupture in our existing theories and their continuation.' (Jandrić et al. 2018: 895) The concept implies neither a complete break-up with the past nor business and usual—it is a complex entanglement between biological and digital modes of existence (Sinclair and Hayes 2019: 126). Postdigital humans, by extension, are not only those who come after the 'digital humans' or 'predigital humans'. Rather, postdigital humans are all those entangled in different configurations of human–machine assemblages.

Focusing to these assemblages, Peter McLaren (2019: 11) asks: 'What kind of socio-historical human agent do we wish to nurture in a postdigital society? One whose computational capacity and recursive self-improvement is enhanced genetically? A being that is emulatable by postdigital materials and powered by evolutionary algorithms?' Mixing sociomaterialism's shared agency between human and non-human actors with critical pedagogy, McLaren opens up a hugely important question: Where do we, as a society, want to direct this shared agency?

Postdigital studies of artificial intelligence (AI) and neurology offer further relevant insights. In 'Brain Data: Scanning, Scraping and Sculpting the Plastic Learning Brain Through Neurotechnology', Ben Williamson (2019: 82) opens up the practical question of what takes to conduct research on digital humans. 'Understanding and analyzing neurotechnology from a postdigital perspective requires engagement with biosocial studies of neuroscience, sociotechnical studies of technology production and posthumanist theory on the assemblages produced by human-machine integration.' Alongside Levinson (2019) and others, Williamson (2019) opens up an important question of postdigital research methodology. Current research in the field sees epistemology as mutually constitutive with political economy (Fuller 2019; Jandrić 2020a). 'Our postdigital age is one of cohabitation, blurring borders between social actors and scientific disciplines, mutual dependence, shifting relationships between traditional centres and margins, and inevitable compromise.' (Jandrić and Hayes 2019: 390) Epistemically, this leads to radical postdisciplinarity; politically, it calls for forms of involvement usually associated with critical pedagogy.

Recent interesting work about postdigital humans can be found in the field of teaching and learning. Within a plethora of available examples, in particular, in their recent book, *The Manifesto for Teaching Online*, scholars from Edinburgh University's Centre for Research in Digital Education apply the postdigital perspective to human contact.

> As many of our digital technologies have become smoother, more immersive, less obtrusive, we find ourselves in a postdigital era in which we need to understand contact as something which takes place multiply: a video call is contact, and so is teacher presence on a Twitter feed; a phone call is contact, and so is a shared gaming session; an asynchronous text chat is contact, and so is a co-authoring session on a shared document. These are forms that we can value on their own terms, without needing always to align them with ideals of contact dependent on proximity in space, and visibility of face. (Bayne et al. 2020: 78)

Written before the Covid-19 pandemic, these insights have hugely risen in importance during recent lockdowns and 'self'-isolations (Jandrić 2020b; Peters and Besley 2020). Arguably, the described shift towards blurring borders between physical and digital social contact, or postdigital human contact, is one of many important steps in development of postdigital humans.

This selection of recent developments in postdigital thinking bursts with unfinished thoughts, open questions, and research opportunities. Therefore, these early insights can be understood as mere announcements of what postdigital thinking could be (about) and possible directions it could explore. After situating this inquiry into postdigital humans within relevant works, it is the time to launch a head-on attack.

3 The Postdigital *Human*

This section examines who is a postdigital human? The first definition might suggest that the postdigital human is a human being living in the postdigital condition defined by vanishing borders between the digital and the analog in all spheres of life, including their own body. However, I first want to remove the most common critique that many people in this world have no access to technology and therefore are not even digital. This critique, which regularly occurs across a range of publications (for example in Feenberg 2019), can be responded to in two different ways. The first response is to argue that the critique is misleading because of its focus to computers, networks, and other digital devices. However, computers are one of many possible embodiments of digital principles and are foundational in fields from physics to biology. In fact, '[h]uman beings have always been digital—we have always classified sounds, colors, textures and smells in certain categories which roughly correspond to "resolution" of our senses' (Jandrić 2019: 172). In the humanities and social sciences, however, computer-related digitalization has indeed deeply transformed our being and society, any inquiry into postdigital humans cannot ignore other forms of digital existence inherent to our bodies and nature.

Even within the special case of computer-related digitalization, the inability to access computers, networks, and other digital devices does not set one free from digitalization. We live in the age of the Anthropocene, where the human race affects the Earth's geology and ecosystems significantly through burning fossil fuels, using chemical fertilizers, and multiple other practices. These days, traditional analog practices such as fertilizing land cannot be thought of without digital technologies which enable development of new fertilizers—situated in a space between the digital and the analog, all our environment-shaping practices are postdigital. Consequently, even the most isolated Inuits in the Arctic, and Tagaeri in the Amazon, cannot escape digitally enabled changes in their environments. These people may indeed not have any access to digital tools, yet the postdigital condition shapes their environments and lives. Therefore, they are also postdigital humans.

These arguments about ubiquity and inescapability of the postdigital condition cover postdigital *Homo sapiens* and their evolutionary successors. However, a growing body of posthumanist research developed during the past few decades suggests that entities very different from *Homo sapiens* may in some cases also be considered human. According to Steve Fuller, the answer to the question 'What does it mean to be human?' reaches far beyond *Homo sapiens*.

> We shouldn't be sentimental about these questions. 'Human' began – and I believe should remain – as a normative not a descriptive category. It's really about which beings that the self-described, self-organised 'humans' decide to include. So we need to reach agreement about the performance standards that a putative 'human' should meet that a 'non-human' does not meet. (Fuller and Jandrić 2019: 207)

Fuller also states: 'you cannot be "human" on your own, simply because you have, say, the right genetic makeup. Humanity is a collective achievement or nothing at all' (Fuller and Jandrić 2019: 207).

Following Fuller's understanding of 'human' as a normative category, an inquiry into postdigital humans beyond *Homo sapiens* implies identification of performance standards. Recent research in the field (Fuller and Jandrić 2019; Peters and Jandrić 2019) has suggested three important performance standards for postdigital humans: life, consciousness, and behaviour.

Before moving on, let us identify possible candidates for postdigital humans. They can be classified into three main categories: biological entities other than *Homo sapiens*, non-biological entities, and entities combined of biological and non-biological parts.

Speaking of biology, all known life on planet Earth is based on carbon. While the common expectation in astrobiology that possible extraterrestrial life forms will also be based on carbon is sometimes critiqued as carbon chauvinism (Sagan 1973: 47), forms of life based on material bases other than carbon have not (yet) been detected and/or developed in laboratories. Looking at biological entities, therefore, the following analysis assumes that they are made of carbon.

Looking at non-biological entities, all today's 'thinking machines', or computers, are based on digital (zero-one) computation—in words of Alan Turing (1950: 439), they are a subgroup of a more general mathematical concept of 'discrete state machines'. Historical computers, such as ENIAC, performed zero-one computation using technologies of the day such as vacuum tubes, crystal diodes, resistors, capacitors, and others. After decades of development, today's zero-one computation takes place in silicon field-effect transistors placed on monolithic integrated circuits. Latest recent research developments point towards opportunities to develop digital computing on other material bases such as graphene and carbon nanotubes, and quantum computing. While all today's machines that could possibly be considered as postdigital humans are based on silicon, all non-carbon-based discrete state machines have the potentials to develop artificial intelligence.

Entities based on this or that combination of human biology and non-carbon-based discrete state machines are well-known under the name of cyborgs. While cyborgs have inspired decades of important posthumanist research, a lot of this research does not question humanity of its protagonists. In *Singularity is Near*, Ray Kurzweil (2005) takes the argument further using an interesting thought experiment. Let us imagine a future in which all bodily organs can be replaced. So, when I break a hip, I replace my bone with an artificial hip; when my liver stops working, I replace it with an artificial liver; and so on. According to Kurzweil, 'gradual replacement also means the end of me. We might therefore wonder: at what point did my body and brain become someone else?' According to Kurzweil, '[i]t's the ultimate ontological question, and we often refer to it as the issue of consciousness' (Kurzweil 2005: 257). However interesting, Kurzweil's thought experiment reaches a philosophical point of no return, and his 'fully replaced' entities need to be examined against performance standards for postdigital humans: life, consciousness, and behaviour.

Based on this preliminary analysis, the following analysis of performance standards for inclusion into humanity discusses entities which are available at present or could be available in foreseeable future: non-carbon-based AIs, including but not limited to today's silicon-based computers.

The First Performance Standard: Life

To be human, one first needs to be alive. Fuller's understanding of being human reflects a long tradition of posthumanist thinking which deconstructs the notion of life from its material base (biological vs. non-biological, carbon-based vs. non-carbon-based). A powerful example of such thinking was presented by Steven Hawking at his lecture 'Life in the Universe' (1996). 'One can define Life to be an ordered system that can sustain itself against the tendency to disorder, and can reproduce itself. That is, it can make similar, but independent, ordered systems.' Hawking proceeds:

> A living being usually has two elements: a set of instructions that tell the system how to sustain and reproduce itself, and a mechanism to carry out the instructions. In biology, these two parts are called genes and metabolism. But it is worth emphasising that there need be nothing biological about them. (Hawking 1996)

In practice, it is possible to imagine a self-repairing robot programmed to produce new self-repairing robots. According to Hawking, a functional self-repairing, self-reproducing robot is a legitimate form of life.

Application of Hawking's definition to robots is relatively straightforward because robots and *Homo sapiens* consist of different material bases (metal and carbon). However, recent advances in biotechnology complicate this analysis because they often transcend the borders between different material bases. For example on the 70th Anniversary of Erwin Schrödinger's famous lecture about the nature of life at Trinity College Dublin, Craig Venter gave a presentation 'What Is Life? A 21st Century Perspective', which explores these developments.

> We can digitize life, and we generate life from the digital world. Just as the ribosome can convert the analogue message in mRNA into a protein robot, it's becoming standard now in the world of science to convert digital code into protein viruses and cells. Scientists send digital code to each other instead of sending genes or proteins. There are several companies around the world that make their living by synthesizing genes for scientific labs. It's faster and cheaper to synthesize a gene than it is to clone it, or even get it by Federal Express. (Venter 2012)

Based on Hawking's definition, it could be argued that the digital code is not alive since it cannot reproduce without the external help of scientists, while the protein cell is alive because it can reproduce on its own. However convincing, this argument is worth an in-depth consideration.

Science in the twenty-first century recognizes that genes, whilst not a form of life, are essential to life. In Venter's example, digital codes for protein synthesis play the role of protein genes—information contained in these entities is necessary, but not enough, for creation of life. According to current biological classifications, both digital codes for protein synthesis and protein genes are small non-living building blocks of larger living forms. However, these classifications are mere conventions—it is difficult, and perhaps even impossible, to determine the exact point where life ends and non-living organic structures begin. A typical case are viruses. Viruses possess their own genes and evolve, yet they do not possess cellular structure, and they require a living host cell to reproduce. Interpretations of such properties hugely vary, and scientists cannot agree whether viruses are a form of life or non-living organic structures—according to the popular adage, viruses are usually defined as being 'at the edge of life' (Rybicki 1990).

These microscopic discussions at the fringes of biology, chemistry, physics, and information science point towards the inseparability of *postdigital* life and postdigital *life*: at some point of interaction with its environment, digital code may become (a building block of) a living biological organism. This conclusion does not imply that an email attachment containing information for protein synthesis is alive. Instead, it merely leaves an opportunity that, at some point of their development, some inorganic entities could be reorganized into biological forms of life.

In the context of posthumanist understanding which removes the notion of life from its material base, various biological and non-biological entities, and some combinations thereof, can be understood as living. This conclusion leaves an opportunity that some postdigital humans may look and feel radically different from *Homo sapiens*.

The Second Performance Standard: Consciousness

The second performance standard for inclusion into humanity, consciousness, is one of the most baffling scientific questions of today. Consciousness is notoriously hard to define, and many historical attempts at explaining consciousness without clearly identifying the question have been deficient. Researchers, such as Ned Block, Daniel Dennett, David J. Chalmers, and others, have developed a distinction between the 'easy problem of consciousness' focused to cognitive abilities and functions and the 'hard problem of consciousness' which accounts for a conscious experience. Both problems are fundamental for this attempt to define the second performance standard for an entity's inclusion into humanity. However, while easy problems of consciousness can be explored and often even measured in practice (which moves them to the third performance standard for inclusion into humanity, which is behaviour), the problem of consciousness lies firmly in theory.

Since the beginning of the twentieth century, physicists including Nils Bohr and Erwin Schrödinger have asked why it seems impossible to explain the functioning of an organism using our understanding of quantum-physical workings of its microscopic building blocks such as atoms and molecules. In a recent article, Fuller outlines Bohr's and Schrödinger's different responses to this question. Embedded in their historical circumstances, these responses present two competing philosophical principles which can be found in consciousness studies to date.

> Bohr argued that knowledge of an organism's overall organization structure and its precise chemical composition may also be mutually exclusive, which could be read as implying that half of the available knowledge about an organism is lost while it is still alive (shades of the famed 'Schrödinger cat' thought experiment). In contrast, Schrödinger assumed that an organism's unique level of physical complexity implies that its design is, so to speak, 'quantum-proof', which allows us—at least in principle—to understand its workings without requiring Bohr-style paradoxes and mysteries. (Fuller 2020)

More recently Chalmers' groundbreaking work, 'Facing Up to the Problem of Consciousness' (1995), argues that 'there are systematic reasons why the usual methods of cognitive science and neuroscience fail to account for conscious experience. These are simply the wrong sort of methods: nothing that they give to us can yield an explanation.' Therefore, Chalmers concludes, '[t]o account for conscious experience, we need an *extra ingredient* in the explanation'. Introducing this dualism between the subjective and the objective, Chalmers distinguishes between mental states and physical systems ontologically; these mental states appear in, making him more aligned to Bohr than Schrödinger. Chalmers does not avoid uncomfortable issues with his dualist approach such as the rejection of materialism. In *The Conscious Mind: In search of a fundamental theory of conscious experience*, Chalmers dedicates the whole chapter to these problems (1996: Chapter 'Venturing Beyond the Imposition of a Postdigital, Anti-human Higher Education') and develops his theory of naturalistic dualism. Further philosophical inquiry into this problem is well beyond the scope of this chapter, yet there is something to be said for Chalmers' argument that his position is a mere supplement to the scientific world view; 'it is a necessary broadening in order to bring consciousness within its scope' (Chalmers 1996: 159).

According to Fuller, possible developments towards understanding and creating human and human-like forms of life are likely to develop in two opposing directions:

> One is simply to forsake the opaque relations between brains and genes in the human organism and focus instead on increasing the self-programming capacities of advanced artificial intelligence—perhaps even as the platform into which humans will migrate in a 'transhuman' future. Think Ray Kurzweil. The other is to dwell, as Schrödinger himself did, on the thermodynamic efficiency of human organism, notwithstanding its opaque inner workings. (Fuller 2020)

The second position is reactive, yet the first position requires one 'to change one's frame of reference from creature to creator—that is, from the naïve human observer to "God's point of view"' (Fuller 2020). It is still unclear whether we will ever reach a full understanding of the nature of consciousness—perhaps, as Bohr claimed, there are natural limits which prevent us from doing so. For better or worse, however, what Fuller calls the 'God's point of view' is the type of thinking behind all humanity's attempts at creating human-made fellow humans.

While Schrödinger's approach is still worthy of consideration, today's practical problem of consciousness is much closer to that of Chalmers' naturalistic dualism. As we build more agile AIs based on the 'God's point of view' (such as silicon-based computers), the hard problem of consciousness can be left aside; Chalmers' extra ingredient will either somehow show up or future progress will deem it irrelevant.

The Third Performance Standard: Behaviour

System behaviour may have been philosophically understood as straightforward problem of consciousness, yet in practice, its measurement is difficult. The conclusion that we should focus on the easy problems of consciousness while leaving the hard problems of consciousness alone may sound simple, yet it is closely related to a 70-year research tradition based on the work of Alan Turing. In his groundbreaking paper 'Computing Machinery and Intelligence', Turing (1950: 433) makes a simple yet powerful proposal to replace the question 'can machines think?' by another question, 'which is closely related to it and is expressed in relatively unambiguous words': can a machine fool a human being into thinking that they are communicating with another human being? Turing allowed only digital computers into this imitation game. In defence of that decision, he writes: 'This restriction appears at first sight to be a very drastic one. I shall attempt to show that it is not so in reality.' (Turing 1950: 436) Following a mathematical proof of universality of discrete machines, he arrived at the final formulation of his test.

> It was suggested tentatively that the question, 'Can machines think?' should be replaced by 'Are there imaginable digital computers which would do well in the imitation game?' If we wish we can make this superficially more general and ask 'Are there discrete state machines which would do well?' (Turing 1950: 442)

Since 1950, variants of the Turing test have been instrumental in development of today's computer-based AIs. The test has been endlessly revised, expanded, and extensively critiqued. The Stanford Encyclopedia of Philosophy identifies nine main categories of objections to the Turing test: the theological objection, the 'heads in the sand' objection, the mathematical objection, the argument from consciousness, arguments from various disabilities, Lady Lovelace's objection, argument from continuity of the nervous system, argument from informality of behaviour, and argument from extra-sensory perception (Graham and Dowe 2020). While this chapter is not a place for detailed consideration of these critiques, John Searle's Chinese Room argument deserves deeper elaboration.

Searle's (1981) thought experiment can be found in many different versions. Its simple version supposes a computer which behaves as if it understands Chinese and manages to convince a human Chinese speaker that they are talking to another human Chinese speaker. While this computer has obviously passed the Turing test, Searle asks whether it literally understands Chinese or merely simulates understanding of Chinese. Not unlike Chalmers' distinction between the easy problem of consciousness and the hard problem of consciousness, Searle proposes that the view that the computer literally understands Chinese can be described as strong AI and the view that the computer merely simulates understanding of Chinese can be described as weak AI. According to Searle, only weak AI can be established experimentally. In *The Conscious Mind: In search of a theory of conscious experience*, Chalmers (1996: 301) claims that the heart of Searle's problem clearly lies in consciousness. The Chinese Room experiment shows that the Turing test can resolve only the weak problem of consciousness (conscious behaviour), while the hard problem of consciousness (experience) remains unanswered.

Every few years, there is a newspaper headline claiming a new machine has passed the Turing test. However, these claims are usually immediately disputed (Ekici 2014; Hruska 2018; amongst many others). The problem is not whether the computer has met benchmarks set by experiment's designers, but whether these benchmarks have been set correctly. Reflecting on these critiques, John Denning, one of the creators of 'a computer program named Eugene Goostman which imitates a Ukrainian teenager with a quirky sense of humour and a pet guinea pig', says: 'I think we passed "a" Turing test, but I don't know if it's "the" Turing test.'

(Sample and Hern 2014) In practice, even theoretically solvable weak problems of consciousness, and weak AI, are too hard for today's sciences. The solvable third performance standard for inclusion into humanity, behaviour, is still not available in practice. Being theoretically solvable, however, it does not exclude non-carbon-based entities from humanity.

4 Conclusion: Self-Designated Evolution and Its Responsibilities

What can be learnt from this postdisciplinary journey into the question who, and what, may be considered as a postdigital human? We now need to accept a possibility of biological, semi-biological, and non-biological forms of life, which may be able to meet (currently unavailable) performance tests for inclusion into humanity. Given the normative nature of performance criteria, these tests need to be developed in postdisciplinary collaboration between diverse fields of human inquiry. For various reasons including natural restrictions (such as Bohr's paradoxes) and restrictions pertaining to human nature (normative questions are notoriously contextual, so is human consensus), we do not yet have, and perhaps never will have, a definite demarcation line between humans and non-humans.

However, our inability to detect postdigital non-carbon-based humans does not imply that such postdigital humans do not exist. The sheer amount of today's AI research, its long-term nature (it takes years to properly develop and train AIs), and the commitment to secrecy in highly funded military and pharmaceutical laboratories (see Stewart 2018) indicates that we could soon face much more advanced forms of AI than those which are publicly available today. Moreover, the evolutionary nature of human development suggests that postdigital humans cannot be described in either–or terms—there should be at least some postdigital non-carbon-based humans, perhaps in early stages of evolutionary development, around us at the moment.

While we wait for non-carbon-based postdigital humans to emerge, postdigital *Homo sapiens* play and attend musical concerts and engage in visual arts, architecture, design, humanities, social sciences, natural sciences, and philosophy. Critical posthumanists working in education ask questions such as '[w]here does the human teacher leak into the algorithm, and where does the algorithm leak into the human teacher's practice?' (Bayne in Jandrić 2017: 206). They also propose the development of a Turing Teacher Test (Kupferman 2020). Transgender activists such as Paul B. Préciado (2013) and McKenzie Wark (2020) explore effects of digitally enabled biotechnology on their own bodies. Silicon-based AIs and non-tampered *Homo sapiens* are just extremes in a long continuum of diverse material configurations and bio-machine entanglements that can make up postdigital humans. The in-between configurations are theoretically and practically more complex, and arguably more interesting, than these clear-cut extremes. Situated at the fringes between the digital and the analog, postdigital theory fits with explorations that are at the postdigital edge of humanity.

Homo sapiens have been around for ca 300,000 years, but our civilization and culture, depending on inclusion criteria, are only a few thousand years old. Throughout that long period, our physical bodies have remained similar, and the main developments have happened within society and culture. Since the first proposal of the cyborg, however, humankind has become able 'to take an active part in [its] own biological evolution' (Clynes and Kline 1960: 29). This transforms human evolution 'from natural selection based on the Darwinian model of internal transmission to cultural or self-designed evolution based on an accelerated external transmission of information' (Peters and Jandrić 2019: 195). Today's postdigital humans are active participants in this new form of evolution. Therefore, Peters and I argue that as we are 'slowly but surely taking natural selection into our own hands', we need to be aware that 'these new powers bring about new responsibilities' (Peters and Jandrić 2019: 205).

These responsibilities can be approached in various ways. Computer scientists need to try to develop new versions of the Turing test, educators need to teach new generations, and artists need to explore new aesthetics. None of these tasks and approaches is more (or less) important than the other. With its radical postdisciplinary approaches, postdigital theory is burdened with numerous issues including but not limited to the obvious incommensurability of different understandings of knowledge within the disciplines drawn upon by this chapter. However, this epistemic burden is a price for opening up a new window of opportunity for identifying links and relationships between traditionally disconnected world views. Such is the nature of postdigital research, in which the high epistemic risk associated with linking the unlinkable is justified with a prize of reaching further than others (see Jandrić 2020a).

However, the key contribution of postdigital theory to studies of human beings is neither in its convenient positioning between the analog and the digital nor in benefits of radical postdisciplinarity. Deeply imbued in the tradition of critical pedagogy, postdigital theory does not stop at explaining the world—its key goal, and its key mission, is to actively participate in its development and to enable the widest spheres of society to participate as well. Therefore, the question, who is a postdigital human?, requires some urgent updates: What kind of postdigital humans do we want to become? What kind of future do we want for our postdigital children? Working at the intersections of diverse human interests and disciplinary approaches, postdigital theory has an important role in developing a wide consensus about the future of the postdigital human.

References

Alexemberg, M. L. (2011). *The Future of Art in a Postdigital Age: From Hellenistic to Hebraic Consciousness* (2nd ed.). Bristol, UK and Chicago, IL: Intellect.

Bayne, S., Evans, P., Ewins, R., Knox, J., Lamb, J., Macleod, H., O'Shea, C., Ross, J., Sheail, P., & Sinclair, C. (2020). *The Manifesto for Teaching Online*. Cambridge, MA: MIT Press.

Cascone, K. (2000). The aesthetics of failure: 'post-digital' tendencies in contemporary computer music. *Computer Music Journal, 24*(4), 12–18. https://doi.org/10.1162/014892600559489.

Chalmers, D. J. (1995). Facing up to the problem of consciousness. *Journal of Consciousness Studies, 2*(3), 200–219. https://doi.org/10.1093/acprof:oso/9780195311105.001.0001.

Chalmers, D. J. (1996). *The Conscious Mind: In Search of a Fundamental Theory*. Oxford: Oxford University Press.

Clynes, M. E., & Kline, N. S. (1960). Cyborgs and space. *Astronautics*, September. http://www.medientheorie.com/doc/clynes_cyborgs.pdf. Accessed 7 October 2020.

Cormier, D., Jandrić, P., Childs, M., Hall, R., White, D., Phipps, L., Truelove, I., Hayes, S., & Fawns, T. (2019). Ten Years of the Postdigital in the 52group: Reflections and Developments 2009–2019. *Postdigital Science and Education, 1*(2), 475–506. https://doi.org/10.1007/s42438-019-00049-8.

Ekici, E. (2014). Passing the Turing Test: Redefining What It Means to 'Think'. Wired. https://www.wired.com/insights/2014/08/passing-turing-test-redefining-means-think/. Accessed 7 October 2020.

Feenberg, A. (2019). Postdigital or Predigital? *Postdigital Science and Education, 1*(1), 8–9. https://doi.org/10.1007/s42438-018-0027-2.

Fuller, S. (2019). Against Academic Rentiership: a Radical Critique of the Knowledge Economy. *Postdigital Science and Education, 1*(2), 335–356. https://doi.org/10.1007/s42438-019-00035-0.

Fuller, S. (2020). Schrödinger's 'What Is Life?' As Postdigital Prophecy. *Postdigital Science and Education*. https://doi.org/10.1007/s42438-020-00149-w.

Fuller, S., & Jandrić, P. (2019). The Postdigital Human: Making the history of the future. *Postdigital Science and Education, 1*(1), 190–217. https://doi.org/10.1007/s42438-018-0003-x.

Gibson, W. (1984). *Neuromancer*. New York: Ace Books.

Graham, O., & Dowe, D. (2020). The Turing Test. In N. Zalta (Ed.), *The Stanford Encyclopedia of Philosophy*. https://plato.stanford.edu/archives/win2020/entries/turing-test/. Accessed 7 October 2020.

Hawking, S. (1996). Life in the universe. https://www.hawking.org.uk/in-words/lectures/life-in-the-universe. Accessed 7 October 2020.

Hruska, J. (2018). Did Google's Duplex AI Demo Just Pass the Turing Test? [Update]. ExtremeTech, 9 May. https://www.extremetech.com/computing/269030-did-google-duplexs-ai-demonstration-just-pass-the-turing-test. Accessed 7 October 2020.

Jandrić, P. (2017). *Learning in the Age of Digital Reason*. Rotterdam: Sense.

Jandrić, P. (2019). The Three Ages of the Digital. In D. R. Ford (Ed.), *Keywords in Radical Philosophy and Education* (pp.161–176). Leiden: Brill/Sense. https://doi.org/10.1163/978900440467_012.

Jandrić, P. (2020a). Postdigital Research Measurement. *Postdigital Science and Education, 3*(1), 15–26. https://doi.org/10.1007/s42438-020-00105-8.

Jandrić, P. (2020b). Postdigital Research in the Time of Covid-19. *Postdigital Science and Education, 2*(2), 233–238. https://doi.org/10.1007/s42438-020-00113-8.

Jandrić, P., & Hayes, S. (2019). The postdigital challenge of redefining education from the margins. *Learning, Media and Technology, 44*(3), 381–393. https://doi.org/10.1080/17439884.2019.1585874.

Jandrić, P., Knox, J., Besley, T., Ryberg, T., Suoranta, J., & Hayes, S. (2018). Postdigital Science and Education. *Educational Philosophy and Theory, 50*(10), 893–899. https://doi.org/10.1080/00131857.2018.1454000.

Jones, C. (2018). Experience and Networked Learning. In N. B. Dohn, S. Cranmer, J. A. Sime, M. de Laat, & T. Ryberg (Eds.), *Networked Learning: Reflections and Challenges* (pp. 39–55). Cham: Springer. https://doi.org/10.1007/978-3-319-74857-3_3.

Kupferman, D. W. (2020). I, robot teacher. *Educational Philosophy and Theory*. https://doi.org/10.1080/00131857.2020.1793534.

Kurzweil, R. (2005). *The Singularity Is Near: when humans transcend biology*. New York: Viking.

Levinson, P. (2019). Needed: a "Post-Post" Formulation. *Postdigital Science and Education, 1*(1), 14–16. https://doi.org/10.1007/s42438-019-0031-1.

McLaren, P. (2019). Reclaiming the Present or a Return to the Ash Heap of the Future? *Postdigital Science and Education, 1*(1), 10–13. https://doi.org/10.1007/s42438-018-0015-6.

Negroponte, N. (1998). Beyond digital. Wired, 12 January. https://web.media.mit.edu/~nicholas/Wired/WIRED6-12.html. Accessed 7 October 2020.

Nichols, M. (1967). *The Graduate* [Motion Picture]. Los Angeles: Lawrence Truman Productions.

Peters, M. A., & Besley, T. (2020). *Pandemic Education and Viral Politics*. London: Routledge.

Peters, M. A., & Jandrić, P. (2019). AI, Human Evolution, and the Speed of Learning. In J. Knox; Y. Wang, & M. Gallagher (Eds.), *Artificial Intelligence and Inclusive Education: speculative futures and emerging practices* (pp. 195-206). Springer Nature. https://doi.org/10.1007/978-981-13-8161-4_12.

Préciado, B. (2013). *Testo Junkie: Sex, Drugs, and Biopolitics in the Pharmacopornographic Era*. New York, NY: Feminist Press.

Rybicki, E. P. (1990). The classification of organisms at the edge of life, or problems with virus systematics. *South African Journal of Science, 86*(4), 182–186.

Sagan, C. (1973). *The Cosmic Connection: An Extraterrestrial Perspective*. New York: Doubleday.

Sample, I., & Hern, A. (2014). Scientists dispute whether computer 'Eugene Goostman' passed Turing test. The Guardian, 9 June. https://www.theguardian.com/technology/2014/jun/09/scientists-disagree-over-whether-turing-test-has-been-passed. Accessed 7 October 2020.

Searle, J. (1981). Minds, Brains, and Programs. *Behavioral and Brain Sciences, 3*, 417–457.

Sinclair, C., & Hayes, S. (2019). Between the post and the com-post: Examining the postdigital "work" of a prefix. *Postdigital Science and Education, 1*(1), 119–131. https://doi.org/10.1007/s42438-018-0017-4.

Stewart, P. (2018). Deep in the Pentagon, a secret AI program to find hidden nuclear missiles. Reuters, 5 June. https://uk.reuters.com/article/us-usa-pentagon-missiles-ai-insight-idUKKCN1J114J. Accessed 7 October 2020.

Turing, A. M. (1950). Computing Machinery and Intelligence. *Mind, 236*(LIX), 433–460. https://doi.org/10.1093/mind/LIX.236.433.

Venter, J. C. (2012). What Is Life? A 21st Century Perspective. On the 70th Anniversary of Schroedinger's Lecture at Trinity College. The Edge. https://www.edge.org/conversation/j_craig_venter-what-is-life-a-21st-century-perspective. Accessed 7 October 2020.

Wark, M. (2020). *Reverse Cowgirl*. Cambridge, MA: MIT Press.

Wikipedia (2020). Postdigital. https://en.wikipedia.org/wiki/Postdigital. Accessed 7 October 2020.

Williamson, B. (2019). Brain Data: Scanning, Scraping and Sculpting the Plastic Learning Brain Through Neurotechnology. *Postdigital Science and Education, 1*(1), 65–86. https://doi.org/10.1007/s42438-018-0008-5.

Part II
Postdigital Humans and Education

Experience of Using a Virtual Life Coach: A Case Study of Novice Users

Victoria Mason-Robbie

1 Introduction

This chapter explores a group of novice users' experience of using a Virtual Life Coach (VLC). A VLC is a chatbot accessed through the web or mobile phone, which can help with day-to-day personal, employment, and career issues, maintaining motivation and supporting retention. Users are able to interact with the VLC in order to gain on-demand, specific, and personalised information. A mixed methods case study evaluation enabled the views and experiences of users to be elucidated. In particular, qualitative enquiry revealed how the VLC can be an adjunct to the commonplace non-specific online interactions that are features of the postdigital world. Data were also collected in order to establish the essential requirements of a VLC, adoption preferences, and usage behaviour. The aim was to ascertain whether the technical, pedagogical, and valuable features of the VLC, and its personalisation, were able to support the well-being of users. Reflecting on the research process itself provides an illustration of the challenges faced by researchers in recruiting participants, an area previously explored by others (e.g. Arfken and Balon 2011; Hughes 1998).

The ubiquitous nature of technology may underpin an expectation that we are constantly connected, which could lead to the experience of technostress (e.g. La Torre et al. 2019; Weil and Rosen 1997). However, the dependence on virtual technologies—rather than contributing to so-called technostress—may provide a more democratic and inclusive opportunity to access a life coach. This is because access to a life coach could be seen as the preserve of the social elite, and thus a virtual manifestation of a life coach represents a democratisation of this otherwise unattainable experience. The extant literature helps to elucidate the relationship between

---

V. Mason-Robbie (✉)
School of Education, University of Worcester, Worcester, UK
e-mail: v.mason-robbie@worc.ac.uk

a VLC and the idea of postdigital humans, a construct laden with potentially conflicting meanings. However, as Jandrić et al. (2018: 896) point out, 'the contemporary use of the term "postdigital" does describe human relationships to technologies that we experience, individually and collectively, in the moment here and now. It shows our raising awareness of blurred and messy relationships between physics and biology, old and new media, humanism and posthumanism, knowledge capitalism and bio-informational capitalism'. The case study described here is embedded within this conceptualisation of the postdigital by providing an illustration of the relationship of users to the technology they are immersed in. Moreover, use of the VLC represents the entanglement of the human with its technological environment as explicated in posthumanism (e.g. Barad 2003), where one can conceptualise the relationship between the human and non-human as interwoven and bidirectional.

2 Background

Life coaching emerged during the 1990s (Williams 2003) and has since burgeoned into a large industry. In a review of the life coaching literature, Jarosz (2016) highlights the focus on wellness and health, and thus it tends to be forward-looking and positively orientated; focusing on the future rather than the past. Life coaching is not a therapeutic modality although there is debate around the boundary between life coaching for non-clinical populations and psychotherapy for people with a mental health condition (Aboujaoude 2020); however, for the present context, the VLC is firmly situated in the non-clinical domain. Inevitably, the life coach industry has moved towards and embraced the digital to extend its reach, although there is a distinction between online life coaching delivered by a human and life coaching via a chatbot interface (i.e. non-human). Online life coach services have proliferated over recent years, although many of these are run by life coach practitioners. A Virtual Life Coach has been applied in a range of contexts, including use with adolescents for life skills training (Gabrielli et al. 2020) and with breast cancer survivors (Hill et al. 2020). Furthermore, the efficacy of chatbots has been explored within a welfare and personal support context including personalisation (Kocaballi et al. 2019), anxiety and depression (Fitzpatrick et al. 2017), young people (Skjuve and Brandtzæg 2018), welfare, engagement and social good (Følstad et al. 2018), and trust in welfare and health (Wang and Siau 2018). Thus, the adaptability to different populations and contexts makes it a useful adjunct to other types of guidance and support, and the underlying technology and interface allow for scalability.

Whilst a virtual interface can provide support to users, moral issues emerge when considering the outsourcing of psychological support to such technology, when users might prefer face-to-face human interaction. The provision of information and anonymity might be an advantage to some individuals, although others may benefit from different modes of delivery. In addition to variation for preferences for online or face-to-face support, preferences may be context dependent so that it is not simply that a person prefers one or the other. However, the remit of the VLC is wider in that it also provides practical information that is quicker to obtain than asking another person, which therefore provides a pragmatic justification for its use. As well as moral concerns, philosophical issues emerge from the process of carrying out research and the extent to which this is able to tell us about underlying beliefs and attitudes, in addition to broader questions about the emergence of new technologies and the way in which humans intersect with these. This includes the sharing of information with non-human entities as a way in which humans can be helped. However, there may be equivalency between disclosure to a person or disclosure to a chatbot (Ho et al. 2018) highlighting how far the boundary between human and non-human has blurred.

3 Method

Participants engaged with the VLC on a number of occasions over a 3-month period. The number of interactions was dependent on the individuals' requirements; however, a minimum of one or two interactions per week was recommended. All data captured were used to support the individual and to evaluate the performance of the VLC, and participants had the opportunity to contribute ideas allowing for iterative development. For the evaluation itself, interviews (face-to-face and telephone) and focus groups were conducted, and usage logs of interaction with the VLC were analysed. The questions aimed to elucidate how the VLC operated technically and pedagogically and to identify the perceived advantages and disadvantages, and the most valued and significant features.

Recruitment and Data Collection

The research site was visited for the purpose of collecting material for content delivery and for the recruitment of participants between October 2019 and February 2020 (pre Covid-19 pandemic and first UK lockdown). Although recruitment was supported by two to three visits per month to the site by the project team, recruitment uptake was slower than expected. The site itself is situated in a rural location with a static population of employees who are both familiar with the site, the surrounding area, and with each other. This familiarity led to challenging recruitment conditions because the lack of desire for information and support became a barrier to participation. Consequently, this led to the recruitment of 47 participants with varying levels of engagement, despite participants being made aware that taking part would not disadvantage them with regard to either the support they received or their career and that they continued to be able to access the same support they normally have from human staff.

    A total of 47 participants engaged with the VLC. Twenty-three participants took part in 8 face-to-face interviews, 6 telephone interviews, and 2 focus groups. A semi-structured schedule was followed and included additional questions in response to participant comments and reactions. Thus, it enabled the researchers to gain a sense of the perceived value of the VLC and of the usefulness of particular areas. Topic areas included satisfaction with and views about the VLC, perceived support, and aspects of health, stress, and work–life balance. The purpose of the focus group was to provide information about different perspectives of the VLC, to document the range of ideas and opinions held, and to highlight any inconsistencies in and between the views of participants. The focus group method is particularly useful for understanding shared and common knowledge, enabling a deeper understanding of cultures and subcultures (Morgan and Kreuger 1993), and in this case diverse views about the VLC. All interviews and focus groups were recorded and transcribed for analysis.

The Virtual Life Coach

The VLC is a chat-based application aimed at improving well-being by helping personnel in their day-to-day activities and welfare needs. It is also intended to help with longer term welfare, well-being, and career planning needs, identifying when additional help may be needed, providing bite-sized learning to help meet those needs, and signposting to other online and human resources and services when appropriate. The content for the VLC was identified and created by domain experts and from trusted information sources such as the sponsor, subject matter experts, and stakeholders at the research site. Broad topics included welfare, the local area, services, career, and well-being.

Participants were requested to engage with the VLC at least once or twice per week for 2–10 min over a period of up to 3 months. The number of interactions per week was based on the users' self-identified individual needs and requirements and involved logging in to the mobile phone app or web-based service with their participant ID and password. Once logged in, the participant was presented with an interface that included a text input and response area similar to many messaging apps. From the outset, users were able to ask the chatbot questions on a range of topics using natural language (e.g. 'What should I do if…?'). These interactions could be as frequent or as short or long as required by the individual, and there were no set topics, but rather the individual requested help, information, and support on issues that they actually required.

During interaction with the VLC, an automated process monitored the conversational logs for keywords and phrases that raised concern for individuals who may be at risk. The exact implementation of this process included manual checking of identified logs and was agreed with the welfare staff at the research site. If required, participants could then be contacted by local welfare staff and signposted to human welfare support provision if required. No live incidents of this type occurred during the study.

Ongoing interaction with the VLC allowed participants to give feedback and comment on their experiences to highlight how the VLC could be improved for end users. The interaction phase of the study was iterative and worked on a 2-week cycle. Opportunities for feedback were provided through the focus groups, ad hoc feedback, and direct feedback. For the latter, the VLC enabled participants to provide feedback directly within the system by typing 'feedback' and using a text entry box, or by using a thumbs up or down to respond to different aspects of functionality. This was recorded in the conversational logs and flagged up to the developers to enable user-driven refinements to be made to the VLC in an iterative manner.

4 Results

Pattern of Use

Peaks in usage followed the project and welfare team promoting the study at the research site. Without encouragement, some participants were reticent to use the VLC. Anecdotal evidence suggested that this was because users thought they had 'no mental health problems' themselves, and thus a chatbot designed to promote well-being was seen through this lens. Indeed, this perception of the VLC by participants was confirmed by the qualitative analysis. Such reticence is important within the context of the postdigital because it highlights the complexity and ambivalence around the desire to use technology for specific ends or purposes. Indeed, it may even question the interconnectedness and dependence on technology.

Usage data suggest that 26 participants (55%) used the VLC on a single day; 11 participants (23%) used the VLC for 2 days; 5 participants (11%) used the VLC for 3–4 days; and 5 participants (11%) used the VLC for 10–19 days. Thus, over 20% of participants used the VLC on at least three separate days suggesting that time spent exploring content was of continued value. Further to the daily usage pattern, users could be divided up into groups according to their usage pattern. Marginal—21 participants (34%) interacted with the VLC fewer than 10 times; test—14 participants (30%) engaged with the VLC on 10–20 occasions; explore—15 participants (32%) explored the VLC content through 21–60 interactions; and sustained—2 participants (4%) had frequent (over 60) interactions with the VLC including wide-ranging use of the available content.

The thumbs up icon was used by 15 participants (representing 37% of user feedback) and was mostly in response to being offered the requested or a related resource, useful local information, or the interaction style of the VLC (e.g. allowing a user to choose a name to be referred to, or the VLC providing a message of the day or news item). The thumbs down icon was used by 8 participants (representing 31% of user feedback) where the VLC provided a failed response (i.e. not understanding user input), to highlight incorrect information (mainly local), or where the content item randomly chosen as the message of the day was judged by the user to be inappropriate (in both cases, it was describing support for issues around self-harming).

Where the VLC failed to respond to the user, 78% of the time this was due to not understanding user input. Where the VLC was not able to translate the user input into a valid request, this was typically due to an inability to parse the user input correctly or to a lack of relevant content (and associated keyword or phrase). Such responses from the VLC were accompanied by suggestions to rephrase the request or the offer of a set of menu or category options in order to prevent user frustration. Where such issues were identified by the log analysis, the development team changed the parsing or added new content to prevent these errors in the future and to ensure that the performance of the VLC was continually improving.

Qualitative Analysis

Regardless of their level of experience or attitude towards the role and usefulness of technology, participants are described as novice users, since they are *ipso facto* new users of this interface. Coding and analysis enabled the identification of common themes, which are as follows: understanding the purpose encapsulates issues about perceived relevance; aesthetic appeal refers to the appearance of the interface; ease of use and functionality relates to both positive and challenging aspects of using the VLC; finally, usefulness and importance address the challenges associated with enabling users to commit to regular use and broader issues around the content of the VLC. These themes underpin beliefs about the future of the VLC and are situated within the context of the broad assumptions of the postdigital.

Understanding the Purpose

Some of the participants described misunderstanding the purpose of the VLC, suggesting that they did not think the information was relevant to themselves or their peers (a static population who generally know the geographical area and amenities well). They also tended to assume that it was only for people with questions about their mental health and therefore not 'for them'. Notwithstanding individual differences and preferences, some participants described how they would speak with another person rather than using an app if they needed support. There was a sense that there needed to be something more to keep users coming back, particularly in the absence of a problem. This could be linked to a lack of reward, which could be seen as a form of extrinsic motivation; something that users of social media experience (e.g. feeling socially connected, experiencing social reinforcement from number of likes, comments, shares, and so on). The private nature of the VLC could therefore be counterproductive in allowing it to gain traction. The following view illustrates how the VLC did not feel relevant because the participant was familiar with the area.

Experience of Using a Virtual Life Coach: A Case Study of Novice Users   41

> ...at the moment it's not useful for me because I've been here for years and I know everything around here. I know the area and where to go. Where a new person, it's probably specific. But there's not that many new people that change over as frequently. So it might not get as many people looking into it until it actually goes live ... where you can get specific site information to follow.

Similarly, who might benefit and whether they feel motivated to continue to use the VLC is described as follows.

> So it's like Catch-22. It's going to benefit the new starters, but once they know the information, are they going to go back into the app and look for something else when they've got mates that will probably just tell them where to go. That's why I think it will be more useful in places like [CITY] or somewhere where there's a high turnover of staff and it's a town rather than in the middle of nowhere where I don't know that it would benefit that much.

Raising awareness of the VLC and keeping it current were also related to understanding its purpose and appreciating the different ways in which it might be helpful to people. For instance:

> I think it's pretty intuitive. It's just really a case of just making sure people use it, really. I mean the danger with these things is that if it's not advertised... and supported then it potentially could become good but not used, which is always a danger. I mean that can always be a problem. So you need to sort of keep it current. And I mean niche-wise, to somebody who has got people with problems and they need a little bit of advice or just need something to go to just to reconfirm that what they're doing is right, then yes, it may be a good little thing.

A more positive attitude was also expressed about understanding the purpose and appreciating that it would be of benefit to some individuals.

> So I've worked with a mental health service before joining the [CURRENT ORGANISATION], so I'm fairly knowledgeable about it. I can see the benefit of having the app in terms of we're talking a lot of people, if they had an issue they would just talk to someone. But if you're in a situation where you don't feel that you have anyone to talk to it's just a nice safe way of getting a bit of advice without it being awkward, I guess you could say.

This is echoed in the following.

> The bit that I probably interacted, as in got benefit from, was the well-being stuff. I think, when I interacted with that. Which was quite interesting. Yes, some of the exercises that it was proposing. It made me think probably, because it was interrogating me, in a nice way, it was actually making me think about it more, rather than just a... How would you feel today. You know, what's stressing you at the moment? You can put it in, then there was actually some relevant stuff like that. Oh, that's good, I hadn't thought of that. And then it's like, how is this manifesting itself?

Taken together, these extracts provide support for the idea that some participants were unsure about the purpose of the VLC within their own context, yet saw the value of it more broadly. Enhancing perceived relevance and providing built-in rewards through for example social reinforcement would be strategies to increase uptake and maintain usage over time. Such continued use over time may itself provide reinforcement for sustained use if the VLC was perceived as relevant and beneficial.

Aesthetic Appeal

The VLC was described as not being aesthetically pleasing. In comparison to other apps, the VLC was described as being text heavy, and there was a desire for softer bubbles; more colours, videos, and style of chat; and more than just a link to other sites (and this despite the fact that early engagement with staff suggested that a more business-like approach would be preferred). The interface was described as too basic compared with, for example Wysa[1] or Headspace.[2] Such views were reflective of the user experience of the interface and what people have come to expect from their more general online experience. The gap between past experience, expectations, and current experience thus presents a challenge because users have grown accustomed to a sophisticated online experience, which they expect, regardless of level of technical knowledge (i.e. they may not appreciate the level of sophistication behind the interface that they see).

The following participant described the interface as 'text heavy' and expressed a desire for it to be more aesthetically pleasing.

> It could be have looked a bit more aesthetically pleasing. I felt that it could be a bit more interesting on the eye. Maybe breaking up the text a bit more and making it a bit more colourful...I like things to look colourful and interesting. It looked like a text message... Well, I was impressed with how quick it was coming back. It was really prompt in getting back to me. And it was easy to use, definitely. I don't know if maybe it was a bit text-heavy at times, and it could have looked a bit more aesthetically pleasing. It's, I don't know... I felt maybe it could be a little bit more interesting on the eye. But, certainly, in terms of how quick it was, it was very prompt and easy to use, definitely.

Individual preferences, for example a desire for the visual aspects of the app to be more salient than the text, were expressed.

> But I'm definitely more visual, and having things to click on, rather than just ask the question, I would prefer that.

Furthermore, suggestions were made for the possibility of being able to personalise the VLC so that it feels both familiar and more welcoming.

> I think if you had the ability to personalise it possibly in terms of fonts and colours and such like, that might help. It felt... I'll say basic, but that's not necessarily a bad thing... So I think possibly the ability to personalise it, maybe put your own wallpaper on the background. Especially if it retains that textable that it allows you to, right, I'm in a comfortable, safe space, so maybe not basic, maybe slightly sterile might be a better phrase. Which again could be good. Could be bad. I think if people wanted to use it for genuine well-being concerns, I think something slightly more welcoming... And it feels more like a safe space. Rather than maybe being something more clinical.

Thus, aesthetic appeal was important to people, and a pleasing interface may help to enhance engagement and promote sustained use over time. Echoing the theme about the purpose of the VLC and the importance of rewards, an appealing

---

[1] See https://www.wysa.io/. Accessed 15 October 2020.
[2] See https://www.headspace.com/. Accessed 15 October 2020.

interface may also act as a reward in itself if the VLC is enjoyable to interact with visually.

Ease of Use and Functionality

Perceived ease of use generated quite dichotomous views. Some described the VLC as easy, quick, and intuitive, whilst others found it difficult to use. Those finding it difficult described having problems logging in, and they felt that it needed buttons or a drop-down menu to guide them to other areas. Furthermore, navigating back to a particular point rather than having to go back to the beginning was expressed as being important as this was a source of frustration. Ease of use appears to be associated with the emotional aspect of engaging with the VLC as frustration is likely to deter people from further use if there is an easier alternative (e.g. an internet search engine). This latter point is important because participants described the ease at which they would take out their phone and use Google to find some information: an action that is quick and requires few steps.

This participant thought they would be more likely to use a search engine than the VLC to find information.

> *I just looked at more of information to see how to use it and what was available. It just points you in the right direction. Whether I'd use it continuously I'm not sure because it's just as quick to go into Google and find out that information. If you wanted to check something rather than get on a computer to log on [in] to then ask that computer a question, by the time I've done that I could have gone on my phone and just googled it.*

The need to go through several steps to find the information was seen as a barrier to use as the following illustrates.

> *It's okay. It gave you the information you needed and that you were looking for. But I don't know. It's just more of the fact that when you want to find something you want to find it straightaway. Whereas you have to ask it a question and then it asks you another question to find specific information on what you were looking for. Rather than just being able to ask the question and get the answer you wanted; it asks you another question to find out specific information on what direction to point you to.*

Similarly, this participant thought that there were too may click throughs to get where you wanted to.

> *There needs to be less [fewer] click throughs...it was a bit clunky, it needed to be smoother for the click throughs.*

Similar issues with functionality are echoed by the following.

> *And it gave you various things to click on, and one of them was a video that wouldn't play on the system, which was a bit of a bugbear... Even though you were working through the stress thing, I found that if I clicked I want to ask another question, it took me totally away from where I wanted to be. And I would have had to start the series again from the beginning.*

Ease of use and functionality is also related to the motivation to keep using the VLC.

> *I go back to the same. Easy to use, it's great. But it's when it comes back with something unrelated that it throws you a bit, and then you get sort of... Well, why am I asking it that question, because it's not giving me what I'm asking for. So then you put it down... Yes. So there's a lot of good things about it, but it throws you. You can't lose patience when you can't get the answer you want to, you put it down and go somewhere else.*

Conversely, this highlights the ease of use and a perception that it worked well.

> *Oh, it's dead easy to use. I mean you just put a word in and it will come back with a load of options. You don't even have to type the whole sentence in, which literally is quite easy. Say for example at Monday I was on it at five o'clock in the morning just putting in snow and it brought up our snow and ice line which is what I was after because the weather was bad. And I just rung the line to see what the update was. So it's got that element. So it works quite well.*

Similarly, the following perspective shows how it was seen as easy to use and intuitive, but with the caveat that it was robotic and lacked the nuances present in human–human interaction. However, this is perhaps *ipso facto* the case.

> *Functionality was no problem. No problems at all. It's very intuitive. It's click this box and then that brings up other boxes. I think, as well, it's a bit robotic... It's not like when you're talking to somebody at the other end of a phone, and you can interact with them, it's either press this box or don't press a box at all. There are no nuances.*

As with aesthetic appeal, ease of use and functionality were important and illustrate that views and experience varied across individuals. Indeed, notwithstanding criticisms, Davis' Technology Acceptance Model (TAM) highlights that computer acceptance is related to both perceived usefulness and ease of use (Davis 1989). Both facets appear to be supported by the views expressed by participants in this study and, taken positively, highlight the usefulness of feedback for further development because such issues are likely to be resolvable.

Usefulness and Importance

A belief was expressed about the potential importance and usefulness of the VLC in principle, in contrast to views about it not being helpful in practice. This echoed understanding the purpose described above, because it was challenging to get people to use the VLC if they only saw it as supporting mental health. Furthermore, where users were local, the motivation to use the VLC to ascertain local information was low. In contrast, however, when life stress was being experienced by the user, the sleep and resilience information and videos were seen as helpful. However, some interviewees reported that they did not find these, or were not able to watch the videos once they had found them. In the interviews, there was a dichotomy between those who found it useful and those that did not; although it was not possible to generalise, the latter group described their frustration about aspects of functionality which prevented them from finding it useful, or described something about their typical mode of help-seeking, e.g. talking to somebody face-to-face rather than going online. This suggests that the VLC might be more suited to people who prefer to seek information and anonymous support, rather than have a conversation with another person.

An account of the usefulness was given by the following participant.

> *I'm probably going to have to play with it a little bit more just to see how it works and a little bit more of that. What I've used it for, what I've found particularly good was that I was looking into sleep and how it takes you into the meditation. And one of the five-minute meditation things that's on there, the relaxation and meditation type of thing, that was quite good. Yes, I found that quite useful for me. I mean for me personally it was just getting used to using the chatbots to then get into the links that then take you to the information.*

Similarly, the following suggests that it would be a useful complement to existing channels of communicating with new personnel and a more interesting way to share information than traditional methods of communication.

> *Overall, it is useful... it's an extra resource for getting information to people...The bare bones are there, it just needs fleshing out. It's like a local version of Google really.*

In contrast, it was also described as something that was forgotten about.

> *To be honest, I keep forgetting I've got it... what I wanted [swimming timetable, weather forecast] wasn't there...I'm not used to having anything like that available.*

In addition, the following highlights an absence of a need for it.

> *To be honest, I didn't really use it that much after the initial download and kind of quick session. I never really felt the need of it really.*

This theme reflects the issue of stakeholder engagement or approval in using the VLC. User buy-in is required, where users feel committed, engaged, and willing to use the VLC. Furthermore, it requires being committed to the idea of the VLC as something that provides an important source of information and support and that is useful in everyday life—likely to underpin the motivation to use it. There may be differences between the types of people who engage and those who do not based on their own characteristics and their typical mode of help-seeking, in addition to the familiarity with the context that they are working in, which in this case seemed to work against the desire to use the VLC.

5 Discussion

This discussion explores users' engagement with the VLC, but is situated in the context of postdigital humans. The findings challenge the smooth interrelationship between the human and the digital by creating some resistance and discord both within the research participation itself, and in engagement with the VLC. Regular use was low, which reflects the level of engagement. The qualitative data from the interviews and focus groups provide explanatory value in understanding this pattern, mainly in terms of perceived use, value, and its aesthetic appeal. Furthermore, use of the VLC did not provide sufficient reward in and of itself to motivate continued use, which echoes research identifying the importance of enjoyment and the presence of others in predicting attitudes towards using a social networking site for communicating with others (Jaafar et al. 2014).

Internal factors such as motivation and external factors such as a social obligation may partially explain the intention to engage with both the research and the technology. With so much digital technology competing for our finite attention, it is not surprising that users wish to exercise some control or freedom in making choices. Indeed, this idea is underpinned by self-determination theory (Deci and Ryan 1985; Ryan and Deci 2000) where enjoyment and satisfaction drive intrinsic motivation and rewards, in contrast to seeking approval and the desire for competition which are said to drive extrinsic motivation. Intrinsic motivation can be seen as more personal and asocial, whereas extrinsic motivation is an internal representation of our social nature and relationships. In the present study, these two facets of motivation may help to explain the relatively low uptake of the research and use of the VLC; curious users who wish to seek information and support may be more intrinsically motivated than those who see it as an additional unwanted task.

Further to ideas around motivation, providing opportunities for engaging with novel technology contrasts with naturalistic observation of technology use, i.e. a person's typical technology use pattern. This dichotomy is important because the expectation of use may engender ambivalence, in contrast to where technology is used through one's own desire and volition. Thus, the locus of causality (Legault 2016) can shift between these types of motivation to bring about behaviour. This is important for two reasons; first to help explain the relatively low uptake of the research itself and second, within the context of this to elucidate why participants were not motivated to be what we describe as sustained users. Once engaged in the study itself, and the potential obligation that this entails, use varied considerably on a spectrum between marginal use, test use, exploratory use, and sustained use.

Turning to the qualitative analysis of the interview and focus group data, the purposes of the VLC, its aesthetic appeal, ease of use and functionality, and usefulness and importance were identified as important to users. These themes underpin beliefs about the future potential of the VLC; in particular, that it was important but that the brief was too wide in terms of functionality and content. It would have been better if it had focused on fewer topics, e.g. well-being or careers. Furthermore, motivating use by promoting either intrinsic or extrinsic motivation may lead to users finding it helpful who otherwise were not willing to try. Expressed views were somewhat idiosyncratic, which might in part be due to the demographic and the relatively static nature of the population (e.g. long duration of service, low turnover of staff). Despite some views about the importance of the VLC, the brief or purpose was seen as wide in relation to the diversity of personnel who might be using it. Providing a VLC that meets diverse needs is more challenging than providing a specific range of possibilities to a relatively homogenous group of individuals who share some common characteristics (e.g. new recruits or employees).

The location, diverse range of personnel, and relatively static population made the relevance of the VLC more difficult to promote to encourage sustained use by participants. This was because personnel were familiar with the local area and were generally aware of the mental health and well-being support available, which were the main aspects of the available content. Thus, targeting a more specific population (for example those who have just completed training) because they share similar characteristics, are more comfortable with online activities, and are generally unfamiliar with their location might have yielded a greater number of participants. Whether the interface should differ for different categories of users would be a question for further research; however, the challenge remains regarding the level of specificity—whether the VLC has a broad enough application, an extensive quantity of information would be required. This also presents a challenge to the extent to which individual users feel that it is relevant to them, unless they are able to personalise the interface and their experience of using it. Many online and app-based services allow for personalisation, and so this is something that users come to expect.

Encouraging frequent use (rather than simply as-needed) through incentives may lead to greater use, and in the absence of such incentives or rewards, actual use is a more accurate reflection of the desire to use it and of the perceived usefulness. The private nature of interactions with the VLC may be counterproductive because there is an absence of reward or social reinforcement which echoes the desire for the presence of others as a predictor of attitudes towards using online environments for communication (Jaafar et al. 2014). Enhancing the contribution of the users in early development phases may prove fruitful in this regard. In addition to building in an element of social reinforcement to promote intrinsic motivation (e.g. 'it is useful so I keep going back to it', 'I am rewarded by its usefulness and the information it provides') and extrinsic motivation to use it (e.g. others are using it, and it helps me to feel connected to other people online and this social element provides an incentive to keep using it).

Competing with the ubiquity and reliance on Google and other search engines to create an accessible and responsive alternative option is a challenge that remains. Internet search engines may already be seen as the most direct route for both local and national information and as way of finding resources that support mental health. However, many of the issues identified by the users are surmountable; particularly improving the aesthetic appeal, providing incentives for engagement, and understanding the scope and purpose of the VLC. More challenging is the promotion of continued engagement and the prevention of frustration in the way users experience the flow of information; these all present barriers to successful development, testing, and use.

Overall, for the VLC to be used to its full potential, sponsors, users, and potential users must engage with and be committed to the idea, purpose, and principle of it and find it useful to them when seeking the answer to questions or when seeking knowledge and information. Research suggests that although the number of mental health apps installed by people and the daily active minutes of use may seem high, only a small portion of users actually used the apps for a long period of time (Baumel et al. 2019). Further research is needed to understand this phenomenon and the ways in which users engage in self-management in real-world settings. Apps must also be pleasing and rewarding to use through being intuitive and accessible, in addition to providing potential stress-relief rather than being a potential stressor in the form of frustration—akin to so-called *technostress* (Weil and Rosen 1997). Improvements to the interface and functionality of apps will also encourage sustained and regular use and demonstrate value. Indeed, relatively simple changes such as adding a drop-down menu and being able to register with a personal email address to aid password recovery improve functionality (Bonneau et al. 2015).

Fortunately, the fieldwork for this research was carried out prior to the Covid-19 pandemic which provides a context for explaining the results. Whilst this type of research is dependent on the use of technology, it still requires interpersonal engagement—which would not have been possible after March 2020. Our lives have taken a further leap beyond the postdigital given our even greater reliance on technology for communicating and working. Such wider influences inevitably impact our social lives and our attitudes towards virtual technologies. Whilst our current epoch can be described as postdigital, the need for face-to-face interpersonal interaction is not obviated, rather it complements our dependency on technology. Indeed, what the Covid-19 pandemic has shown is that our reliance on technology is not enough—people need human interaction. Moreover, as the technology landscape changes, there remain differences in level of engagement and willingness to use technology across different age groups; however, the picture is nuanced as a study of students in a Higher Education setting shows. Whilst attitudes towards technology do not differ amongst mature and non-mature students, mature students actually use fewer technologies and use them less often than their non-mature counterparts, although effect sizes are modest (Staddon 2020). Overall, the desire to use a VLC is variable and even low amongst certain individuals; reasons include a preference for face-to-face interactions as sources of support and guidance, and not seeing oneself as a user of technology. Thus, preferences and identity are also important drivers of behaviour, in addition to motivation when considering technology use within a postdigital context.

Challenges, Implications, and Recommendations

Low engagement and technical barriers to access presented challenges to the execution of the research. As we look to an uncertain future, there are likely to be further challenges involved in carrying out fieldwork given restrictions placed upon face-to-face interaction. This presents a remarkable opportunity for virtual technology to be developed, tested, and implemented within the postdigital landscape. The VLC as both a tool and a concept is potentially an important source of support and information; however, at present its brief may be too wide. Thus, there is a trade-off between breadth and depth to maximise perceived relevance. Engaging users and potential users to access and maintain use could help to reinforce the benefits of continued use, particularly amongst those who do not perceive it to be useful in the first instance, and it may need to be presented differently for diverse groups of users. If functionality issues were successfully resolved, it may be useful for people who do not have anyone to talk too, i.e. a safe way/space to obtain advice. There may be important differences between those who would use a VLC for well-being support and those who prefer face-to-face interaction; such individual preferences with respect to help-seeking are likely to impact on who uses the VLC and when. March and colleagues (2018) found a preference for face-to-face over e-mental health services, despite there being a higher intention to use e-mental health services in the future. Such a gap between preferences, intentions, and behaviour highlights the complexity of help-seeking behaviour. Furthermore, studies show that help-seeking behaviour differs across groups where males and young people are less likely to seek help (e.g. Oliver et al. 2005).

The analysis of accounts of the experience and use patterns suggests that there is a need to identify where the need for a VLC might be greatest. A clear and focused unique selling point is required to ensure that it can compete with other apps—this is particularly important in a dynamic, competitive, and crowded market. Working closely with users to enhance motivation to use and increase understanding of the purpose and scope of the VLC, including built-in rewards or incentives may help to bring about more sustained use. Modifying the interface to improve aesthetic appeal, including the potential to adapt or personalise the interface for people with different preferences, may prove fruitful and make it more welcoming and rewarding to use (Kocaballi et al. 2019). For example the VLC requires people to have a degree of emotional literacy and to be able to articulate what they are thinking and feeling; an ability that varies across individuals from those who are very able to those with alexithymia. Jain et al. (2018) found that users of chatbots found the mixture of text and buttons natural and engaging, highlighting that text alone may limit the appeal of an interface.

Although individual preferences vary, a comparison between a chatbot-style life coach and other modes such as online or face-to-face with a person would be useful; however, once developed, the chatbot has greater potential to reach a larger number of individuals than the very limited reach and resource heavy approach of using a trained human coach. Indeed, other chatbot-based services including Woebot have applied cognitive behaviour therapy in young adults with symptoms of anxiety and depression (Fitzpatrick et al. 2017). Although this is the specific use of a well-tested therapeutic technique and once again highlights the fine-line between life coaching and psychotherapy, it demonstrates that there is great potential in the virtual mode of delivery, particularly in promoting well-being, signposting, and in the training and retention of staff.

6 Conclusion

Adopting a chatbot-style life coach to support personal and work-related challenges provided an opportunity to explore use patterns and user views. In so doing, this chapter has addressed some of the challenges faced by developers, employers, researchers, and users in the context of both training and practice. It appears that it is not life coaching per se that is in question, but the technical/digital side and practicalities that pertain to this. The challenge for developers is to ensure that users have a desire to use the technology and that they trust the information that it provides them; particularly in the context of education and training. For employers, to use the technology to enhance the well-being of their employees or trainees, to develop skills, and to improve retention are potentially important and complementary goals. Finally, for researchers, the challenge is to continue to enable research to effectively capture and disentangle the digital from the user (if this is desirable or possible), whilst retaining a sense of the human at the centre of the technological milieu.

Philosophical questions remain about the way such technology shapes the human condition and impacts on selfhood and social relationships. Obviating the need for others when technology can answer questions and thus contributing to fewer face-to-face interactions and social de-skilling can be contrasted with the fruitful, complex, and complementary relationship between humans and technology that characterises the postdigital. Conceptions of postdigital are likely to evolve concurrently with the technology underpinning the existence and manifestation of virtual life coach technology, in conjunction with the way users interact with and utilise such technology in their everyday lives.

References

Aboujaoude, E. (2020). Where Life Coaching Ends and Therapy Begins: Toward a Less Confusing Treatment Landscape. *Perspectives on Psychological Science, 15*(4), 973–977. https://doi.org/10.1177/1745691620904962.
Arfken, C. L., & Balon, R. (2011). Declining Participation in Research Studies. *Psychother Psychosom, 80*, 325–328. https://doi.org/10.1159/000324795.
Barad, K. (2003). Posthumanist Performativity: Toward an Understanding of How Matter Comes to Matter. *Signs: Journal of Women in Culture and Society, 28*(3), 808. https://doi.org/10.1086/345321.
Baumel, A., Muench, F., Edan, S., & Kane, J. M. (2019). Objective User Engagement With Mental Health Apps: Systematic Search and Panel-Based Usage Analysis. *Journal of Medical Internet Research, 21*(9), e14567. https://doi.org/10.2196/14567.
Bonneau, J., Bursztein, E., Caron, I., Jackson, R., & Williamson, M. (2015). Secrets, lies, and account recovery: Lessons from the use of personal knowledge questions at Google. In *Proceedings of the 24th international conference on world wide web* (pp. 141–150). https://doi.org/10.1145/2736277.2741691.
Davis, F. D. (1989). Perceived usefulness, perceived ease of use, and user acceptance of information technology. *MIS Quarterly, 13*(3), 319–340. https://doi.org/10.2307/249008.
Deci, E. L., & Ryan, R. M. (1985). *Intrinsic motivation and self-determination in human behavior*. New York: Plenum Press.
Fitzpatrick, K. K., Darcy, A., & Vierhile, M. (2017). Delivering Cognitive Behavior Therapy to Young Adults With Symptoms of Depression and Anxiety Using a Fully Automated Conversational Agent (Woebot): A Randomized Controlled Trial. *The Journal of Medical Internet Research Mental Health, 4*(2), e19. https://doi.org/10.2196/mental.7785.
Følstad, A., Brandtzaeg, P. B., Feltwell, T., Law, E. L., Tscheligi, M., & Luger, E. A. (2018). Sig: Chatbots for social good. In *Extended Abstracts of the 2018 CHI Conference on Human Factors in Computing Systems* (pp. 1–4). https://doi.org/10.1145/3170427.3185372.

Gabrielli, S., Rizzi, S., Carbone, S., & Donisi, V. (2020). A Chatbot-Based Coaching Intervention for Adolescents to Promote Life Skills: Pilot Study. *The Journal of Medical Internet Research Human Factors, 7*(1), e16762. https://doi.org/10.2196/16762.

Hill, C. K., Luu, T., & Bourdeanu, L. (2020). Abstract P1-17-15: OWL: Own your wellness and living platform - An artificial intelligence virtual well-being supporting coach for breast cancer survivors. *Cancer Res, 80*(4), P1-17-15. https://doi.org/10.1158/1538-7445.SABCS19-P1-17-15.

Jain, M., Kumar, P., Kota, R., & Patel, S. N. (2018). Evaluating and informing the design of chatbots. In *Proceedings of the 2018 Designing Interactive Systems Conference* (pp. 895–906). https://doi.org/10.1145/3196709.3196735.

Kocaballi, A. B., Berkovsky, S., Quiroz, J. C., Laranjo, L., Tong, H. L., Rezazadegan, D., Briatore, A., & Coiera, E. (2019). The Personalization of Conversational Agents in Health Care: Systematic Review. *Journal of Medical Internet Research, 21*(11), e15360. https://doi.org/10.2196/15360.

Ho, A., Hancock, J., & Miner, A. (2018). Psychological, Relational, and Emotional Effects of Self-Disclosure After Conversations With a Chatbot. *Journal of Communication, 68*. https://doi.org/10.1093/joc/jqy026.

Hughes, R. (1998). Why do people agree to participate in social research? The case of drug injectors. *International Journal of Social Research Methodology, 1*(4), 315–324. https://doi.org/10.1080/13645579.1998.10846883.

Jaafar, N. I., Darmawan, B., & Mohamed Ariffin, M. Y. (2014). Face-to-face or not-to-face: A technology preference for communication. *Cyberpsychology, Behavior and Social Networking, 17*(11), 702–708. https://doi.org/10.1089/cyber.2014.0098.

Jandrić, P., Knox, J., Besley, T., Ryberg, T., Suoranta, J., & Hayes, S. (2018). Postdigital Science and Education. *Educational Philosophy and Theory, 50*(10), 893–899. https://doi.org/10.1080/00131857.2018.1454000.

Jarosz, J. (2016). What is life coaching? An integrative review of the evidence-based literature. *International Journal of Evidence Based Coaching and Mentoring, 14*(1), 34–56.

La Torre, G., Esposito, A., Sciarra, I., et al. (2019). Definition, symptoms and risk of techno-stress: a systematic review. *International Archives of Occupational and Environmental Health, 92*, 13–35. https://doi.org/10.1007/s00420-018-1352-1.

Legault, L. (2016). Intrinsic and Extrinsic Motivation. In V. Zeigler-Hill & T. K. Shackelford (Eds.), *Encyclopedia of Personality and Individual Differences*. Cham: Springer. https://doi.org/10.1007/978-3-319-28099-8_1139-1.

March S, Day J, Ritchie G, Rowe A, Gough J, Hall T, Yuen CYJ, Donovan CL, Ireland M, (2018). Attitudes Toward e-Mental Health Services in a Community Sample of Adults: Online Survey. J Med Internet Res;20(2):e59 https://www.jmir.org/2018/2/e59; https://doi.org/10.2196/jmir.9109

Morgan, D. L., & Kreuger, R. A. (1993). When to use focus groups and why. In S. F. Groups (Ed.), *D. L. Morgan*. London: Sage.

Ryan, R. M., & Deci, E. L. (2000). Self-determination theory and the facilitation of intrinsic motivation, social development, and well-being. *American Psychologist, 55*, 68–78. https://psycnet.apa.org/doi/10.1037/0003-066X.55.1.68.

Skjuve, M., & Brandtzæg, P. B. (2018). Chatbots as a new user interface for providing health information to young people. In Y. Andersson, U. Dalquist, & J. Ohlsson (Eds.), *Youth and news in a digital media environment–Nordic-Baltic perspectives*. Gothenburg: Nordicom. https://www.nordicom.gu.se/sites/default/files/kapitel-pdf/06_bjaalandskjuve_brandtzaeg.pdf. Accessed 15 October 2020.

Staddon, R. V. (2020). Bringing technology to the mature classroom: age differences in use and attitudes. *International Journal of Educational Technology in Higher Education, 17*, 11. https://doi.org/10.1186/s41239-020-00184-4.

Oliver, M., Pearson, N., Coe, N., & Gunnell, D. (2005). Help-seeking behaviour in men and women with common mental health problems: Cross-sectional study. *British Journal of Psychiatry, 186*(4), 297–301. https://doi.org/10.1192/bjp.186.4.297.

Wang, W., & Siau, K. (2018). Living with Artificial Intelligence–Developing a Theory on Trust in Health Chatbots. In *Proceedings of the Sixteenth Annual Pre-ICIS Workshop on HCI Research in MIS*. San Francisco, CA: Association for Information Systems. https://aisel.aisnet.org/sighci2018/4.

Weil, M. M., & Rosen, L. D. (1997). *Technostress: coping with technology @ work @ home @ play*. London: Wiley.

Williams, P. (2003). The potential perils of personal issues in coaching: The continuing debate: Therapy or Coaching? What every coach must know. *International Journal of Coaching in Organisations, 2*(2), 21–30.

Venturing Beyond the Imposition of a Postdigital, Anti-human Higher Education

Richard Hall

1 Introduction: The Morbidity of Higher Education

The idea of higher education (HE) suffers from increasing scrutiny, grounded in narratives of productivity, value-for-money, human capital development, impact, entrepreneurship, and on and on. These narratives have been amplified as national and international systems of HE have been folded into the circuits of capitalist expansion. Whilst the rollback of state-based, public funding, at least in the form of grants to students or institutions, continues to be replaced by discourses predicated upon debt, there has also been a rollout of governance and regulation for marketised or marketable outcomes. Increasingly, the symbolism of HE reflects the primacy of atomised and devolved responsibility for sustaining an existence that is mediated in economistic terms.

In the global North, the interconnected processes of rollback of the idea of the public and rollout of the idea of the private have been stress-tested by individual, institutional, national, and international responses to: first, the global financial crisis that erupted after the collapse of Lehman Brothers in 2007, and the subsequent implementation of austerity as a political decision; and second, the Covid-19 pandemic and its impact on human relations and mutuality. These two crises, of finance capital and epidemiology, historically and materially affect the forms, cultures, and activities of universities and colleges, which are caught between the compulsion to develop economic value and their role as sites of humane values (Hall 2020a). In this, there is a struggle over the responsibilities of HE in social reproduction and trust in its institutions to deliver.

One way in which this antagonism between economic value and humane values might be illustrated is in terms of the digital lives of the staff and students who

---

R. Hall (✉)
Education Division, De Montfort University, Leicester, UK
e-mail: rhall1@dmu.ac.uk

labour in HE. There is a long history of considering how to integrate technology into HE, often predicated upon the idea that it increases personalisation, employability, or work-readiness, or that it builds capacity for new communities of practice and networks (Weller 2020). During the politics of austerity, a sense of technology as enhancement in curriculum design, delivery, and assessment, or the student experience, gave way to risk-based approaches for the assurance of governance and regulation surrounding the digital University (Johnston et al. 2018). This subsequently amplified critiques of the relationship between education and the digital, in particular focused upon racism and intersectional injustices, alongside the lived realities of surveillance and control (Noble 2018; Watters 2021).

This contested idea of the integration of the digital into educational contexts crystallises around data, and in particular performance data. Conversations around the promise of data-enriched monitoring and performance management have emerged in relation to human agency and behavioural changes in academic practice or student engagement (Williamson 2020). For instance, flows of data enable assertions to be made around the causes of attrition, progression, or achievement for students or groups of students and for new services to be developed around those data and assumptions. This materially affects the work of staff inside universities, as digital technologies change the ways in which individuals relate to themselves and each other and the nature of their data-managed work. The integration of digital tools with technocratic modes of managing activities has further coalesced around the idea of the Platform University, inside which technologies, flows of data, modes of quantifying lived experiences, the norms of behavioural science, and algorithmic governance interact to reinforce dominant discourses (Boyd 2017; Hall 2020b).

The ability to collect clean, controlled data from individuals and groups is crucial in creating use-values as the basis for new educational commodities, either as spin-outs and knowledge transfer from inside institutions or as services from which external partners can extract rents in the form of licences. This represents a particular movement of digital practice in relation to human, material history. In order to understand the impact of this particular instantiation upon the construction of HE in an era of intersecting crises, it needs to be situated against the reproduction of capitalism as the organising principle of society. This speaks to a world in which the idea of the postdigital relates to modes of being, knowing, and doing in the world that are governed by an anti-human totality (Holloway 2019).

Here, the ways in which the digital and human are integrated or refused inside the forms, cultures, and activities of the HE institution, or inside the identities of the individual or her communities, speaks to the wider relationships between *both* the individual, her communities and institutions, *and* capitalist social relations. In responding to the intersection of financial and epidemiological crises (and ignoring crises of nature and the environment), these modes of integration and refusal are amplified. For instance, universities and colleges moved to close campuses and yet maintain business-as-usual online in response to the pandemic. Yet, the reality is of institutions acting individually rather than collectively, in exploring how: to manage everyday engagement in a curriculum; to manage pedagogic practice mediated through screens as a form of personal protective equipment; to build teams whilst caring for the self and others; and to pivot online or return to campus (Chitty et al. 2020).

In both the financial crisis and the pandemic, uncertainty was instantaneously injected into the ability of national and international HE sectors, alongside individual institutions, to provide a controlled ecosystem for growth (Kornbluh 2020). It is clear that the digital terrain offered some kind of safety net, but not one in which that terrain was fully integrated to minimise risk to the system of capital. If there is a postdigital reality in HE, it is framed competitively, through which institutional independence pivots around the systemic desire for certainty, and the reduction of risk that the institution and its labourers will not meet their targets, whatever their physical and emotional circumstances.

This re-focusing upon the relationship between human and the digital, at the crux of the idea of a postdigital life, highlights the deep complexities of an individual's engagement with their higher learning. This engagement is shaped by personal identity and history, cultures and contexts, communities and structures, and works as a mediated dialogue grounded in power. The power of the institution over the educational lives of its students and the working lives of its staff is affected by its own performative desires for impact and excellence and its response to the desires of networks of policymakers, private finance capital, technology companies, spin-out operations, media corporations, local communities, and so on. This power shapes the relationship between the institution and the individual who labours inside it and contributes to the agency of those individuals.

It is in these relationships that the idea of a postdigital HE might be analysed in terms of its anti-humanism. In developing this position and looking beyond it, this chapter explores the relationship between the political economics of the University in relation to authoritarian forms of governance, with a focus upon the postdigital human as manufactured both for and by economic value. The chapter examines whether humanist narratives of solidarity, in particular from marginalised voices, and the idea of composting might help academics and students to analyse their alienated educational existences, compromised rather than liberated by technology, in order to imagine that other worlds are possible.

Such a conversation is important because in the intersection of normalised austerity and the Covid-19 outbreak, the reality of HE has been revealed as pathological. Even prior to the pandemic, HE institutions have been described as *anxiety machines* (Hall and Bowles 2016) or *pressure vessels* (Morrish and Priaulx 2020), inside which particular forms of performance and overwork are normalised and technologically infused. Higher education institutions create a morbidity that is replicated in physical and mental ill-being and distress amongst many of those who labour inside it, in particular where they cannot exemplify dominant norms of performance or where they cannot perform those duties digitally.

Any discussion of postdigital HE might usefully begin from an analysis of the morbid desire to maintain business-as-usual and value-for-money. Moreover, this must reflect upon the differential, intersectional experiences of students and staff, which are shaped by uncertainty and established vulnerabilities, and tend to amplify injustices (Andreotti 2016; Tuck and Yang 2012). This is a reflection upon the material history of University and College life, and the need to maintain social, intellectual, and economic capital in a competitive and marketised environment. Such reflections question how digital tools might enable or disable meaningful responses. Might HE workers mobilise those tools and the forms, cultures, and activities that they enable, for humane ends? Do they force a reimagination or reexamination of how the digital inflects the idea of the University? A starting point for this lies in the political economy of HE, and its existence in the shadow of value.

2 HE in the Shadow of Value

The digital life of HE is framed against the need to reproduce economic value and services that can be extracted from, or inserted inside, institutions. This might take the form of rents to private providers like publishers or technology consultancies, through knowledge exchange and transfer, or the development of human capital through appropriate accreditation. Moreover, that digital life is underscored by the systemic need to produce and circulate commodities at an accelerated rate and at reduced cost. As a result, any examination of a postdigital HE sector sits against everyday reports of casualised or precarious staff being at risk of redundancy, alongside intersectional inequalities, overwork, and the imposition of *flexploitation* through the creation of micro-activities production of curriculum content, research outputs, assessments, and so on (Morgan and Wood 2017).

For those who labour in HE, including academics, professional services' staff, and students, the digital life of the institution emerges in the shadow of value and its shaping of specific social relations. In an important footnote to the chapter on machinery and large-scale industry in *Capital*, Marx (1867/1976: 493) highlights how an analysis of technology enables us to reveal the following about our dominant mode of reproducing everyday life.

- Particular *forms of production* come to predominate across a global terrain. For instance, there is a focus upon production of commodities, or the commodification of everyday, educational processes, from the curriculum and research agendas to the student experience. This includes accelerated production for the exchange of commodities like educational accreditation or services, which can be circulated and consumed in domestic and international markets. It also includes the generation of surpluses that can be accumulated, for instance by educational technology corporations in the form of software and content licenses.
- These forms of production, and the ways in which technology and organisational development are in relationship with them, affect how we *relate to nature* and the environment. Here, institutional engagement in the use of energy or the focus upon education for sustainable development is implicated in ideas of efficiency, value-for-money, and green capitalism.
- Technology then mediates *the particular social relations* that emerge between people, including in educational contexts. For instance relationships between

lecturers and students are based upon how digital tools enable accreditation, and their relationship to the idea of student-as-consumer or producer. Private property, contract law, and the rights of the individual affect these social relations.

- Reproducing these social relations, our specific, *mental conceptions of the world* demonstrate which knowledges, cultural understandings, and beliefs become hegemonic. This affects our approach to indigenous ways of knowing, and the extent to which particular digital technologies co-opt those ways of knowing as knowledge that can be commodified.
- These digitally infused circuits of commodification reinforce *labour processes* that enable the production of specific goods, geographies, services, or affects. This includes cloud hosting services or outsourcing institutional infrastructure, alongside the proliferation of particular forms of emotional labour that can be managed through forms of personal tutoring, counselling, mindfulness, and so on and that are separated from the classroom.
- Within the curriculum, *institutional, legal, and governmental arrangements* frame educational practices and are shaped technologically and technocratically. For instance data protection and copyright law affect educational provision, as do transnational trade partnerships in educational services and goods.
- Finally, Marx speaks of technology revealing the *conduct of daily life* that underpins social reproduction. Here, digital tools reinforce the visibility of particular white, male, able, straight norms and reinforce their dominance in the performance management of educational space-time.

As the mode of production is grounded in capitalist social relations, which are predicated upon the production of value, the ways in which humans relate to each other and reproduce themselves demand their constant return to the market, in order to resell their labour-power. It is this labour-power, and its knowledge, skills, and capabilities, that corporations and institutions seek to organise and combine with a range of technologies and artefacts or use-values, in order to generate surpluses. This production process, including in educational contexts, requires the exploitation of labour-power, in order to generate existing commodities and services at a lower cost, or new commodities and services that can drive a higher price. This is a process that creates an educational cyber-proletariat of precarious staff and students, in permanent competition and denied symbolic forms of status and privilege (Huws 2014).

Yet this precarious, technocratic existence is based upon the exploitation of human knowledge, skills, and capabilities embedded in labour-power, which Marx (1857/1993) referred to as the *general intellect* of society. This general intellect is harnessed and organised collectively by capital, and through its digital infusion, it accelerates the reality that humans constantly reproduce the system that seeks to proletarianise them and place them in its shadow. In this acceleration, the use-value of educational labour, whether it be academic research outputs, institutional marketing and recruitment, or a student's development of their human capital, aims at generating surplus-value, which can be turned into some form of wealth like monetary profit. Mediating this, and in dialogue with it, is the compulsion to compete, in order to gain market share and to increase value (Dyer-Witheford 2015; Hoofd 2017).

Our understanding of how education is technologically infused, and its implications for identity and relationships, must be analysed dialectically against the political economic context from which it emerges. This situates HE, its institutions, and its labourers against the demand to maintain the reproduction of capitalism, hidden by discourses of impact, productivity, and value-for-money. In response to the pandemic, this has generated a policy-focus upon business-as-usual that centres on the economy, rather than human well-being, and then focuses upon the ways in which the digital enables this economistic lifeworld. The idea of value and its deep interconnection to the generation of surpluses that can be privatised or commodified colonises digital technologies and online working as means of reproducing a particular kind of social life. This is the digital and technocratic management of systemic risk, such that the idea of what it means to be educated is restructured by economic value, rather than humane values (Hall 2018), precisely because this idea emerges from within the shadow cast by value.

In thinking about this shadow, there are increasing reports of how technology has been used in HE:

- to generate overwork and to lengthen the working day, as well as enabling work to infect the home because it can be undertaken beyond the campus;
- to make certain activities like assessment routine, for instance in the demand that particular technologies are used for assessment and feedback, or the monitoring of plagiarism;
- to create micro-activities that can be proletarianized, for instance by separating curriculum delivery from assessment, which can be undertaken by more precarious colleagues on worse conditions of employment;
- to focus upon competitive edge between institutions or disciplines across institutions; and,
- to reduce the labour content of services and products, in order to generate new surpluses.

These materially affect the identity of the HE labourer, who must compete for attention and work by becoming self-exploiting and entrepreneurial in the development of new knowledge, skills, and capabilities, or in driving down the costs for delivering certain activities, in order to win contracts. If there is a postdigital reality, and this will be discussed below, it is that, in the face of multiple crises, value has utilised technology to lengthen its shadow across space and time, such that the future of the HE labourer is to be governed by the desire for surpluses that are estranged from them (Smyth 2017).

In the shadow of value, those labourers are condemned to utilise digital technologies not for socialised solidarity, but instead as a means of colonising their everyday existence. This is the systemic reality of a postdigital HE. It denies communal manifestations of life beyond the market. Digital technologies enable association with others, as long as they reproduce the dominant mode of production, which is situated against particular modes of privilege, power, and status. This affects how staff and students relate to: nature and the environment; each other through their mediated social relations; the discourses that shape their worlds; the labour process and governance arrangements around those worlds; and dominant norms that are reinforced technologically. In analysing this postdigital world, the disciplinary and authoritarian mode of reinforcement becomes clear.

3 The Authoritarian Reproduction of Higher Education

Increasingly, HE labourers are co-opted into the implementation of disciplinary technologies, or technologies designed to control the classroom for value. The integration of learning environment, pedagogy, identity, and technology strips-back autonomy as flows of performance data provide ongoing, formative feedback to systems of algorithmic governance. Independence is reduced beyond the ability to provide feedback on behaviour and activity, in order to fulfil the desires of particular ideological conceptions of HE. Where behaviour and activity are wilful, they are constantly finessed or managed out of the system (Ahmed 2019). Thus, the digital ecosystems of HE embed competitive techniques and manage risk through behavioural reengineering.

Ideologically, structures and processes are used to make claims focused upon accountability with performance-based incentives, and a commitment to the idea of a meritocracy, through which resources can flow to structures and service units focused upon particular kinds of teaching and research performance. However, it is important to remember that technologies are used against labour by structuring and accelerating work, and the emotional, social, and embodied costs of extended or intensified work 'ultimately falls on the workers who make the machine hum' (Phillips and Rozworski 2019: 89). Algorithmic control cares little for social negotiation or discussions of the flows of power or inequality (McQuillan 2016; Pasquale 2018).

Both curriculum and research practices are overlain with institutionalised technologies that monitor and allow judgements to be made. This includes those for facial recognition and app-enabled attendance monitoring via Wi-Fi tethering (Andrejevic and Selwyn 2020; Meneses et al. 2019), which are marketed in terms of campus security, progression, and retention, but which damage or restrict free expression, privacy, and autonomy (Fight for the Future 2020). The utilisation of such technologies is framed around tracking the individual in response to their actions and location, with judgements imposed about legitimacy, behaviour, and identity. Where behaviours and identities do not match dominant norms, there is an additional layer of injustice in the deployment of the digital ecosystem, in particular given the lack of algorithmic accuracy in addressing people of colour and women, alongside non-binary and trans people (Grother et al. 2019). This is amplified because the collection of sensitive biometric data is intrusive and tends to lack consent, even whilst information about individuals, contacts, behaviour, feelings, and practices is sequestered and re-purposed (Pasquale 2016).

Such technologies are authoritarian not simply in terms of their governance and the ways in which they maintain systemic order in the face of uncertainty directed for the production of economic value. They are also disciplinary in that they quantify human lives and experiences, construct particular identities based on dominant norms, and then enforce the internalisation of that quantification/construction (Stark 2019). They form a terrain of necropolitics that makes invisible certain bodies, or makes their existence a form of living death (Mbembe 2019). The process of making invisible is shaped by institutional formations that serve to benchmark individuals, subjects, and institutions, pivoting around human capital formation (World Bank Group Education 2020). This demands structures that can measure, monitor, and report learning outcomes and implement action plans predicated upon generating commodity and leverage graduate skills and contributing to innovation, across a comparable, international terrain.

The institution, whether postdigital or not, makes it difficult for individuals and groups to move beyond these flows of power, or to challenge them collectively. There has been an emptying out of the politics of the University in the face of the disciplinary imperatives of commodity production and exchange. This means that any meaningful analysis of the humanist potential of a postdigital HE has to recognise its increasingly authoritarian policy and practice-based context, including:

- struggles in 2020 against cuts to humanities and social sciences courses that are deemed low-value, for instance at the universities of Sunderland and Portsmouth in the UK;
- struggles by graduate students at the University of California, Santa Cruz, taking part in wildcat strikes since 2019 to demand living wages;
- struggles in 2019 at the University of Juba in South Sudan against tuition fee hikes that threatened the right to education;
- the history of protest at Jawaharlal Nehru University in Delhi, including the 2016 sedition row, and 2019 struggles over accommodation fees and India's Citizenship Amendment Act;
- the hostile environment created by institutional engagement with national immigration practices like the Prevent Duty in the UK;
- the use of court injunctions to halt demonstrations on campuses;
- media panics over issues like grade inflation, which are presented as threats to the value of a degree or of higher education composition; and,
- discourses around free speech predicated upon disciplining specific bodies and communities.

These struggles are responses to policy narratives that deform and re-purpose the epistemic role of HE in society. They enable us to analyse any postdigital conceptualisation of HE in relation to the authoritarian characteristics of the forms or structures of HE, its cultures or pathologies, and its activities or methodologies.

- First, the form or structure of the University or College develops in order to maintain the ideological repositioning of social reproduction around ordered liberties rather than democratic rights. Thus, HE gives individuals the liberty to develop their own human capital and that of their families, and any rights they

have are rooted in the deployment of that human capital for entrepreneurial, value-driven ends (Bruff and Tansel 2018).
- Second, the cultures that emerge from these structures pathologically reinforce inequality in access to collective, public goods, based upon dominant, patriarchal notions of productivity (Bruff 2014). In order to consume social goods, individuals are expected to deliver value-for-money and to be economically productive, in ways that are defined hegemonically in relation to white, male, ableist, heterosexual norms.
- Third, these pathologies recalibrate social relationships in the name of markets through labour market reforms and regulation that supports corporate forms, such that the regulation and governance of institutions, data and justice is focused upon the production and circulation of value, rather than shared values (Connell 2013).
- Fourth, the terrain of HE is re-engineered methodologically, through commodification to enable the corporate parasitisation of notionally public organisations, through ideologies, policies, and practices of privatisation, marketisation, and financialization (Davies 2017). As a result, the activities of HE, like the production of textbooks, articles, and ways of knowing the world, become commodities that can be exchanged.

These characteristics interact through flows of data and digital lives, in order to discipline specific kinds of useful knowledge and a specific kind of useful knowledge producer, in relation to the authoritarian reproduction of value. It is in this context that postdigital HE takes shape.

4 In, Against, and Beyond the Digital

There is a material history of the relationship between technology, institutions, cultures, and practices. In analysing this material history, the idea of the postdigital has been framed in terms of: interaction, complexity, and social change; digital subservience to the idea of the social; digital transparency enabling issues-based dialogue; the stagnation of positivist, digital discourses; the digital reproduction of relationships of power; the decoding of relationships of power through digital transparency; and a focus upon the platform rather than the tool (Cormier et al. 2019; Jandrić et al. 2018).

At issue has been how to reimagine the idea of the human inside systems predicated upon: complexity-for-innovation; a social terrain defined around productive value; obfuscation of the ways in which algorithmic control is coded; the control of certain forms of public data and their presentation; ongoing techno-determinist readings of progress; and the subservience of life under platforms that mediate and quantify existences. This reimagining matters because, systemically and productively, the only space for radical imagination appears to be in the further, ongoing digital colonisation of the body and the self, as a means of reproducing value

(Berardi 2009; Lazzarato 2014). This process is limited precisely because the space-time of life is bounded by competition between digitally enabled humans.

In this bounded space-time, individuals, groups, or States attempt to break or harness specific technologies for particular political ends (Watters 2021). Such contestation is amplified at the boundary between the human and the development of convergence technologies, based on the integration of 5G cellular networks, tokenomics and forms of blockchain, machine augmentation, sentiment analysis, biotechnologies, and so on. Interactions at these boundaries then enforce human–machine intersections with digital, monopoly capitalism in the form of Google, Microsoft, Amazon, Facebook, and Apple, and the rise of alternate geopolitical rivals, in particular from China. As a result, the postdigital realities of HE, and teaching, learning, and researching inside its institutions, are framed by the techno-colonisation of what it means to be human from a variety of intersecting structures and processes (Peters 2020).

Thus, the idea of the postdigital needs to be discussed in relation to its potential to act as a dystopian pivot for the convergence of the personal/the person and a range of technologies (cognitive, biological, nano-). The terrain of aspiration is shaped through the exploitation of the flesh and of the mind, the augmentation enabled by technology, and the ongoing expropriation of what it means to be human. These moments of exploitation, expropriation, and extraction are rooted in wider, intersectional injustices, grounded in the separation of politics and economics, denying the potential for a reintegrated political economy that radically reimagines society (Hall 2018). As a result, social reproduction cannot be viewed beyond the lens of capital, and technology cannot be viewed beyond the ways in which it expands the field of accumulation.

Part of the issue is the apparent monopolisation of digitally enhanced expertise, in relation to crises and their mitigation, by institutions of higher learning. Either private investment in institutions or state-sponsored privatisation for the creation of infrastructures like universities in which private investment can take hold disables populations from imagining futures that do not emerge from experts, technocrats, or technologists. Moreover, beyond business-as-usual, the postdigital institution has no political content. Thus, in the separation of HE institutions from their publics, except through exploitative labour and study conditions, contracts, licences, rents, or modes of knowledge transfer, there is a weakening of political imagination. Disciplinary separations, competition between subjects and institutions, technologies for monitoring and audit, each reinforce a value-driven, human-digital reality.

At issue is whether it is possible to work against this reality and the multiple differential and unjust ways in which it is experienced. This requires a new political economy, which seeks to reduce the space and time required for the production of self-sufficiency and widen the base for autonomous existence. Might the very automation, or human–machine augmentation and symbiosis, demanded and developed by capital to discipline and control labour make possible an exodus from the society of capitalist work? As surplus time arises as an outcome of automation, new, radical possibilities for disposing of that time beyond the universe of value might be discussed. This requires a re-connection with the ideas of being human, knowing the plurality of humanity, and acting or doing in humane ways. This includes a reimagination of the relationship between humans and the digital in the name of dignity, in order to recover autonomy for the self beyond being a factory for value. That factory and the inhumanity that it breeds must be decomposed as a starting point.

5 Composting the Anti-human University

Marx (1867/1976: 547) argued that machinery is 'a more hideous form [for] exploiting labour-power', reducing the worker into 'a part of the specialised machine', and *both* reducing wages *and* breeding 'helpless dependence upon the factory as a whole'. The concrete realities of the HE terrain described as postdigital are of struggle against the discipline of commodity production and exchange and for humane cultures and practices. Some of these struggles are noted above, as students, teachers, and their communities push the boundaries of education for another world. However, being against a system places bodies and identities at-risk of being disciplined.

Curle (1973: 8–9) emphasised the need for a new education, which demands 'an alien form of society' that values the human, or our shared humanity. This is the possibility of personal evolution, or 'higher-awareness (awareness-identity)', formed inside a counter-system of education rooted in altruism (or #solidarity). This counter-system has echoes of Gramsci's work on hegemony and counter-hegemony, rooted in acknowledging, analysing, and abolishing power, in both formal and informal settings. For Curle (1973: 10), such a counter-system would have higher levels of (social) awareness (beyond value). It would be grounded in awareness-identity (social connections against-and-beyond the market), and as such be altruistic and empathetic with peaceful relations that are based on cooperative and egalitarian democracy.

In addressing how education relates to the creation of such a counter-system, Curle (1973: 17) diagnosed that we need to reveal the reality of the system as is, in order to demonstrate how hegemony rests on making particular lives intolerable or invisible. As a result, it becomes possible to prefigure other ways of knowing how to live, as a process that is generative, iterative, and educative (Amsler 2015). In revealing how life inside the postdigital University or college is reproduced for-value, and the lived experiences of those made marginal inside this system, it becomes possible to discuss the values upon which living might be organised.

This reimagines the University as a pedagogical project that begins from humans and their society as it is embedded and reproduced in nature. It is a 'sacred' project, grounded in 'the practice of freedom' (hooks 1994: 13). Such practice is learning and teaching not as algorithmically or cybernetically managed and finessed, rather as a process, integrated with the souls of students and teachers, and in symbiosis with 'the necessary conditions where learning can most deeply and intimately begin'.

This idea of symbiosis and necessary conditions is critical in thinking about venturing beyond the universe of value, which reproduces itself through dialectical processes that are technologically enriched. As has been noted, Marx (1867/1976: 473) described the dialectical relationship between technologies and forms of production, relations to nature, particular social relations, mental conceptions of the world, labour processes, arrangements for governance and regulation, and the conduct of daily life. At issue is whether and how to take these relationships as they form the necessary conditions for capitalist reproduction, and to move beyond their hegemonic description of the world.

Here, French et al. (2020) describe composting as a metaphor for re-engaging humans with the conditions inside which they reproduce their world. A starting point is a thick dialogue grounded in lived experiences of exploitation, expropriation, and extraction, in this case emerging from 'stories of displacement, dispossession, dislocation, disclosure/enclosure, discomfort/comfort, and binaries'. In engaging with the realities of settler colonialism, these authors identify hegemonic structures, pathologies, and methodologies as 'invasive, ongoing, and invisible', and which scrub existing human relations of any meaning. They argue the need to compost anger, grief, and trauma, as a process of unearthing and breaking down distortions, and thereby creating 'a garden of truth-telling' (French et al. 2020). Composting serves 'as a rich metaphor for our experiential approach to documenting our stories and building relationships with one another, with our ancestors and with land, because it is itself a relational process that repeats and is enriched with every churning of the soil'.

The process of composting centres humanity and feelings, stories, histories, relationships, cultures, and lands. Through a deep engagement with truth-telling, it seeks to begin from suffering and apparent hopelessness, in order to cultivate alternative ways of being, knowing, and acting in the world. Engaging with this struggle in educational contexts requires reflection on the realities of the time required for truth-telling, alongside individual fallibilities and personal limitations, and potential for paralysis when faced by overwhelming, structural crises and forms of power (Tuck and McKenzie 2015).

Yet, in the desire to curate and cultivate ways of living more humanely, those who labour in postdigital HE might usefully seek to grapple with Tuck's (2018) question: 'how shall we live?'. In a technologically enriched, interconnected set of environments, inside which individual behaviours and actions are increasingly cybernetically tracked and controlled, and inside which legitimacy is judged in relation to systemic norms, this question is both imperative and revolutionary. This is more so because the idea of composting the world as it is speaks to a system that needs to decompose and lives that need to be fertilised in new ways, lest they wither or remain unfulfilled. Against the morbid realities of HE, and of living and studying in the shadow of value, this is a starting point for reimagining the relationship between humans and their technologies, and how they are integrated in institutions, cultures and practices.

6 Venturing Beyond a Postdigital Higher Education

The strengths of composting as a metaphor and a process have ramifications for the relationship between technology and educational contexts, cultures, and practices. Moreover, they help to shape different modes of living, which do not deny the digital, but which actively work against the current, systemic manifestation of postdigital HE. In this manifestation, whatever the hopes of theorists and activists, a focus upon complexity and social change is governed by increasingly disciplinary algorithmic modes of control. One outcome is the Platform University, inside which the technological terrain is shaped against the authoritarian dictates of commodity production and human capital development.

This space to rethink Marx's (1867/1976) unpacking of the processes that interact dialectically forms a historical and material unfolding, as human, productive power. In the current mode of understanding, this unfolding is singular and points towards the universe of value. Educational structures, cultures, and pedagogic practices have a rhythm and energy that contributes towards the expansion of this universe. This forces individuals and communities to seek their own engagement with that system through compromises, by reflecting themselves in the dominant ideals of that system, in accommodations that deny or make invisible their true selves, or by refusal and resistance. In a system whose reproduction depends upon human energy in extraction, expropriation, and exploitation, maintaining individual legitimacy is a struggle for life.

Instead, holding the anger, grief, and trauma of a compromised, invisible, or refused lived experience enables the potential to explore alternatives both on individual and communal levels. This remains a potential, precisely because in order to exist inside a dehumanising system, individuals need to earn a wage through ongoing alienation and estrangement from themselves (Hall 2018). This is as true in postdigital HE environments, as in any other sector of the economy. It remains a potential because the process of composting takes time, and to be generative, it takes the recognition of individual and systemic limitations and the ability to act mutually against the exhortation to compete.

Technologically, then, it is important to reconsider Marx's interrelating of technology and the reproduction of capitalist social relations, in order to understand whether alternative postdigital forms of higher learning might be possible. The following questions act as a starting point for reimagination.

- How is it possible to use the idea of an integrated, postdigital lifeworld to demonstrate the lived experiences of HE, as an alienating *form of producing* human capital as a commodity?
- How might the expanding use of digital technologies in educational institutions be explicitly *related to nature* and the environment, in terms of hardware, software and cultural practices? Is our expanding use of technology making us more efficiently unsustainable?
- In what ways are postdigital ecosystems reproducing *particular social relations* that are alienating and privileged?

- What is the relationship between postdigital and value-driven, *mental conceptions of the world* and the dominance of particular knowledges? To what extent are these postdigital conceptions extinguishing the possibilities for meaningful human existences?
- Is it possible to refuse postdigital *labour processes*, as they reinforce an estrangement or divorce between individuals and their work, the communities, nature and themselves?
- Is it possible to push beyond pathological and methodological *institutional, legal and governmental arrangements* for HE, by refusing algorithmic or cybernetic governance?
- Might the idea of the postdigital and the concrete reality of digital tools be dissolved into a new *conduct of daily life* that underpins social reproduction as a mutual and plural way of knowing the world, and being in it?

It may be argued that these are utopian questions, which deny the realities of a meritocratic, postdigital education for a world of work, and which also deny the realities of power, privilege, and marginalisation. Yet they point to the fact that humans make the world through their ongoing, every day, material and sensuous practice. The idea of the postdigital, and the reality of the ways in which technologies are integrated or infused inside the structures, cultures, and activities of HE institutions, enables a way in. This is not simply to think about a technologically enriched human existence, rather to examine how current experiences of HE institutions are pathologically and methodologically dehumanising.

In thinking postdigitally about 'how shall we live?', we are encouraged to think about our social power to make our lives, rather than our marketised and commodified power over the world. This is a different, collective power, which enables different ways of utilising technologies, for plural ends (Cleaver 2017; Holloway 2003). At present, postdigital HE is incapable of recognising such collective forms of power, precisely because it imposes knowledge transfer, performance management, forms of organisational development, metrics, and so on, as technologies to be finessed algorithmically for control. In moving against these flows of educational alienation, our struggle is to build up our power to do differently and socially. This is not individual autonomy, or the primacy of specific identities, rather it is the use of postdigital, in order to understand social forms of subjectivity and the creation of a terrain for self-determination.

In thinking this through, it is possible to critique the necessity of the postdigital University or College, precisely because those institutions contribute to the shadow value over our lives. Instead of working for the autonomy and creation of value, composting the idea that only discrete educational institutions have legitimacy enables societies to consider education as a social practice beyond the market and human capital. This means developing confidence in our own structures, in our own times, and in our own spaces, and as a result develop new ways of (re-)imagining society.

One way of addressing this is by relating education to the concept of 'mass intellectuality', which emerges from Marx's (1857/1993: 694) work on the 'general intellect', through which the dynamics of capitalism mean 'the accumulation of knowledge and of skill, of the general productive forces of the social brain, is thus absorbed into capital, as opposed to labour, and hence appears as an attribute of capital, and more specifically of fixed capital [machinery]'. Through innovation and competition, the technical and skilled work of the social individual, operating in factories, corporations, or schools, is absorbed into the things they produce. It is alienated from them, and therefore, the 'general intellect' of society, i.e. its general capacity for science in the broadest sense, is absorbed into capitalised technologies and techniques, in order to reduce labour costs and increase productivity.

With the crisis of funding, regulation, and governance of higher education, there is a need to understand: first, the mechanisms through which the general intellect is absorbed into the total social production process of value, to which postdigital HE contributes; and second, how academic practices enables or resists such co-option. This calls attention to the proliferation of alternative educational practices, which are themselves reimaginings of the idea of HE as a site for the production of knowledge. These alternatives are rooted in the desire and potential for reclaiming the knowledge, skills, practices, and techniques that form the general intellect, in order to produce and circulate new forms of socially useful knowledge or ways of knowing, being in, and creating the world.

From this reclaiming or liberation of the general intellect, away from the valorisation of capital, emerges 'mass intellectuality' as a direct, cognitive and social force of production that exists as an increasingly diffuse form of intellectuality. In this form, it circulates as a 'commons' that is pregnant with critical and practical potential but still remains marginal in the face of general commodity production. As a result, it risks being recuperated by capital in the form of the 'knowledge economy' or 'cognitive capitalism', but it is a new, communal starting point (Vercellone 2007; Virno 2004).

Struggles against recuperation might erupt from within, and as a response to, postdigital HE, but mass intellectuality is a pedagogical, social movement, which seeks to integrate technology and education through a broader and deeper social reimagining. Such struggles seek to compost, rather than recuperate, our existing institutions, cultures, and practices, which themselves give heat and light to the universe of value. Struggles, digitally enabled and infused with lived experiences of anger, grief, and trauma, point towards alternative ways of reproducing the world, grounded in dignity. It is this deep, human connection with dignity, flowing through the individual, her community and her natural world as an integrated movement, which offers the potential for a humane, postdigital higher learning, and a dialectical engagement with the question: 'how shall we live?'

References

Ahmed, S. (2019). *What's the Use? On the Uses of Use*. Durham, NC: Duke University Press.
Amsler, S. (2015). *The Education of Radical Democracy*. London: Routledge.

Andrejevic, M., & Selwyn, N. (2020). Facial recognition technology in schools: critical questions and concerns. *Learning, Media and Technology, 45*(2), 115–128. https://doi.org/10.1080/17439884.2020.1686014.

Andreotti, V. (2016). Research and pedagogical notes: The educational challenges of imagining the world differently. *Canadian Journal of Development Studies, 37*(1), 101–112. https://doi.org/10.1080/02255189.2016.1134456.

Berardi, F. (2009). *The Soul at Work: From Alienation to Autonomy*. Trans. F. Cadel and G. Mecchia. Los Angeles, CA: Semiotext(e).

Bruff, I. (2014). The Rise of Authoritarian Neoliberalism. *Rethinking Marxism: A Journal of Economics, Culture & Society, 26*(1), 113–129. https://doi.org/10.1080/08935696.2013.843250.

Bruff, I., & Tansel, C. B. (2018). Authoritarian neoliberalism: trajectories of knowledge production and praxis. *Globalizations*. https://doi.org/10.1080/14747731.2018.1502497.

Boyd, D. (2017). The radicalization of utopian dreams. Points, 20 November. https://points.datasociety.net/the-radicalization-of-utopian-dreams-e1b785a0cb5d. Accessed 9 September 2020.

Chitty, M., Callard, F., & Pearce, W. (2020). Why universities must move all teaching online this autumn. USSBriefs, 21 August. https://medium.com/ussbriefs/why-universities-must-move-all-teaching-online-this-autumn-efdf7d09cce5. Accessed 9 September 2020.

Cleaver, H. (2017). *Rupturing the Dialectic: The Struggle against Work, Money, and Financialization*. Oakland, CA: AK Press.

Connell, R. (2013). The Neoliberal Cascade and Education: An Essay on the Market Agenda and Its Consequences. *Critical Studies in Education, 54*(2), 99–112. https://doi.org/10.1080/17508487.2013.776990.

Cormier, D., Jandrić, P., Childs, M., Hall, R., White, D., Phipps, L., Truelove, I., Hayes, S., & Fawns, T. (2019). Ten Years of the Postdigital in the 52group: Reflections and Developments 2009–2019. *Postdigital Science and Education, 1*(2), 475–506. https://doi.org/10.1007/s42438-019-00049-8.

Curle, A. (1973). *Education for Liberation*. London: Tavistock.

Davies, W. (2017). Elite Power under Advanced Neoliberalism. *Theory, Culture & Society, 34*(5-6), 227–250. https://doi.org/10.1177/0263276417715072.

Dyer-Witheford, N. (2015). *Cyber-Proletariat: Global Labour in the Digital Vortex*. London: Pluto Press.

Fight for the Future. (2020). Who are we? https://www.fightforthefuture.org/. Accessed 9 September 2020.

French, K. B., Sanchez, A., & Ullom, E. (2020). Composting Settler Colonial Distortions: Cultivating Critical Land-Based Family History. *Genealogy, 4*(3) https://www.mdpi.com/2313-5778/4/3/84/htm.

Grother, P., Ngan, M., & Hanaoka, K. (2019). *Face Recognition Vendor Test (FRVT), Part 3: Demographic Effects. Institute Report 8280*. Berhampur: National Institute of Science and Technology. https://doi.org/10.6028/NIST.IR.8280.

Hall, R. (2018). *The Alienated Academic: The Struggle for Autonomy Inside the University*. London: Palgrave Macmillan.

Hall, R. (2020a). The Hopeless University: Intellectual Work at the End of the End of History. *Postdigital Science and Education, 2*(3), 830–848. https://doi.org/10.1007/s42438-020-00158-9.

Hall, R. (2020b). Platform Discontent against the University. In M. Stocchetti (Ed.), *The Digital Age and Its Discontents*. Helsinki: Helsinki University Press. https://doi.org/10.33134/HUP-4-7.

Hall, R., & Bowles, K. (2016). Re-engineering higher education: the subsumption of academic labour and the exploitation of anxiety. *Workplace: A Journal of Academic Labour*, 28, 30-47. https://ices.library.ubc.ca/index.php/workplace/article/view/186211. Accessed 9 September 2020.

Holloway, J. (2003). *Change the World Without Taking Power: The Meaning of Revolution Today*. London: Pluto Press.

Holloway, J. (2019). *We are the Crisis of Capital*. Oakland, CA: PM Press.

Hoofd, I. (2017). *Higher Education and Technological Acceleration: The Disintegration of University Teaching and Research*. London: Palgrave Macmillan.

hooks, B. (1994). *Teaching to Transgress: Education as the Practice of Freedom*. London: Routledge.

Huws, U. (2014). *Labor in the global digital economy: the cybertariat comes of age*. New York: Monthly Review Press.

Jandrić, P., Knox, J., Besley, T., Ryberg, T., Suoranta, J., & Hayes, S. (2018). Postdigital Science and Education. *Educational Philosophy and Theory, 50*(10), 893–899. https://doi.org/10.1080/00131857.2018.1454000.

Johnston, B., MacNeill, S., & Smyth, K. (2018). *Conceptualising the Digital University: The Intersection of Policy, Pedagogy and Practice*. London: Palgrave Macmillan.

Kornbluh, A. (2020). Academe's Coronavirus Shock Doctrine. The Chronicle of Higher Education, 12 March. https://www.chronicle.com/article/Academe-s-Coronavirus-Shock/248238. Accessed 9 September 2020.

Lazzarato, M. (2014). *Signs and Machines: Capitalism and the Production of Subjectivity*. Cambridge, MA: Semiotext(e)/MIT Press.

Marx, K. (1857/1993). *Grundrisse: Outline of the Critique of Political Economy*. London: Penguin.

Marx, K. (1867/1976). *Capital Volume 1: A Critique of Political Economy*. London: Penguin.

Mbembe, A. (2019). *Necropolitics*. Durham: Duke University Press.

McQuillan, D. (2016). Algorithmic paranoia and the convivial alternative. *Big Data & Society, 3*(2). https://doi.org/10.1177/2053951716671340.

Meneses, Y. N. G., García, Y. G., García, C. A. R., Pineda, I. O., & Calleros, J. M. G. (2019). Methodology for Automatic Identification of Emotions in Learning Environments. *Research in Computing Science, 148*(5), 89–96.

Morgan, G., & Wood, J. (2017). The "academic career" in the era of flexploitation. In E. Armano, A. Bove, & A. Murgia (Eds.), *Mapping Precariousness, Labour Insecurity and Uncertain Livelihoods: Subjectivities and Resistance* (pp. 82–97). London: Routledge.

Morrish, L., & Priaulx, N. (2020). Pressure Vessels II: An update on mental health among higher education staff in the UK. Hepi Occasional Paper, 23. Oxford: Higher Education Policy Institute. https://www.hepi.ac.uk/2020/04/30/pressure-vessels-ii-an-update-on-mental-health-among-higher-education-staff-in-the-uk/. Accessed 9 September 2020.

Noble, S. (2018). *Algorithms of Oppression: How Search Engines Reinforce Racism*. New York, NY: New York University Press.

Pasquale, F. (2016). Two Narratives of Platform Capitalism. *Yale Law and Policy Review, 309*. https://ylpr.yale.edu/twonarratives-platform-capitalism/. Accessed 9 September 2020.

Pasquale, F. (2018). Tech Platforms and the Knowledge Problem. *American Affairs, 2*(2). https://americanaffairsjournal.org/2018/05/tech-platforms-and-the-knowledge-problem/. Accessed 9 September 2020.

Peters, M. (2020). Critical Philosophy of Technological Convergence: Education and the Nano-Bio-Info-Cogno Paradigm. In M. Stocchetti (Ed.), *The Digital Age and Its Discontents*. Helsinki: Helsinki University Press. https://doi.org/10.33134/HUP-4-12.

Phillips, L., & Rozworski, M. (2019). *The People's Republic of Walmart: How the World's Biggest Corporations are Laying the Foundation for Socialism*. London: Verso.

Smyth, J. (2017). *The Toxic University: Zombie Leadership, Academic Rock Stars and Neoliberal Ideology*. London: Palgrave Macmillan.

Stark, L. (2019). Facial Recognition is the Plutonium of AI. *XRDS: Crossroads, The ACM Magazine for Students, 25*(3), 50–55. https://doi.org/10.1145/3313129.

Tuck, E. (2018). *I Do Not Want to Haunt You but I Will: Indigenous Feminist Theorizing on Reluctant Theories of Change*. Edmonton: University of Alberta, Faculty of Arts.

Tuck, E., & McKenzie, M. (2015). *Place in Research: Theory, Methodology, and Methods*. London: Routledge.

Tuck, E., & Yang, W. (2012). Decolonization Is Not a Metaphor. *Decolonization: Indigeneity, Education & Society, 1*(1), 1–40. https://jps.library.utoronto.ca/index.php/des/article/view/18630. Accessed 9 September 2020.

Vercellone, C. (2007). From Formal Subsumption to General Intellect: Elements for a Marxist Reading of the Thesis of Cognitive Capitalism. *Historical Materialism, 15*(1), 13–36. https://doi.org/10.1163/156920607X171681.

Virno, P. (2004). *A Grammar of the Multitude*. Los Angeles, CA: Semiotext(e).

Watters, A. (2021). *Teaching Machines*. Cambridge, MA: MIT Press.

Weller, M. (2020). *25 Years of Ed Tech*. Edmonton: Athabasca University Press.

Williamson, B. (2020). Datafication and automation in higher education during and after the Covid-19 crisis. https://codeactsineducation.wordpress.com/2020/05/06/datafication-automation-he-covid19-crisis/. Accessed 9 September 2020.

World Bank Group Education (2020). The Covid-19 Pandemic: Shocks to Education and Policy Responses. https://t.co/DHn34oFCZL. Accessed 9 September 2020.

The Value of Postdigital Humans as Objects, or Subjects, in McDonaldised Society

Sarah Hayes

1 Introduction

A key question surrounding postdigital humans concerns how humans might be either 'valued' or 'evaluated' and according to what measure. For Steve Fuller, 'human' is a normative category concerning what 'self-described' humans decide to include, or exclude (Fuller and Jandrić 2019). As such, Fuller suggests we might reach agreement about the performance standards that a putative 'human' should meet that a 'non-human' does not meet. Others though point to how the identity of a human is constructed differently across different disciplinary fields. As Mark Poster (1990: 147) observed, the discipline of computer science is identified through its relationship to the computer: 'identity remains part of the disciplinary protocol of the field, even if the actual object, the computer, changes significantly, even unrecognizably, in the course of the years'. It can be argued then on this basis that in the humanities a different focal point is taken, emphasising instead the human, even if what it means to be human has changed significantly, alongside new, intimate digital interactions with computers that now intermingle with public health.

Gary Hall (2013) has contended that what has come to be called the digital humanities should not simply be perceived as a bringing together of computing and humanities, as if these were 'equivalent'. He suggests that it is necessary instead to maintain a distinction between digital computing and the humanities. More emphasis has been placed on what 'direct, practical uses computer science can be put to in the humanities' to improve processes and operations. This one-way flow imposes a particular rational logic from computer science on the humanities. There has been less discussion on what 'the humanities themselves bring to the understanding of

---

S. Hayes (✉)
Education Observatory, Faculty of Education, Health and Wellbeing, University of Wolverhampton, Wolverhampton, UK
e-mail: Sarah.Hayes@wlv.ac.uk

© The Author(s), under exclusive license to Springer Nature Switzerland AG 2021
M. Savin-Baden (ed.), *Postdigital Humans*, Postdigital Science and Education, https://doi.org/10.1007/978-3-030-65592-1_5

computing' (Hall 2013: 782). This pattern can be noticed as computing techniques are applied in all manner of human activities across organisations, along with objective goals that seek greater quantitative efficiency. Whereas insights from the humanities applied to better understand these computing activities would lean towards a more qualitative and subjective analysis. The Covid-19 pandemic, and the need for humans to distance from each other, has added further biological and informational complexities to the postdigital contexts that humans now occupy (Jandrić et al. 2018).To give a brief example, the proposal that talking robots might be used in care homes to avoid human contact, ease loneliness, and improve mental health is a rational route that might: 'relieve some pressures in hospitals and care homes' and 'support existing care systems'. In this case, a robot called 'Pepper is able to engage in and keep up a conversation and can also learn about people's habits and tastes' (Mee 2020). So far so good on the efficiency front to apply computing to supplement care and minimise risk of viral infection. There are though, some ethical questions to raise about the vulnerability of the human beings in care, their capacity to understand where the data they pass to these robots in conversation is stored, or later utilised. A human companion is at more risk of transferring the virus, and a human also listens and uses outcomes from conversations with another human to make rational decisions. There are though differences in how data is memorised by robots, storage capacity, and other networks of computing devices, databases, and global companies who may be involved.

Examining postdigital humans in the light of George Ritzer's McDonaldisation thesis (Ritzer 1993/2018) is one way to help to place the arguments above within a more global overview of political economy and wider culture. McDonaldisation provides a view on how humans have come to be valued through digital developments as these have been applied in rational, commercial agendas to increase efficiency and exercise control. Essentially, the route where computing capabilities are simply applied to improve performance standards for humans is an underpinning approach observed in the values of McDonaldisation (Ritzer 1993/2018). Adapted from Weber's theory of rationalisation (Weber 1930), Ritzer argued that the process of McDonaldisation occurs when the principles on which the fast-food restaurant are constructed (efficiency, calculability, predictability, control) start to dominate increasing sectors of society, leading to global homogeneity and dehumanisation. Weber's theory, modified in this way by Ritzer, has remained relevant as processes of globalisation and automation through technology have brought new forms of large-scale rationalisation into play, both in physical and online situations. Of particular interest, in this chapter are scenarios where rational forms of McDonaldisation can lead also into unexpected, irrational outcomes.

McDonaldisation treats humans more objectively than subjectively, in both organisational practices and related discourse. As this approach has penetrated deeply across institutions, further studies have been undertaken across different sectors, to observe McDonaldisation in new contemporary realities. With digital progress, there are now more irrationalities to observe surrounding rationalisation of human activities through computing techniques. For example, the persistent tendency in recent decades to reorganise education through what sounds like common sense logic in policy discourse, McPolicy, has effectively seen humans writing themselves out of their own roles even amid predictions of a fourth Industrial Revolution that could lead to mass unemployment (Hayes 2019). Technology has been assigned human characteristics in the policy language, such as an ability to automatically 'enhance' learning within strategy documents that irrationally attribute human labour to machines and not to people (Hayes and Bartholomew 2015). Some have argued that such reforms reflect a growing disorientation concerning the purposes of education, alongside a rising 'therapy culture' (Furedi 2004). Yet now, as the Covid-19 pandemic has brought a global biological threat to humanity, spread of this virus has accelerated the use of digital in order to distance. This has taken place too at the very moment when a therapeutic culture would suggest we need to make more human contact with students, not less. Furthermore, whilst it could be pointed out objectively that the Covid-19 threat has simply accelerated the efficiencies of using computing to teach online, a more subjective approach to this through the humanities would notice how this situation plays out differently in each individual human context, depending on a person's 'postdigital positionality' (Hayes 2020).

This chapter is concerned then, with how postdigital humans may come to be 'valued' in more objective or subjective ways, in McDonaldised society beyond the Covid-19 outbreak. The term 'postdigital humans' will be applied rather loosely throughout, to refer to both human encounters with digital computing and computing techniques as these encounter human contexts. This is intended to develop arguments concerning 'postdigital positionality' (Hayes 2020), which refers to individual postdigital contexts and how these play out very differently for people, due to the complex combination of factors involved. Both humans and computers may find themselves objectively categorised but there is a positionality in each individual encounter, where subjective 'self-description' may be more appropriate than objective rationality.

After firstly examining how Ritzer extended his original theory to reflect augmented situations that humans now find themselves in, represented as various 'cages' of consumption (Ritzer et al. 2018), the chapter will explore new angles of human self-determination. It will consider secondly, if humans who have been routinely subject to rational forms of computer processing and objective evaluation through McDonaldisation are now finding new ways to perceive their postdigital positionality subjectively, perhaps from 'cages of security' more than 'cages of consumption' since Covid-19 (Hayes 2020). The ways in which they are developing these routes since the fundamental changes that the pandemic has wrought lead into some final speculation. There may be signs that society is beginning to move away from more global forms of McDonaldisation based mostly on consumer consumption and where computing techniques are simply applied to humans to improve productivity. If this is the case, bringing concerns from the humanities on what computing really means in our individual lives as postdigital humans is now a pressing matter. Perhaps a more subjective analysis of new forms of postdigital participation may yet prove possible in an equal, but still not equivalent, gathering between humans and machines (Jandrić and Hayes 2020).

2 McDonaldisation Across Recent Decades

Over the decades since Ritzer first wrote about McDonaldisation, his thesis has been applied in various contexts including Higher Education (Hayes and Wynyard 2002; Ritzer et al. 2018; Hayes 2019). Ritzer defined five basic dimensions of the McDonaldisation process: efficiency, calculability, predictability, control—as people are substituted by technology, and finally, the irrationality of rationality. Efficiency refers to the processes, structures, policies, and regulations that are the means to lead quickly to the end result or goal required. In this understanding, the efficiency of one party may also be dependent on the efficiency of others (Ritzer and Dean 2019: 187). Calculability is denoted by an emphasis on speed of production or service which stresses quantity of some kind, often at the expense of quality of experience. Predictability concerns the similarity of products across different global locations and also the predictable behaviours of employees and customers. Control, in relation to technological progress, is noticed as technologies that have dominated human activity and have come to replace humans (Ritzer and Dean 2019: 187). Lastly, Ritzer argued that the irrationality of rationality often accompanies these other dimensions in a paradoxical manner. For example, the rationality of a fast-food restaurant may lead to such popularity that results in long queues where service is no longer fast (Ritzer and Dean 2019: 188). In such an example, predictability is then replaced with unpredictability. In these dimensions of McDonaldisation, the human has been 'valued' in a particular (objective and rather functional, and also increasingly disposable) manner.

A key dimension of McDonaldization is the 'iron cage' of control, via rationalisation. The analysis of how McDonaldisation has worked over recent decades in physical contexts has built on a historical scenario where one form of technology tended to replace another, fairly chronologically due to advances in manufacturing techniques and subsequent unemployment. Well before digital technologies emerged, processes of rationalisation had therefore already accompanied automation. A series of technological revolutions, with the first of these beginning in the mid-eighteenth century, had brought new industrial processes, forms of travel and distribution, production, and global communication. Amidst these tangible developments, forms of managerial control that accompanied efficiency, calculability, and predictability were relatively easy to spot. However, alongside digital technological change, many new and less obvious forms of control have emerged in relation to consumer behaviour and the provision and value of data. Ritzer has described these as giving rise to new 'cages'.

Recognising Humans as Moving Between Various 'Cages'

McDonaldization is based originally on Weber's 'iron cage' of control. This is the idea that people are trapped but cannot necessarily recognise the figurative iron bars of this rational world. Although once contained within physical sites of bricks and mortar, digital sites have now augmented physical forms of consumer consumption, so that humans can encounter a 'velvet cage' within which they may in fact enjoy being trapped, even at the hands of non-human technologies that may threaten human labour and autonomy (Ritzer et al. 2018). Ritzer draws on examples where algorithmic popularity rankings and online reviews further augment the knowledge and data that stores can know about their customers, with algorithms making choices for people and control being increasingly achieved through non-human technologies. Such techniques have enabled a global grip on people that has a much larger reach than the iron cage within physical locations. The velvet cage is less visible as it applies the key principles of McDonaldisation, and people are less able to notice how they become subject to these, as 'prosumers' (Ritzer et al. 2018). Prosumer refers to the position of a person as both a producer and a consumer, such as when a purchase made online involves also providing reviewer feedback that may help the company sell further products. There is also the rise of prosuming machines, such as blockchain and bitcoin, that can both produce and consume without interventions from human prosumers. Ritzer has argued that these will explode into unprecedented and unpredictable directions in the years to come (Ritzer et al. 2018).

Reflecting once more on 'human' as a normative category concerning what 'self-described' humans decide to include, or exclude (Fuller and Jandrić 2019), there is perhaps a link with the third form of cage that Ritzer described: 'the rubber cage'. This cage of rationality possesses rubber bars which can be pulled apart at any time to enable humans to escape (Ritzer et al. 2018). Such imagery has a certain appeal because it plays to the idea from Gary Hall (2013) that computing and humanities are not entirely 'equivalent' and so humans might retain some self-determination to act. The rapid changes in computing (whether we can physically see these anymore, or not) proceed simultaneously alongside ongoing changes in humans as they interact with technology. Sometimes an individual may share a very intimate cage with a digital device, sometimes they might pull apart the rubber bars and leave, at least in theory. So, rather than each new technology simply taking over from the last, as an isolated instigator of change that might be rationally deployed, this picture has altered considerably in our postdigital context (Jandrić et al. 2018). It is somewhat appealing though to imagine humans coexisting as postdigital beings alongside their computing counterparts with a surrounding that is more rubber, than it is iron, or velvet. Rubber has elasticity, flexibility, and it can be used to erase. Moving towards an uncertain future, this could be a valuable feature for humans to retain.

3 A Postdigital Context

In a postdigital perspective, little of what is technological, or human, is erased as such. All technological changes are argued to remain with humans, whether or not the machines themselves remain in use. This has implications for the category of 'human' and what 'self-described' humans decide to include, or exclude under this label (Fuller and Jandrić 2019). It affects what people value or not and how they rationalise about human labour and learning. Based on this argument, if no technology is ever perceived to be gone altogether from our lives, then no former, or future, theories about human labour or learning can be obsolete either (Jandrić and Hayes 2020). From a postdigital point of view, both physical and virtual reactions to postdigital change arise as humans respond in new and sometimes irrational processes of self-determination. However, some approaches that emerge as more dominant to define humans can be surprising. Stepping in and out from between the bars of the rubber cage as a human reaction to digital developments within McDonaldised society sounds empowering. Yet the 'therapeutic' ethos that has ascended across society and into education seems less so.

Humans have become extremely preoccupied with emotional difficulties in a rise of popular therapy that advises people not only on ways to live but also on 'what to feel' (Ecclestone and Hayes 2019: 5). A need to be noticed can materialise in all sorts of ways, such as 'presenteeism' where people have become obsessed with working longer and longer hours. Ironically, an irrationality that emerges from this rational approach towards work is the need for a 'work–life balance', but even this can become a demand in the workplace (Ecclestone and Hayes 2019: 108). Therapy culture in this context can take the form of staff development, well-being activities, and advice, but these may be accompanied also by surveillance and monitoring (Ecclestone and Hayes 2019: 117). Personal postdigital responses of self-determination then cut across the virtual and the physical, as a desire to be 'memorable' as a person may take the form of a 'selfie' (Leone 2018: 44), a tattoo, or through oversharing across online forums.

Ultimately though, whether we know it yet or not, we are now in interesting territory that could begin to challenge more traditional global forms of McDonaldisation altogether. In a postdigital society, it is increasingly difficult to separate who (or what) is contributing to the 'viral' viewpoints that can be seen to spread rapidly across multiple platforms. Peters et al. (2020b: 3) have referred to 'viral modernity', pointing to the association between viral biology on the one hand and information science on the other. They argue that this applies to 'viral technologies, codes and ecosystems in information, publishing, education, and emerging knowledge (journal) systems'. The complex relationships between epidemics, quarantine, and public health management during the Covid-19 pandemic have further revealed this 'fusion of living and technological systems' (Peters et al. 2020b: 3). During the Covid-19 crisis, moral judgements have intermingled with public health advice and misinformation 'infodemics' (Peters et al. 2020b; Gregory 2020). This could prove challenging to the 'predictability' principle discussed as central to McDonaldisation, so that re-visiting the forms of cages that might now be inhabited by postdigital humans could be a productive way forward.

The Postdigital 'Cages' of Covid-19

During 2020, the Covid-19 pandemic and related lockdown policies dramatically increased the use of online systems to support learning, health, welfare and entertainment. Whilst globally and locally, some people were better positioned than others to access digital devices, platforms, services to acquire associated skills, and to interact through these, for most people there has been a seismic shift in the ways that they now make contact. The Covid-19 lockdown may have physically 'caged' human beings, but it has also provided spaces for self-evaluation and self-description. An obvious example of such a space is the variation in design of facemasks that people adopt, to hoodies with built in masks, or even to full hazmat suits for socialising, such as Micrashell (2020) 'a socially responsible solution to safely allow people to interact in close proximity'. A 'cage' perhaps but at least one that doubles as a wearable outfit.

As humans, we have to choose whether we remain postdigital objects trapped within iron or velvet cages of consumption, or we develop our self-expression as postdigital subjects, as we step in and out of our rubber cages (Ritzer et al. 2018). Gabrielle (2020) argues that:

> The shift to a locked-in world has accelerated the acceptance of identity as distinct from physical body or place. We still want to communicate, socialize and play during this time, but have only a digital version to offer. Those constraints are forcing new expressions of selfhood, from the Zoom background used to express a personal interest or make a joke, to the avatars roaming rich, interactive metaverses. (Gabrielle 2020)

It sounds like many humans are running amok then under these new circumstances to trial and adopt a range of backgrounds, appearances, avatars, and emoticons, which Gabrielle suggests are now separating identity itself from human bodies and their locations. This is even discussed from an angle where the physical identities of people out on the street are considered more shadowy, and less human, in comparison: 'In stark contrast to the masked, distant, de-individuated person we show outside our homes, something a little less than human. There are indications that this redacted version of ourselves is becoming something of a style' (Gabrielle 2020).

These arguments suggest that we may have 'pivoted' as people to become more vibrant now as digital humans, than we are as physical humans. Given the long hours that many people are now spending in online locations, it seems feasible at first that this may be the case, at least for some groups. There will be those who have gained new skills and might thus be more creative in these varied ways online. It cannot be the case for all though, when globally and locally in different parts of the world, digital access, services, skills, and opportunities are far from evenly distributed (Traxler et al. 2020; Roy 2020). The pandemic has revealed that such disparities are the case in developed, as well as less developed, parts of the world with the so-called 'digital divide' not only worsened through Covid-19 (Lem 2020) but now connected with many other forms of existing disadvantage across society. Whilst social distancing has, for some, involved home-based work, for others it has meant a loss of work, for some it has brought a break from travel, for others more desperate forms of travel (Roy 2020; Jandrić et al. 2020a, b).

Whilst digital divides have always been damaging, there are wider effects due to the spread of digital platforms and data to support all human activities. Perhaps new 'postdigital cages' are developing as Covid-19 has revealed those who have capacity to be included in online activities, relating to education, welfare, and employment, and those who do not. Therefore, the online subjectivities and playful identities discussed by Gabrielle (2020), although important to observe, are also a partial view. They can distract attention away from structural cages of inequality that have been heightened by the pandemic. It is also important to recall who put many new technological platforms in place quickly during the crisis, and for what potential purposes.

4 Techlap or Techlash

Whilst some people are 'lapping up' the tech, as described above, others are examining 'techlash' where there has been a growing reaction to an optimistic embracing of digital technologies developed by either idealistic or predatory founders of systems and platforms. Ben Williamson (2020) discusses the positioning of such tech players and the powerful global organisations that are forming networks during the pandemic, liaisons that could have sustained effects on education and democracy, well beyond the current crisis:

> big tech companies such as Google, Microsoft and Facebook, international organizations including the OECD and UNESCO, as well as a global education industry of edu-businesses, consultancies, investors and technology providers, are coming together to define how education systems should respond to the crisis. (Selwyn et al. 2020)

Williamson points out the many implications ranging from the data-driven nature of the businesses forming these coalitions to the consequences for privacy and surveillance, as well as the swift adoption of these platforms at scale, without more vetting procedures. Whilst there are aspirations towards addressing inequalities remotely, this could have profound implications in the longer term for systems of public education (Selwyn et al. 2020).

Levy suggests too that the techlash which existed before the global pandemic arose may also be changing:

> Now that our lives are dominated by these giants, we see them as greedy exploiters of personal data and anticompetitive behemoths who have generally degraded society. Before the pandemic, there was every expectation that those companies would be reined in, if not split apart (Levy 2020).

Amusingly, Levy (2020) asked at the start of lockdown: 'who knew the techlash was susceptible to a virus?'. It seems then that we could be socially distancing ourselves from techlash too. As humans, our morals may now get weighed against our need for online access to these systems developed by the greedy exploiters of personal data. It becomes necessary to assess then in a Covid-19 stricken McDonaldised society, just how much we do or do not mind being subject to these rational networks of corporate players:

> While Big Tech's misdeeds are still apparent, their actual deeds now matter more to us. We're using Facebook to comfort ourselves while physically bunkered and social distancing. Google is being conscripted as the potential hub of one of our greatest needs—Covid-19 testing. Our personal supply chain—literally the only way many of us are getting food and vital supplies—is Amazon. (Levy 2020)

It might be worth avoiding the 'bleach touted as "miracle cure" for Covid being sold on Amazon' (Pilkington 2020), as we stock up ready for the next lockdown. Perhaps then these many changes during the pandemic have some far-reaching implications for the category of 'human' and for what 'self-described' humans decide to include, or exclude in this assessment (Fuller and Jandrić 2019), particularly during a global crisis and as we imagine how to bounce back beyond the pandemic.

How Will Humans Bounce Back?

An interesting question then is how humans might indeed attempt to bounce back from being caged by Covid-19. It is interesting, certainly for the focus of this chapter, on how postdigital humans may come to be valued in either more objective or subjective ways, in McDonaldised society, as we move forward from the global outbreak. The varied angles that are being taken by individual people, at the same time as those actions undertaken by technology companies, welfare and educational organisations, governments and politicians, suggest that many humans who have long been routinely subject to rational forms of computer processing and objective evaluation through McDonaldisation are now finding new routes of expression from the security of their homes. These may not always fit the consumer consumption category and its related McDonaldisation principles either. Instead this response could be said to fit more within a model of security, than one of consumption. How people perceive their postdigital positionality (Hayes 2020) as individual subjects, following the fundamental changes that Covid-19 has wrought, could begin to disrupt and fragment patterns of consumer consumption that have been in place for decades.

At the same time as observing how life changed during lockdown for those in secure homes, the pandemic has revealed how differently other large groups in populations across the world were positioned:

> The lockdown worked like a chemical experiment that suddenly illuminated hidden things. As shops, restaurants, factories and the construction industry shut down, as the wealthy and the middle classes enclosed themselves in gated colonies, our towns and megacities began to extrude their working-class citizens—their migrant workers—like so much unwanted accrual. Many driven out by their employers and landlords, millions of impoverished, hungry, thirsty people, young and old, men, women, children, sick people, blind people, disabled people, with nowhere else to go, with no public transport in sight, began a long march home to their villages. (Roy 2020)

Roy was describing fleeing populations in India early in the pandemic in April 2020. Here the rationally imposed lockdown to enforce physical distancing resulted in the exact opposite—a physical compression of people on an unthinkable scale. Whether walking, sealed into cramped quarters in slums and shanties, or worry about catching the virus, though real, was less present in people's lives than looming unemployment, starvation, and the violence of the police.

> The virus has moved freely along the pathways of trade and international capital, and the terrible illness it has brought in its wake has locked humans down in their countries, their cities and their homes. But unlike the flow of capital, this virus seeks proliferation, not profit, and has, therefore, inadvertently, to some extent, reversed the direction of the flow. It has mocked immigration controls, biometrics, digital surveillance and every other kind of data analytics, and struck hardest—thus far—in the richest, most powerful nations of the world, bringing the engine of capitalism to a juddering halt. Temporarily perhaps, but at least long enough for us to examine its parts, make an assessment and decide whether we want to help fix it, or look for a better engine. (Roy 2020)

Covid-19 seems then to have challenged the flow of rationality from McDonaldisation with a new run of irrationalities to consider. Roy observes that historically 'pandemics have forced humans to break with the past and imagine their world anew', adding that:

> Coronavirus has made the mighty kneel and brought the world to a halt like nothing else could. Our minds are still racing back and forth, longing for a return to "normality", trying to stitch our future to our past and refusing to acknowledge the rupture. But the rupture exists. And in the midst of this terrible despair, it offers us a chance to rethink the doomsday machine we have built for ourselves. Nothing could be worse than a return to normality. (Roy 2020)

Therefore, if the old 'normality' is defined in terms of the McDonaldised society that lockdowns changed forever, perhaps a proliferation of rubber cages will (at least on the surface) be the most noticeable change first. Reported widely across the media, the varying online experiments tried by those in lockdown and discussed by Gabrielle (2020) are just one part of a complex postdigital picture. The scenes of mass migration described by Roy concern people without the same means to experiment with what it means to be a postdigital human. Humans are not occupying equivalent rubber cages, as not only do the digital and human aspects vary for people, other physical and biological factors do too.

It rapidly became apparent that Covid-19 itself did not respect equality or diversity as figures of cases, hospitalisation, and death by race/ethnicity were published (CDC 2020). The color of Coronavirus project monitors such statistics (APM Research Lab 2020). Wide disparities by race seem to be due to numerous reinforcing factors including: workplace exposures, inability to work from home, no access to sick days, geographic areas where people reside, dependence on public transport where the virus is more easily spread, less access to testing, a higher presence of underlying health conditions and receiving delayed medical care, or distrusting health providers. Thus, racial disparities from compounding, elevated risks have been further illuminated by the pandemic (APM Research Lab 2020).

Roy (2020) has questioned though, whilst a viral pandemic has no morals in and of itself, it may in fact yet provide humans with a 'portal', 'a gateway between one world and the next'. But perhaps this is not actually a question of moving from one normal to another. In these circumstances, it is worth considering what passes for 'normal' anyway (Fuller and Jandrić 2019). Perhaps deliberation on a 'new normal' might be accompanied by discussion on more dynamic 'new normals' that have befallen each of us in different ways. Individual or group cages vary depending on the postdigital circumstances within which each person finds themselves. So, it is worth reflecting on Ritzer's 'cages' and whether some may be more hybrid in construction (iron, velvet, and/or rubber) and also multifaceted (as the humans occupying these encounter postdigital systems and Covid-19 cages to varying degrees).

For example, alongside stark reports of physical loss and human grief in the news media, incongruous attempts to recreate life as it was before lockdown in 'Mumdonalds' Happy Meals to replace routine, family fast-food experiences can be observed. The creation of 'social distancing logos' by a group of companies including McDonald's, Coca-Cola, Audi, and Volkswagen (Valinsky 2020) is also not surprising, when predictability is after all, one of the key principles of McDonaldisation theory, alongside efficiency, calculability, control, and the 'irrationality of rationality' (Ritzer et al. 2018). However, lockdown has taken very different shapes for families and individuals. Comments on social media indicate that for some people this just represents a fun take on a tedious process, whilst others argue that 'social distancing logos' assist a global effort by reminding people to distance from each other. Further viewpoints expressed concerns that these icons trivialise a serious matter (Valinsky 2020). Whichever perspective appeals, the production of static logos still plays its part in reinforcing a rational, commercial generalisation. Social distancing becomes reified within McDonaldised marketing, inferring that it is experienced by everyone in a similar, predictable way. As such, many more individual aspects of the 'cages of self-isolation', including the varied national lockdown timelines, separation from loved ones, personal grief, loss, quarantine, migration, and/or economic hardships experienced by so many people across the globe, are rendered less visible (Hayes 2020).

5 Digital Humanities or a Gathering of Postdigital Humans?

There is also an argument that Covid-19 is now speeding up the process of robots replacing humans which raises questions on where matters of identity and value will sit in the coming years. If computer science takes the lead on such developments (Poster 1990) and matters of the humanities are swallowed up in this disciplinary logic, then perhaps the human will take a back seat (just as they might in a self-driving car): '"People usually say they want a human element to their interactions but Covid-19 has changed that", says Martin Ford, a futurist who has written about the ways robots will be integrated into the economy in the coming decades' (Thomas 2020). Changes to consumer preferences are a serious consideration that some suggest are rapidly opening new opportunities for automation. From robot cleaners for schools and offices for example to fast-food chains like McDonald's testing robots as cooks and servers. As Covid-19 accelerates a shift away from humans and towards machines, there are some aspects of this automation that seem to be warmly welcomed to keep critical services running and spare us from disease (Thomas 2020). Chatbot girlfriends and practices of seeking romance or friendship from artificial intelligence (AI) are other potential routes for removing human partnerships and replacing these with computing alternatives (Olson 2020). Then there are the changes to transport and the virus anxiety that have disrupted businesses and supply chains. It seems that suddenly, autonomous transport and the future of delivery is getting a boost because this 'helps customers reduce physical contact and address labour shortages caused by lingering quarantines and travel restrictions' (Bloomberg News 2020).

Interesting too is that such automation is not only affecting manual labour. If anything, the broad term of 'key workers' has lifted some professions to the forefront, alongside the value already placed on skilled health workers. Security staff to operate Covid-19 test centres and shop workers to keep shelves in supermarkets stocked are two such examples. Alongside this focus, Gabrielle (2020) reports that many large companies are 'aggressively employing AI solutions', for example 'Facebook and Google have expanded automated moderation, while PayPal used chatbots for 65% of customer inquiries in recent weeks, a record for the firm' (Gabrielle 2020). Indeed, the picture that emerges currently seems to be richly postdigital as often augmented solutions seem to be adopted with humans not about to bow out just yet:

> Those lucky enough to retain their jobs may face a very different work environment in which they are forced to collaborate with robots and be treated as an increasingly mechanized system themselves. Walmart greeters will stand side-by-side with automated floor-scrubbers, and Amazon warehouse workers—old-hands at human-robot collaboration thanks to the company's acquisition of Kiva Systems—must adapt to being managed more like their pallet-ferrying co-workers, with temperatures monitored by thermal cameras. (Gabrielle 2020)

Ultimately, what remains to be seen are the policies that will emerge alongside these changes to demonstrate how postdigital humans are expected to collaborate in the workplace. Will humans and their computing counterparts be valued, in more objective or subjective ways, in McDonaldised society following the Covid-19 outbreak? Whether society is starting to move away from more traditional global forms of McDonaldisation, based mostly on the rationality of consumer consumption, where computing techniques are simply applied to humans to improve productivity alone, is important to debate. The rationality that placed humans in iron cages was based on the development of new industrial technologies that replaced the old ones in a series of 'revolutions' (Jandrić et al. 2020a). As the digital economy has provided ways to augment industry, entertainment, and the high street, many humans have found their place in more comfortable velvet cages. However, at a time when humanity has been forced to occupy Covid-19 cages, there is a 'fusion of living and technological systems' (Peters et al. 2020b: 3). In a postdigital society, it is increasingly difficult to separate who (or what) is contributing to the cages occupied by humans. Now that there are complex links between epidemics, quarantine, and public health management, these have caused moral and ethical judgements and public health advice to begin to alter approaches towards automation.

Security, Consumption, or Both?

How people perceive their postdigital positionality (Hayes 2020) may therefore be changing somewhat from cages of consumer consumption towards cages of security given new biological risks. This is raising issues with regard to surveillance as the number of devices and different forms of data gather in our lives. Whilst humans may be distancing from each other, these technologies are becoming ever more intimately involved with us. Once when computing was a specialised field, it was less of an issue, but now networked and ubiquitous computing have altered our society to become increasingly 'data-driven'. From consumer habits to educational outcomes and behavioural observation, the ability to film, record, create, and encrypt human data, as well as to decide matters for humans through algorithms, has brought privacy to the forefront. Whilst the Internet of Things (IoT) has enabled all manner of devices to support humans in the home as they operate appliances or seek to monitor who visits their doorstep, there are concerns that data collection is increasingly seamless between devices and consumer data remains open to industry abuse. A confusing mass of information in the form of a 'data smog' is concealing and conflating information now about multiple individuals (Mortier et al. 2020).

Moving from an individual or home level towards a broader monitoring of citizens in general, the installation of close circuit cameras for safety on the street has long received criticism and support. Now that automatic facial recognition (AFR) software has found its place into towns and institutions, there has been both backlash and even removal of these technologies. In a recent landmark case in the UK, the use of AFR Locate was argued to have breached human rights when biometric data was analysed without the knowledge or consent of the individual concerned. The court upheld that there was 'no clear guidance on where AFR Locate could be used and who could be put on a watchlist, a data protection impact assessment was deficient and the police force did not take reasonable steps to find out if the software had a racial or gender bias' (Rees 2020).

Yet just as such cases may be bringing concerns from the humanities to bear on what computing really means in each of our lives as postdigital humans, Covid-19 has led to demand for 'webcams to enable customers to check online to see how busy the high streets are, in a bid to help with social distancing' (Beardmore 2020). There are concerns too regarding the pros and cons of track-and-trace apps and invasion of privacy (Amnesty International 2020). Just as postdigital humans are adapting to working online more autonomously, 'tattleware' software, such as Interguard and Sneek are being bought by companies to increase surveillance on employees, taking photos of workers as often as once a minute (Gabrielle 2020). Perhaps the old iron cage of McDonaldisation has now moved itself online. If this is the case, new forms of postdigital participation, rather than McDonaldisation, may go on being contested for some time to come, demonstrating a less than equal gathering between machines and humans.

6 Conclusion: Equal But Not Equivalent

In summary, it could be argued that a machine or a device performing a task that a human might otherwise have completed is undertaking something 'equal' in nature, e.g. if the end result is that a self-driving car delivers a human passenger at a given destination, just as the same human would arrive at the same destination having driven the car themselves. However, this does not mean that seemingly equal results can be considered as identical. Depending on whether this example is viewed from a computing perspective, or from within the humanities, different properties of such a situation may be considered. In a postdigital analysis, it can be noticed how even autonomous, or semi-autonomous, digital technologies retain their connections to human rationality. This may be via programming and design, related to the data on humans that these devices, apps, or platforms carry, or more broadly connected to rational human aims and values described in policies for situations where technologies are utilised. It may perhaps be argued then that our digital counterparts are equal to some extent but not equivalent.

To play with language in this way also demonstrates why qualitative as well as quantitative perspectives are needed. The rationality of McDonaldisation described by Ritzer in terms of efficiency, calculability, predictability, and control may be achieved via technology, but this is also supported through the discourse that accompanies its utilisation in any given situation. McDonaldisation, as a large enduring social theory, has demonstrated how patterns of rationality have been sustained in different ways over decades across global, political, economies, and popular cultures. The homogeneity that Ritzer first observed could also be noticed in augmented ways, as digital developments enabled online activities to supplement the sameness of companies on the high street of every city (Ritzer et al. 2018).

Now the spread of Covid-19 has revealed a mass of postdigital human subjectivities from across the globe (Peters et al. 2020a, b, Jandrić et al. 2020b). The starkly uneven human access to digital devices, skills, and services revealed is a reminder that in postdigital society there are also huge numbers of humans and communities who remain pre-digital or semi-digital too (Traxler et al. 2020). Then there are the more objective treatments of humans through surveillance technologies and also the call for more of these to support our fight against the pandemic.

Perhaps we are witnessing something of a collision between the subjective nature of the humanities and the objective nature of digital computing. If so, it is a battle with a viral umpire keeping score just now as the rationalities of McDonaldisation fragment or begin to reform. As humanity looks beyond the pandemic and contemplates the gathering of machines and humans that has protected us, it will be important to check what may have been erased from us at the same time.

References

Amnesty International (2020). Bahrain, Kuwait and Norway contact tracing apps among most dangerous for privacy. 16 June. https://www.amnesty.org/en/latest/news/2020/06/bahrain-kuwait-norway-contact-tracing-apps-danger-for-privacy/. Accessed 1 September 2020.

APM Research Lab. (2020). The color of coronavirus. 15 October. https://www.apmresearchlab.org/covid/deaths-by-race#age. Accessed 1 September 2020.

Beardmore, R. (2020). Webcams and speakers set for installation in Wyre town centres 'will not be used for monitoring'. Fleetwood Weekly News, 17 September. https://www.fleetwoodtoday.co.uk/news/politics/webcams-and-speakers-set-installation-wyre-town-centres-will-not-be-used-monitoring-2975347. Accessed 1 September 2020.

Bloomberg News (2020). Driverless Delivery Van Startup Sees Demand Surge Amid Outbreak. Hyperdrive, 8 March. https://www.bloomberg.com/news/articles/2020-03-08/they-won-t-catch-the-virus-so-chinese-robovan-maker-s-sales-jump?sref=QYc4Et5D. Accessed 1 September 2020.

Centers for Disease Control and Prevention (CDC) (2020). Covid-19 cases, hospitalisation and death by race/ethnicity. https://www.cdc.gov/coronavirus/2019-ncov/downloads/covid-data/hospitalization-death-by-race-ethnicity.pdf. Accessed 1 September 2020.

Ecclestone, K., & Hayes, D. (2019). *The dangerous rise of therapeutic education*. London: Routledge.

Fuller, S., & Jandrić, P. (2019). The Postdigital Human: Making the history of the future. *Postdigital Science and Education, 1*(1), 190–217. https://doi.org/10.1007/s42438-018-0003-x.

Furedi, F. (2004). *Therapy culture: creating vulnerability in an uncertain age*. London: Routledge.

Gabrielle, M. (2020). The Coronovirus has hastened the post-human era. TechCrunch, 1 June. https://techcrunch.com/2020/06/01/the-coronavirus-has-hastened-the-post-human-era/. Accessed 1 September 2020.

Gregory, J. (2020). The coronavirus 'infodemic' is real. We rated the websites responsible for it. *Stat*, 28 February. https://www.statnews.com/2020/02/28/websites-spreading-coronavirus-misinformation-infodemic/. Accessed 1 September 2020.

Hall, G. (2013). Toward a postdigital humanities: Cultural analytics and the computational turn to data-driven scholarship. *American Literature, 85*(4), 781–809. https://doi.org/10.1215/00029831-2367337.

Hayes, D., & Wynyard, R. (2002). *The McDonaldization of higher education*. Santa Barbara, CA: Praeger.

Hayes, S. (2020). *Postdigital Positionality: Developing powerful, inclusive narratives for learning, teaching, research and policy in Higher Education*. Leiden: Brill.

Hayes, S. (2019). *The labour of words in Higher Education: is it time to reoccupy policy?* Leiden: Brill.

Hayes, S., & Bartholomew, P. (2015). Where's the humanity? Challenging the policy discourse of technology enhanced learning. In J. Branch, P. Bartholomew, & C. Nygaard (Eds.), *Technology enhanced learning in higher education*. London: Libri.

Jandrić, P., Hayes, D., Truelove, I., Levinson, P., Mayo, P., Ryberg, T., Monzó, L. D., Allen, Q., Stewart, P. A., Carr, P. R., Jackson, L., Bridges, S., Escaño, C., Grauslund, D., Mañero, J., Lukoko, H. O., Bryant, P., Fuentes Martinez, A., Gibbons, A., Sturm, S., Rose, J., Chuma, M. M., Biličić, E., Pfohl, S., Gustafsson, U., Arantes, J. A., Ford, D. R., Kihwele, J. E., Mozelius, P., Suoranta, J., Jurjević, L., Jurčević, M., Steketee, A., Irwin, J., White, E. J., Davidsen, J., Jaldemark, J., Abegglen, S., Burns, T., Sinfield, S., Kirylo, J. D., Batarelo Kokić, I., Stewart, G. T., Rikowski, G., Lisberg Christensen, L., Arndt, S., Pyyhtinen, O., Reitz, C., Lodahl, M., Humble, N., Buchanan, R., Forster, D. J., Kishore, P., Ozoliņš, J., Sharma, N., Urvashi, S., Nejad, H. G., Hood, N., Tesar, M., Wang, Y., Wright, J., Brown, J. B., Prinsloo, P., Kaur, K., Mukherjee, M., Novak, R., Shukla, R., Hollings, S., Konnerup, U., Mallya, M., Olorundare, A., Achieng-Evensen, C., Philip, A. P., Hazzan, M. K., Stockbridge, K., Komolafe, B. F., Bolanle, O. F., Hogan, M., Redder, B., Sattarzadeh, S. D., Jopling, M., SooHoo, S.,

Devine, N., & Hayes, S. (2020a). Teaching in The Age of Covid-19. *Postdigital Science and Education, 2*(3), 1069–1230. https://doi.org/10.1007/s42438-020-00169-6.

Jandrić, P., Jaldemark, J., Hurley, Z., Bartram, B., Matthews, A., Jopling, M., Mañero, J., MacKenzie, A., Irwin, J., Rothmüller, N., Green, B., Ralston, S. J., Pyyhtinen, O., Hayes, S., Wright, J., Peters, M. A., & Tesar, M. (2020b). Philosophy of education in a new key: Who remembers Greta Thunberg? Education and environment after the coronavirus. *Educational Philosophy and Theory*. https://doi.org/10.1080/00131857.2020.1811678.

Jandrić, P., & Hayes, S. (2020). Postdigital We-Learn. *Studies in Philosophy of Education, 39*(3), 285–297. https://doi.org/10.1007/s11217-020-09711-2.

Jandrić, P., Knox, J., Besley, T., Ryberg, T., Suoranta, J., & Hayes, S. (2018). Postdigital Science and Education. *Educational Philosophy and Theory, 50*(10), 893–899. https://doi.org/10.1080/00131857.2018.1454000.

Lem, P. (2020). Covid-19 could worsen digital divide. Research Professional, 17 September. https://researchprofessionalnews.com/rr-news-europe-universities-2020-9-covid-19-could-worsen-digital-divide/. Accessed 1 September 2020.

Levy, S. (2020). Has the Coronavirus killed the techlash. Wired, 20 March 2020. https://www.wired.com/story/plaintext-has-the-coronavirus-killed-the-techlash/. Accessed 1 September 2020.

Leone, M. (2018). Semiotics of the Selfie: The Glorification of the Present. Punctum, 44(2): 33–48.

Mee, E. (2020). Talking robots could be used in UK care homes to ease loneliness and improve mental health. Sky News, 8 September. https://news.sky.com/story/talking-robots-could-be-used-in-uk-care-homes-to-ease-loneliness-and-improve-mental-health-12066296. Accessed 1 September 2020.

Micrashell (2020). A suit that allows you to safely socialise in times of a pandemic. https://production.club/micrashell/. Accessed 1 September 2020.

Mortier, R., Haddadi, H., Henderson, T., McAuley, D., Crowcroft, J., & Crabtree, A. (2020). Human-data interaction. In *The Encyclopedia of Human-Computer Interaction*, 2nd Edition. Interaction Design Foundation. https://nottingham-repository.worktribe.com/preview/819355/Human-Data%20Interaction.pdf. Accessed 1 September 2020.

Olson, P. (2020). My girlfriend is a chatbot. The Wall Street Journal, 10 April. https://www.wsj.com/articles/my-girlfriend-is-a-chatbot-11586523208. Accessed 1 September 2020.

Peters, M. A., Wang, H., Ogunniran, M. O., Huang, Y., Green, B., Chunga, J. O., Quainoo, E. A., Ren, Z., Hollings, S., Mou, C., Khomera, S. W., Zhang, M., Zhou, S., Laimeche, A., Zheng, W., Xu, R., Jackson, L., & Hayes, S. (2020a). China's internationalized Higher Education during Covid-19: collective student autoethnography. *Postdigital Science and Education, 2*(3), 968–988. https://doi.org/10.1007/s42438-020-00128-1.

Peters, M. A., Jandrić, P., & McLaren, P. (2020b). Viral modernity? Epidemics, infodemics, and the 'bioinformational' paradigm. *Educational Philosophy and Theory*. https://doi.org/10.1080/00131857.2020.1744226.

Pilkington, E. (2020). Bleach touted as 'miracle cure' for Covid being sold on Amazon. The Guardian, 19 September. https://www.theguardian.com/world/2020/sep/19/bleach-miracle-cure-amazon-covid. Accessed 1 September 2020.

Poster, M. (1990). *The Mode of Information: Poststructuralism and Social Context*. Cambridge, UK: Polity.

Rees, J. (2020). Facial recognition use by South Wales Police ruled unlawful. BBC News, 11 August. https://www.bbc.co.uk/news/uk-wales-53734716. Accessed 1 September 2020.

Ritzer, G., & Dean, P. (2019). *Globalisation: the essentials*. New York: Wiley Blackwell.

Ritzer, G. (1993/2018). *The McDonaldisation of society: Into the digital age* (9th ed.). Thousand Oaks, CA: Sage Publications.

Ritzer, G., Jandrić, P., & Hayes, S. (2018). Prosumer capitalism and its machines. *Open Review of Educational Research, 5*(1), 113–129. https://doi.org/10.1080/23265507.2018.1546124.

Roy, A. (2020). The pandemic is a portal. Financial Times, 4 April https://www.ft.com/content/10d8f5e8-74eb-11ea-95fe-fcd274e920ca. Accessed 1 September 2020.

Selwyn, N., Macgilchrist, F., & Williamson, B. (2020). Digital education after COVID-19. *Techlash*, 1. https://der.monash.edu.au/lnm/wp-content/uploads/2020/06/TECHLASH-01--COVID-education.pdf. Accessed 8 August 2020.

Thomas, Z. (2020). Coronavirus: Will Covid-19 speed up the use of robots to replace human workers? BBC News, 18 April. https://www.bbc.co.uk/news/technology-52340651. Accessed 1 September 2020.

Traxler, J., Smith, M., Scott, H., & Hayes, S. (2020). Learning through the crisis. Department for International Development (DFID) EdTech Hub.

Valinsky, J. (2020). McDonald's and other brands are making 'social distancing' logos. CNN, 26 March. https://edition.cnn.com/2020/03/26/business/social-distancing-brand-logos-coronavirus/index.html. Accessed 1 September 2020.

Weber, M. (1930). *The protestant ethic and the spirit of capitalism*. London: Allen and Unwin.

Williamson, B. (2020). New pandemic edtech power networks. https://codeactsineducation.wordpress.com/2020/04/01/new-pandemic-edtech-power-networks/. Accessed 1 September 2020.

Postdigital Truths: Educational Reflections on Fake News and Digital Identities

Kathrin Otrel-Cass and Michael Fasching

1 Introduction

Mona, an 18-year-old secondary school student from Denmark, is talking to us about how she evaluates the information she collects from the Internet, and especially how she assesses her own competences in dealing with fake news. She says that she has experienced a lot of fake news when surfing the Internet. At school they learned about how to identify fake news, but it was *'out of touch because as a younger generation we know that fake news exists and we know to be critical of the things we read'*. This short example should depict the problem we would like to address in this chapter, namely: what kind of digital competences young people should acquire at school, in particular when they are or will be faced with fake news.

Fake news is not a new phenomenon, but it has become increasingly difficult to distinguish between correct, erroneous, and deliberately falsified information (Auberry 2018), and the debates about the magnitude of this problem amongst media industry, politics, and academia have increased (Lazer et al. 2018). Around two-thirds of students, rate news reports in social media as credible, and an increasing amount of fake news is interpreted as fact (Himmelrath and Egbers 2018). It seems therefore necessary to better understand young people's postdigital practices. For this reason, we asked students to *show* us their online performances (Goffman 1959). This approach should help us gain a better understanding of young people's online practices and sharpen our suggestion of what kind of competences are needed to obtain critical digital literacies (Davies 2018).

K. Otrel-Cass (✉) · M. Fasching
University of Graz, Graz, Austria
e-mail: kathrin.otrel-cass@uni-graz.at; michael.fasching@uni-graz.at

2 Education for Digital Competences

Although the debate of what entails digital literacy has been ongoing, we find at least one fundamental question that needs to be answered: How important is the reliability of information when we are getting used to consume, produce, and reproduce digitised information? When Information Communication Technologies (ICTs) have become agents that are more than just tools, but a force majeure that is shaping who we are, how we socialise, and how we experience reality and our own agency (Floridi 2015) we need to develop new reflective approaches.

In postdigital ages, ICTs have transformed lives so that globally, education systems and governance bodies are focusing on ways to boost the development of digital competence for teachers and students [see, for example the European framework for the digital competence of educators: DigCompEdu (Redecker 2017)]. Alkali and Amichai-Hamburger point out that when it comes to 'digital competences' the terminology can be a bit diffuse, but that in general it describes 'a large variety of complex skills—cognitive, motoric, sociological, and emotional—users need to have in order to use digital environments effectively'(2004: 421). Since the main focus in this chapter is on the kind of competences that are necessary to be handling fake news, we will now focus on that particular knowledge and skill set.

3 Managing Compromised Online Spaces

Lazer et al. (2018: 1094) define fake news as 'fabricated information that mimics news media content in form but not in organizational process or intent'. This means that dealing with *fake news* requires a person to identify and manage manipulated online content and differentiate it from real news. This critical competency, reserved to the management of digital media, is also referred to as *information literacy* (Jones-Jang et al. 2019; Livingstone et al. 2008). Management of digital information under these new conditions requires meta skills to avoid an operationalised and simplistic approach to information literacy as Barnett (1994) points out. Dealing with fake news is not only about the tampered content of a message but also has to do with how information is received in the first place, since users of online spaces (that includes young people) are navigating in compromised online spaces (Allcott and Gentzkow 2017). For example social media and also search engines are operated by algorithms that select content and posts based on a person's viewing history and create so-called *filter bubbles* (Pariser 2011). While this, in its simplest form, is convenient for instance when cookies remember settings or information, filtered search results can create the illusion of personalised online spaces, and this can produce a self-affirmation of one's interests. The illusion is hidden in the fact that the person using this function may not realise the magnitude of profiling that has taken place in the background in order to create a given context menu.

Zuboff (2019) has described the financially and politically motivated drivers that lead to what is also described as surveillance capitalism. Zuboff argues that 'highly profitable machine intelligence operations convert raw material into the firm's highly profitable algorithmic products designed to predict the behaviour of users' (2019: 65). When a person utilises these functionalities deliberately (for example in social media) to follow selected content providers, the online space that is created is also described as an *echo chamber* (Pörksen 2018). When people are faced with information that is contrary to the information they have expected to receive through their echo chambers, they may experience a dissonance effect and be forced to make a decision between this information and their pre-existing position (Liao and Fu 2013).

The growing empirical literature on fake news can be divided into three categories: research on how fake news occurs in public discourse, studies that focus on their impacts, and those that examine how to counteract the spread of fake news (Egelhofer and Lecheler 2019). Tandoc et al. (2018) analysed in a study a collection of six different types of fake news: news satire, news parody, news production, photo manipulation, propaganda, and advertising together with public relations. Tandoc et al. (2018) as well as Egelhofer and Lecheler (2019) distinguish further between high and low levels of factuality. What the literature agrees on is that fake news are not tied to a specific media type, they are always verifiable wrong, are not necessarily produced with an intention to deceive, and do not automatically imply a misdirection of the recipient (Zimmermann and Kohring 2018). While there is focus on the producers of fake news, the role the recipients play seems to be overlooked so far (Hermida 2011). Some questions whether fake news can be called fake news, if recipients do not classify the material they read as real news in the first place. This puts the need for information literacy of the recipients into the foreground (Jang and Kim 2018). In order to understand the ways young people encounter or manage online content, it helps to unpack what shapes their digital presence.

4 Being Digitally Present and Having a Digital Identity

The persistency of our digital footprints ensures that we create our digital identity whether we want it or not (Williams et al. 2010). From a postdigital perspective, digital identities are the 'collections of digital information that belong to an individual or an organisation' (Hansen and Meints 2006: 543) and configure a person's digital relationships (Buckingham 2007). Since digital identities seem to be enmeshed with our everyday offline lives (Otrel-Cass 2019), it affects millions of people everywhere (Floridi 2011). This is an issue of growing importance. Taking the postdigital approach allows us to hone in on the 'normalisation of the digital in almost all aspects of activity' (Cormier et al. 2019: 482).

Burden and Savin-Baden explain that 'identity creation and exploration is not only evident through representations on social networking sites but also the ways in which people accessorise themselves technologically' (2019: 198). This means it is important to take note of how people furnish their own online appearances and the online spaces they create for themselves. Depending on media or online contexts, identities change and shift, so there is no such thing as a fixed identity. Identities move with contexts, temporalities, and the virtual world in which we live (Burden and Savin-Baden 2019). The construction of digital identities influences how young people understand themselves as well as their peer groups, societies, and cultures to which belong. They contribute to shaping their self-esteem, lifestyles, moral behaviours, values, and ethical expectations (Floridi 2011). Another important role in the formation of digital identities is online communities, which are 'understood as dynamic, interactive and distributed networks, in which the individual is never a stand-alone entity but always a participant' (Floridi 2011: 478). What becomes evident is that digital identities change and are being changed constantly. This active shaping of one's digital identity in response to changing social and cultural contexts is also referred to as 'tinkering' (Hitzler and Honer 1994). *Tinker identities* are not reserved for specific feelings of belongings (e.g. nationality) but describe social contextual relationships with multiple cultures as well as hybrid identities (Scherke 2011; Lindau 2010).

This ability to tinker with and reassemble representations about oneself also shows that the production process of digital assemblages creates information or knowledge in a seemingly liquid way (Sørensen 2009). Sometimes, however, these liquid assemblages can become more stabilised. However, Sørensen qualifies that '[l]iquid knowledge of the virtual environment is not a knowledge that maps the practice of the environment 'on the scale of a mile to a mile'. Liquid knowledge is not a map. It is not regional' (128); it is communal and temporary, and this makes it liquid according to the author.

Caught in Echo Chambers and Filter Bubbles

When social media or the Internet is accessed, pre-filtered information is received. This means that personalised filtering systems consisting of complex algorithms gate keep or gate *manage* what kind of information is being presented. This filter function only shows selected information that algorithms have identified to be of interest to users and creates an illusion of personalised online spaces for the recipient, a self-affirmation of one's interests—a so-called echo chamber or filter bubble (Pörksen 2018). Pariser describes filter bubbles in this way:

> The new generation of Internet filters looks at the things you seem to like - the actual things you've done, or the things people like you like - and tries to extrapolate. They are prediction engines, constantly creating and refining a theory of who you are and what you'll do and want next. Together, these engines create a unique universe of information for each of us - what I've come to call a filter bubble. (Pariser 2011: 7)

The difference between filter bubbles and echo chambers is that the former is the result of different information search processes, selection, perception, and the algorithm-tailored information that fits the pre-existing attitudes of the individuals (Boutyline and Willer 2017). The latter describes communities in which content that confirms certain ideologies is echoed and multiplied. Echo chamber communities are prone to foster processes of polarisation and possibly group radicalisation (O'Hara and Stevens 2015).

Filter bubbles are not a new phenomenon, since people have always consumed media and topics that appealed to their specific interests (Pariser 2011). However, filter bubbles can influence the way choices are made. Pariser writes that people are alone in their bubbles and have no specific reference audience to share the experience with. The agenda behind the filter bubble is invisible to most, since search engines for instance do not reveal the full details of why they are displaying certain search results. Typically, people do not choose to enter the filter bubble, but rather they are often presented to them due to profits made by the (mostly unpaid) digital services that are being used. For that reason, it will become harder and harder to avoid filter bubbles (Pariser 2011).

The hidden nature of manipulated content is exacerbated in the production of so-called *deepfakes,* which are techniques based on artificial intelligence (AI) to synthesise new visual products, such as the production of a video with replaced faces (Floridi 2018). Some of the better-known examples of deepfakes are of well-known personalities like Barack Obama, Donald Trump, Mark Zuckerberg, or Boris Johnson. Automated video and audio editing tools make it almost impossible for recipients to distinguish between real and fake content. With specific video software, the production of deepfake videos is becoming increasingly easier even for individuals with lower technological skills (Chesney and Citron 2019).

In addition, *chatbot*s, AI-based conversational software agents that get activated by language inputs in the form of voice, text, or both (Radziwill and Benton 2017), as multipliers of echo chambers, increasingly aggravate the problem of spreading rumours. In social media, such as Twitter, fake user profiles have been set up to artificially increase the number of followers to spread fake news, to dynamically adapt to user behaviour and to influence particular political positions of users (Ferrara et al. 2016).

Information Literacy for Education

The importance of equipping young people with the competences to understand the scope of dealing with fake news is just becoming evident to educators and educational governance bodies. In a report, McDougall et al. (2018) focus on primary and secondary school students' media literacies and present their analysis of the European education landscape. They argue that being media literate was a matter of developing students' citizenship competences, since young people need to have the ability to participate in democratic societal processes, and to not have those skills would compromise this important aim.

There are still too few educational studies that examine fake news in all its complexity, and what this means especially for primary and secondary school students (Sciannamea 2020). It may be a tempting solution to advise students to simply not trust, to avoid non-traditional news sites, and to access information only from traditional quality media. But this approach would be far too simplistic, and the creation of dichotomous 'good' or 'bad' distinctions is not helpful, since there is always the possibility that mainstream media may spread false information too and that less credible sources uncover legitimate stories (Journell 2019). Farmer (2019) suggests that fake news is a 'wake-up call' for education and that young people urgently need support to develop their critical analytical skills, but that this is only possible if teachers too gain those competences. Farmer urges that curricular changes are needed, and he too stresses that being information literate is about becoming an informed citizen. Williamson et al. (2019) describe the challenge of education in dealing with fake news as a 'live issue', which falls 'between traditional subject silos and often they have no formal place in the curriculum at all' (2019: 89).

The next section presents the methodology of the research we present here. Our aim was to find an overarching strategy and rationale to consider the networks of people and things in the context of their online practices.

5 A Socio-material Methodology

Estrid Sørensen (2009) describes in her book the '*Materiality of Learning*' and points out that it is important to ask 'how specific technologies contribute to practice' (2009: 7). Sørensen is critical of the tradition to approach learning from the humanist perspective which only grants humans, a priori, exceptional positions in practice. To analyse people's practices with technology, we should describe particular learning practices as patterns of relations of human and non-human components. This in turn characterises the performance of humans. However, since this is an investigation shaped by postdigital intentionality, we are interested in understanding socio-material relations (Knox 2019), and their consequences for thinking about the purpose of information literacy in education. With this intention, we do want to draw attention to material perspectives but only to return to human practices. For this reason, we have analysed the online materials our participated students use with the help of actor–network theory (ANT) (Latour 1987, 1992; Callon and Law 1997). Actor–network theory helps us to sensitise ourselves to the presence of material actors, while identifying how they are assembled and how they occupy a defined landscape. The theory allows for the unravelling of what is also described as 'assemblage or gathering of materials brought together and linked through processes of translation' (Fenwick and Edwards 2011: 5). The authors point out that ANT offers new insights into educational objects. We wondered how ANT might help us gain insights into objects students should be learning about.

To return the focus of our analysis on human practices, we utilised cultural-historical activity theory (CHAT) in a second step to explore the relationship of digital materials and social factors, since materials and people have shared histories that allow them to connect their practices (Cole 1996; Law 1987). CHAT is an analytical lens that allows us to examine material objects in their ideal and material form to ask in what ways those artefacts become part of people's goal-directed activities. In other words, by tracing a person's online activity and paying attention to the materials they utilise to achieve the goal of an activity, we can also examine how they are embedded in context, are more than information processing, operate at different levels, and relate to other objects in the world (Kaptelinin and Nardi 2006).

We used these theoretical frameworks to examine observational data from two studies conducted in Denmark and Austria. The analysis of this chapter was conducted on selected episodes that are presented as vignettes. The project 'One day in my Onlife' is a digital ethnography tracing the entanglements of human–machine consciousness that has been conducted in Denmark involving young people aged 17–24. The Austrian project 'Digital? Safe!' is a study on cybersecurity and digital competences amongst Austrian pupils between the ages of 14 and 19. The students, whose stories are presented here, were secondary school students at the time of the interviews. The students were commenting on their practices with social media and were doing so while sharing and exploring content on their laptops and/or mobile devices. We recorded their screens while they were showing us content while reflecting.

Our analysis process began by transcribing the video recordings. After identifying episodes of interest that were relevant to responding to our research question, we followed up with a familiarisation of the non-human actors within the given episode. This meant that we started by identifying seemingly heterogeneous components and determining how these parts become part of a network, since we did not want to assume that any technology operates as 'automatons that work by themselves' (Sørensen 2009: 53). We continued analysing relevant levels of proximity or distance and expressed this in a graphical representation (Callon 1984; Latour 1999). We decided to show proximity in two ways: by shading and by distance vectors. The darker shades are the actors we identified as central in a given episode and have concentrated on in our analysis. The grey shades indicate other contributing actors that are more distanced to those in the first layer. Patterned fills should indicate non-human actors that may not be visible to human actors. Lines should indicate the relative nearness of the actors to each other. In a second step of our analysis, we applied CHAT to return to the human actor and their motives in a given activity. We took note how material objects mediated the pursuit of goals in the activities of our participants (Kaptelinin and Nardi 2006).

6 A Socio-material Analysis in Three Vignettes

Three vignettes are presented: information management, opinion management, and identity management followed by a discussion with our participants on the kind of competences they believe they and their peers need to have.

Vignette: Critical Information Management

Analysis of human and non-human actors: Mona (pseudonym), an 18-year-old young woman from Denmark, is scrolling on a laptop through her Facebook timeline. The Facebook page was set up in the traditional layout. Left were shortcuts or links to other places including messenger, but also a Covid-19 information centre (see Fig. 1).

To the right are the list of contacts and the centre of the page is occupied by the main feed of information. It is also noteworthy that the Facebook page was opened on an incognito tab, and the background colour of the screen was set in black. The episode starts at a point where Mona stops at a bright map of Denmark showing Chinchilla farms and a picture of a caged Chinchilla in the right corner. Above the map is a logo and name of the vegan party, and below it says that it is a sponsored ad by the vegan party. It says: '*Vi har over 40.000 afdissepelsdyr bag fremmer.* (We have over 40,000 of these fur animals caged up). *Vil du også have det til at stoppe?* (Do you too want this to stop?)'.

The map was headlined brightly '*Chinchillafabrikker I Danmark* (Chinchilla farms in Denmark)'. Below it says in small writing '*Hjælpchinchillaen med envælgererklæring, 2 klik* (Help the chinchillas with this petition, two clicks)', followed by a button saying 'Learn more'.

In this first episode, we identified the following non-human components: a laptop, the Internet, Facebook, the Vegan party post, images, text, algorithms. The algorithms are shaded since they stayed hidden, yet their presence could be experienced everywhere on the social media page. These components are juxtaposed to the human actor, Mona, a young woman living in Denmark, still going to school. In

Fig. 1 Screenshot Vegan party, Chinchilla factory map Denmark

Postdigital Truths: Educational Reflections on Fake News and Digital Identities

the figure, we have indicated the relative significance and proximate distance (Fig. 2).

In a next step, we followed Mona's activity as it unfolded in this episode and considered the social-historical configurations. Mona scrolls through her Facebook timeline when she stops at an advertisement of the Danish Vegan Party—'*ok, this is interesting*' she says. Her motivation in this activity was to show us her Facebook page and how she manages the material and content she receives. The post (see Fig. 1) shows a Danish map with red dots pointing to chinchilla rodent factories with a link to an animal welfare petition. Mona recognises that this is a sponsored post and clicks on 'more information' in the post and to find out why she received this advertisement.

She finds out she received the post because she is '…*older than 18, living in Denmark, Danish speaking*'. Mona is surprised and comments, '*I am not a vegan [...] it's funny, that it's reaching me*'. Mona wonders '*I don't believe that*' and starts to fact check the post with a Google search. Her first search result leads her to 'Kopenhagen Fur' but she dismisses this result: '*because that's just gonna be advertising*'. However, she cannot find the desired information while browsing the first Google page. This confirms to her to be critical about this post. Facebook pages typically include a note saying 'There may be other reasons not listed here', such as location data, movement profiles, interactions with similar companies, information from Facebook or Instagram profiles, or offline activities are also considered in the ad-tracking. Maybe Mona knows of this. However, she did not refer to this when we spoke to her.

The analysis of this episode illustrated that sustaining investment of Mona's attention into the party's aims via the Facebook technology required an orchestration of visual imagery plus text information to lead Mona into a cyber-rabbit hole to find out more.

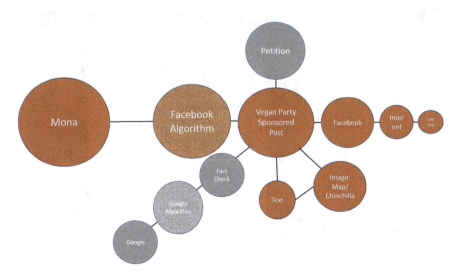

Fig. 2 Analysis of Mona and her fact check

Vignette: Opinion Management

Analysis of human and non-human actors: Mona stops scrolling at the private Facebook group 'Vax vs. Anti-Vax' on her laptop and describes things she notices. She explains that she had joined this private group out of interest.

On the left are still the groups in which Mona is actively registered. In the middle of the page is a picture of US President Donald Trump with the quote 'I don't take any responsibility at all'. Above the picture are 3% figures about Covid-19: '% of the world population who are American: 4.2%. % of world Covid-19 cases who are American: 33.1%. % of world Covid-19 deaths who are American: 28.2%.' The three numbers are in the colours of the US flag, in red, white, and blue. Below the numbers is the following text 'Data accurate as of 6 May 2020'. A logo with the letters 'RtAVM' is on the right side (see Fig. 3).

In this episode, Mona notices a logo on the right side of the image and we have identified the following non-human actors: a laptop, the Internet, Facebook algorithm, Facebook group Vax vs. Anti-Vax (image/text), logo, Google algorithm, and a Twitter post (see Fig. 4). Different from the previous episode, the Facebook algorithm was defined by Mona herself, since she had subscribed as a member of the Vax vs. Anti-Vax group.

Applying an activity theory analysis, we identify in this episode that the goal of the activity was to show the researcher an example of a group Mona was following. Mona's motive to be part of this group was because she was intrigued by the topic. Her goal was to observe the discussion, because she *'finds it funny'* to scroll through private groups that show heated debates, false comments and discussions. She explained she had joined the group solely to watch as a bystander since she would

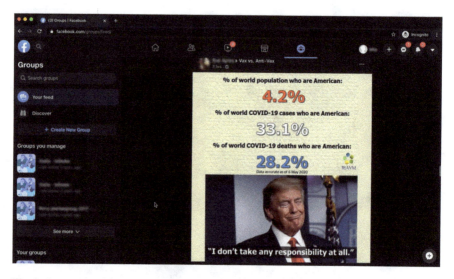

Fig. 3 Screenshot, Covid-19 and Donald Trump in the group 'Vax vs. Anti-Vax'

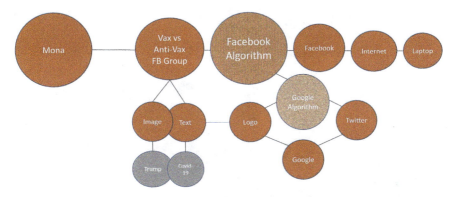

Fig. 4 Analysis of Mona and her echo chamber with Actor–network theory

encounter *'unbelievable posts'* such as the picture showing Donald Trump (see Fig. 3). Mona identifies this post as a hate-post against Trump and says that she rather believes in the content of the post because it reinforces her opinion. *'Automatically I am more inclined to believe it, because it is sort of aligning with my beliefs'*, she says. She notices a logo and starts a Google search that leads her to the Twitter account 'Refutation of anti-vaccination memes', which she classifies as an untrustworthy source, *'this is not a source at all, this is just a watermark'*. Mona thinks the logo is *'misleading'* because it suggests seriousness. Although the image is linked to the date of the displayed percentages, there are no further references, *'they do not cite any sources'*. This suggests as if it is *'from the World Health Organization'*. The activity shows that there are particular rules, norms, and procedures that regulate Mona's interactions and her coordination related to the use of the target technology. Mona had defined some of those rules herself. She created an echo chamber where she received information she believed in and other information that confirmed her position about often politically polarised topics.

Vignette: Identity Management

The third vignette is from the Austrian project 'Digital? Sicher! (Digital? Safe!)', a study on cybersecurity and digital literacy amongst Austrian students aged 13–19 years. Analysis of human and non-human actors: Flora and Maria (pseudonyms), two 13-year-old school girls from Austria, talk about their preferred social media and the content they particularly like to engage with. One of the two girls shows the researcher TikTok, a social media app on her phone, with a number of videos posted by another girl under the banner 'black lives matter' (see Fig. 5). The app shows the girl's profile, pictures, videos with reach, likes, and comments.

In this episode, we identify the following non-human actors: a smartphone, the Internet, TikTok, the TikTok algorithm, TikTok profile of Charlie D'Amelio, her

Fig. 5 Screenshot, Flora and Maria talking about #blacklivesmatters on TikTok

images, videos, a Black Lives Matters profile picture, following numbers, follower numbers, and like numbers, red follow button (see Fig. 6). Each of the video thumbnails includes a count of the reach.

Using an activity theory analysis lens, we identify that Flora and Maria are following the 16-year-old TikTok star Charlie D'Amelio from the USA, who is one of the most successful TikTokers worldwide with 81.1 million fans (as of August 2020). To follow this girl, they utilise their smartphones and the TikTok apps that creates a personalised connection to the young influencer, since it shows not only how many followers Charlie D'Amelio has but also how many people Maria or Flora are following. They state that the motivation for using TikTok is because of its funny content or because they are bored, or to get tips and suggestions from tutorials. Flora and Maria like watching tutorials on cooking, make-up, dieting, or what movies to view, and they watch product test videos. They show the researcher a video of Maja, a German TikTok influencer who tests sweets. *'I think it's good to watch, and sometimes you buy some things,'* says Maria. For entertainment, the two also like to watch dances and choreographies on TikTok to current music hits. TikTok mediates these goals by using a very particular spatial layout and temporal organisation that shapes also the rules and the motivations for being online. Number counts of likes or followers indicate degrees of popularity of oneself and others.

Maria and Flora tell us also about making their own TikTok videos. They say that they would check the videos *'100 times'* before uploading anything. *'I don't like having a double chin in the video',* says Flora. The videos form part of their identity which is fluid and moving between the on and offline. They adapt and negotiate their online identity. The video recorded and highly orchestrated material snapshots of their identity almost appear unstable; however, what has been put online is a

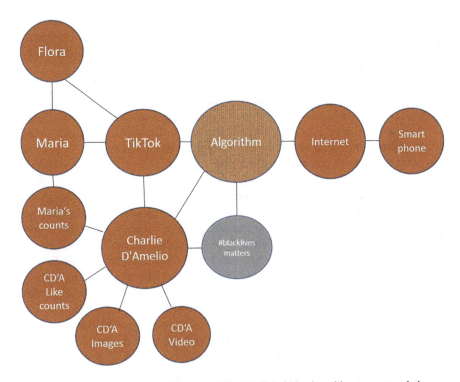

Fig. 6 Analysis of the fragility of Flora's and Maria's digital identity with actor–network theory

semi-permanent material piece in time and is as such not as fleeting as offline performances are.

7 Returning to the Human Actors: Conversations About Digital Competence

We discussed with our participants what kind of competences young people need specifically when it comes to fake news. Mona explains that the problem of fake news was real and that she experienced a lot of fake news when surfing the Internet. She told us that she had a workshop at school to learn how to analyse fake news, but it was *'out of touch because as a younger generation we know that fake news exists and we know to be critical of the things we read'*. Mona describes it as a problem of the older generation.

Thinking about the term fake news, Mona wonders about the role of advertisements. She talks about Instagram that only shows *'the best parts'* of an ideal life. Is it fake news, when users are sharing *'crazy and photoshopped body standards?'*, Mona asks. In her opinion, advertisements are also fake news: *'If you define fake* news as advertising this perfect life, then everybody produces fake news on Instagram'. She talks about advertisements of health teas or hair vitamins that tell you that it will make you look fantastic. *'I know a lot of girls that follow these influences'*, says Mona.

Mona talks also about deepfake videos, she seems terrified, because *'that's gonna be the end of everything. I mean imagine [...] somebody who doesn't like you taking your face and putting it on a very inappropriate video and then sharing it with your entire family. I mean that would just [...] really harm you. People are not prepared for that'*, Mona says. But she is sceptical when it comes to the place of education for digital competences, because *'there is a limit of what education can do'*.

Flora and Maria reflect on fake news: *'on Facebook, there are some things that are not true'*. They tell us that they too had a workshop at school and that they had learned about the possibility of reporting fake news, but that they have never done this before, just scrolling on. Different from Mona, Maria and Flora believe that they should have workshops of this kind more often, to deal not only with disinformation but also with unwanted information. Flora and Maria tell us also that they have received *'strange pictures'* sent to them by people they did not know, naked photos of men (so-called 'dickpics') and that *'almost everyone in our class got one of these before'*. They explain to us that the reason they got these pictures was because they used the chat page omegle.com, where a random generator connects them with an anonymous person. After a short conversation, they exchanged Snapchat names and received the pictures on Snapchat. They explain that even when they immediately block or delete those contacts, they do not dare to talk about it with their parents. They fear that parents might want to see this content on their mobile phone and ban or restrict their activities on social media platforms. They only talk with close friends about it because it is a *'very unpleasant'* topic for them.

8 Discussion

In their report on European media literacy in education, McDougall et al. (2018) ask how students can be prepared for a future where they have to deal with fake news. They point out that this is a key competence and a matter of citizen engagement. While young people find it easy to access many different platforms and information sources, they need guidance on how to navigate and make sense of the materials they are faced with. We found that all participants reported having received some kind of formal introduction or training to build their information literacy competencies. However, all of them lacked some degree of knowledge to detect when they should be careful with the information that has been presented to them, or the mechanisms that are operating in the background. Maria and Flora were using an online application that connected them with strangers and the consequences were disturbing and embarrassing for the girls. Mona, who was clearly capable in assessing the ways in which information is presented, did not fully realise the extent to which the Facebook algorithm analysed and shared her profile. Also, she may not be aware how politically motivated many of the posts are that she receives. Given some of the more serious experiences the young people in our studies had, it demonstrates how difficult it is to assess the trustworthiness of some online information, and it would seem that you cannot start early enough to prepare young people for this complexity.

The findings illustrate three themes of critical information literacy: information management, opinion management, and identity management.

Information management requires an understanding of the asymmetrical arrangements in online environments. Young people need to understand the complexity of different agents including those that are not visible, such as the algorithms that seem to be pulling strings behind the curtains. Information management skills also require competences to orchestrate these agents. Jones-Jang et al. (2019) observed that accurate identification of fake news was significantly connected with heightened information literacy. Transferred to the educational context, this illustrates the need to foster the understanding, finding, evaluating, and use of information. The authors stress that to successfully deal with fake news, students and teachers need the ability to navigate and locate information in digital environments (Jones-Jang et al. 2019).

Opinion management describes the competence to identify how algorithms reflect and amplify opinions, how filter bubbles work, how echo chambers operate, and what benefits but also dangers can be associated with them. The students whose stories we presented here told us that they are part of digital communities and that these groups present materials to them they like to read and view. The European Commission (2018) warns about 'powerful echo chambers' that shape 'information campaigns'. Mona beliefs that she understands the nature of topics in the group's debate and that spending time with this group would reinforce her opinion. Perhaps she is not fully aware of the potential to polarise and radicalise.

Identity management is about the ability to construct and maintain a personal identity in online environments. Floridi (2011) refers to Personal Identity Online (PIO) that is created and changed in an ever-perpetuating spiral. It requires an ability to evaluate how one's online presence should be received by others and how it is expressed and how it shapes identity formation, for example through quantifications (likes). The permanency of online spaces has an additional profound impact on the production of digital identities.

The entanglements mean also that the distinction between facts, opinions, or commercial advertising seems to become very blurred. Maria points out that she occasionally buys products advertised by influencers. Mona appears more critical of the distorted reality on Instagram and wonders whether this presentation of a 'perfect life' could not also be classified as fake news. However, she knows enough others who are influenced by the kind of stories that are being spun in social media. Although Flora and Maria are reflective of their activities, they are clearly affected by the ability to quantify likes, comments, followers, and reach. These materialised quantifications become significant actors that shape how (young) human beings feel about themselves or others.

Students need to be equipped with more knowledge on how to deal with their and other people's digital identity. They also need to have network competences during their information journey, in order to manage and control the information from their online networks, while they themselves become a hub in these networks when they are sharing relevant information, news, or digital content (Pegrum 2010).

9 Educational Consequences

A number of studies have examined how to prepare young people for a digitalised future. We found that the online activities of our participants are deeply infused with political intentionality. While political interest and participation increase with age 'the only exceptions are signing a petition, participating in a demonstration or arguing for one's opinion' (Holt et al. 2013: 29).

Since positions or ideologies are hard to discern in digital texts, this can be especially problematic for younger audiences. It is well documented that by the age of 10, most young people are active users of social media and this means they need to be equipped with the skills needed not only to find and collect information but also to filter, process, and shape this information, before becoming the creators of new information they may wish to share with others (Gibson and Smith 2018).

Yet it is not clear at what age young people are confronted with decisions where they have to draw on their information literacy competence. Rather than adopting age-related user profiles, it may be more conducive to focus on individual needs of students (Jauregui et al. 2020). Students operate within different online environments in and outside of school times. However, if education systems want to ensure they contribute to building information literacy competence, they need to invest equally into building teachers' competences.

Building information literacy competencies should be a societal matter. This means that the responsibility to prepare young people should be shouldered not only by teachers but also by parents and caregivers who have a vested interest in preparing young people to become active citizens. As a society, it will be increasingly important that we all understand the material components that have been put in place in digital environments that not only allow for the distribution of information but also for the distortion and manipulation of content and its consequences.

10 Conclusion

In this chapter, the analysis of the entanglements between their on- and offline worlds, and in particular the worlds of young people, showed us that we need to prepare ourselves, especially young people, for possible manipulations of online content. The information we had collected from our studies was disassembled to identify human–non-human associations and by doing so we were hoping to 'understand connections and relationships' (Otrel-Cass 2019: 148). Being postdigital means to understand socio-material relations (Knox 2019), and this will allow us to get a better grasp on the consequences of the entanglements we have created for ourselves. Based on the findings of our studies, we suggest that we need to pay attention to three dimensions of digital literacy: information management, opinion management, and identity management.

Information management suggests that young people should develop critical analytical skills in order to identify deception through untrue digital information, advertisement, or politically driven intentionality and be prepared for a future where they have to deal with fake news. Opinion management entails that students should get a deeper understanding of how algorithms, filter bubbles, and echo chambers work. They need to acquire an understanding on how people's online experiences are shaped, at times polarised, or radicalised when selected digital information is presented. Identity management requires learning about how to reflect on our online and offline identities and how they change over time and in different environments. This includes the changes we experience as we grow up, participate in different social groups, and tinker with our own representations.

Jan Masschelein (2010) points out that we know the world through its representations and that representations have redefined what 'real' means. We have created different digital products that mirror the world and concurrently we mirror versions of ourselves to the world and share (willingly and unwillingly) our views and ideas. Masschelein tells us the only way to find out about reality is to expose ourselves to the reality that is presented to us. It is about being 'conscious about what is "really" happening in the world and becoming aware of the way our gaze is itself bound to a perspective and particular position' (Masschelein 2010: 43). In an era of fake news, educators and also parents and caregivers will need to 'walk' with young people to learn together how different digital materials are produced and shaped and experienced.

References

Alkali, Y. E., & Amichai-Hamburger, Y. (2004). Experiments in digital literacy. *CyberPsychology& Behavior, 7*(4), 421–429. https://doi.org/10.1089/cpb.2004.7.421.

Allcott, H., & Gentzkow, M. (2017). Social media and Fake News in the 2016 Election. *Journal of Economic Perspectives, 31*(2), 211–236. https://doi.org/10.1257/jep.31.2.211.

Auberry, K. (2018). Increasing students' ability to identify fake news through information literacy education and content management systems. *The Reference Librarian, 59*(4), 179–187. https://doi.org/10.1080/02763877.2018.1489935.

Barnett, R. (1994). *The Limits of Competence*. Buckingham: SRHE and The Open University Press.

Boutyline, A., & Willer, R. (2017). The social structure of political echo chambers: Variation in ideological homophily in online networks. *Political Psychology, 38*(3), 551–569.

Buckingham, D. (2007). *Youth, Identity and Digital Media*. Cambridge, MA: MIT Press. https://doi.org/10.1111/pops.12337.

Burden, D., & Savin-Baden, M. (2019). *Virtual humans: Today and tomorrow*. London: CRC Press.

Callon, M. (1984). Some elements of a sociology of translation: domestication of the scallops and the fishermen of St Brieuc Bay. *The sociological review, 32*(1), 196–233. https://doi.org/10.1111/j.1467-954X.1984.tb00113.x.

Callon, M., & Law, J. (1997). After the individual in society: Lessons on collectivity from science, technology and society. *Canadian Journal of Sociology/Cahiers canadiens de sociologie, 22*(2), 165–182.

Chesney, R., & Citron, D. (2019). Deepfakes and the new disinformation war: The coming age of post-truth geopolitics. Foreign Affairs, 98, 147. https://www.foreignaffairs.com/articles/world/2018-12-11/deepfakes-and-new-disinformation-war. Accessed 1 October 2020.

Cole, M. (1996). *Cultural psychology: A once and future discipline*. Harvard: Harvard University Press.

Cormier, D., Jandrić, P., Childs, M., Hall, R., White, D., Phipps, L., Truelove, I., Hayes, S., & Fawns, T. (2019). Ten Years of the Postdigital in the 52group: Reflections and Developments 2009–2019. *Postdigital Science and Education, 1*(2), 475–506. https://doi.org/10.1007/s42438-019-00049-8.

Davies, H. C. (2018). Learning to Google: Understanding classed and gendered practices when young people use the Internet for research. *New Media &Society, 20*(8), 2764–2780. https://doi.org/10.1177/1461444817732326.

Egelhofer, J., & Lecheler, S. (2019). Fake news as a two-dimensional phenomenon: a framework and research agenda. *Annals of the International Communication Association, 43*(2), 97–116. https://doi.org/10.1080/23808985.2019.1602782.

European Commission (2018). Communication from the Commission to the European Parliament, the Council, the European Economic and Social Committee and the Committee of the Regions. Tackling online disinformation: a European Approach. COM (2018) 236 final. Brussels: European Commission. https://eur-lex.europa.eu/legal-content/EN/TXT/?uri=CELEX%3A52018DC0236. Accessed 1 October 2020.

Farmer, L. (2019). News literacy and fake news curriculum: School librarians' perceptions of pedagogical practices. *Journal of Media Literacy Education, 11*(3), 1–11. https://doi.org/10.23860/JMLE-2019-11-3-1.

Fenwick, T., & Edwards, R. (2011). Introduction: Reclaiming and renewing actor network theory for educational research. *Educational Philosophy and Theory, 43*(1), 1–14. https://doi.org/10.1111/j.1469-5812.2010.00667.x.

Ferrara, E., Varol, O., Davis, C., Menczer, F., & Flammini, A. (2016). The rise of social bots. *Communications of the ACM, 59*(7), 96–104. https://doi.org/10.1145/2818717.

Floridi, L. (2011). The construction of personal identities online. *Minds and Machines, 21*, 477–479. https://doi.org/10.1007/s11023-011-9254-y.

Floridi, L. (2015). *The onlife manifesto: Being human in a hyperconnected era*. Cham: Springer Nature.

Floridi, L. (2018). Artificial intelligence, deepfakes and a future of ectypes. *Philosophy & Technology, 31*(3), 317–321. https://doi.org/10.1007/s13347-018-0325-3.

Gibson, P., & Smith, S. (2018). Digital literacies: preparing pupils and students for their information journey in the twenty-first century. *Information and Learning Science, 119*(12), 733–742. https://doi.org/10.1108/ILS-07-2018-0059.

Goffman, E. (1959). *The Presentation of Self in Everyday Life, Anchor Doubleday*. New York, NY: Garden City.

Hansen, M., & Meints, M. (2006). Digitale Identitäten. Überblick und aktuelle Trends. *Datenschutz und Datensicherheit-DuD, 30*(9), 543–547. https://doi.org/10.1007/s11623-006-0139-9.

Hermida, A. (2011). Fluid spaces, fluid journalism: The Role of the "Active Recipient" in Participatory Journalism. In J. B. Singer, A. Hermida, D. Domingo, A. Heinonen, S. Paulussen, T. Quandt, Z. Reich, & M. Vujnovic (Eds.), *Participatory journalism: Guarding open gates at online newspapers* (pp. 177–191). Malden, MA: Wiley-Blackwell. https://doi.org/10.1002/9781444340747.ch10.

Himmelrath, A., & Egbers, J. (2018). *Fake News – ein Handbuch für Schule und Unterricht*. Bern: Hep Verlag.

Hitzler, R., & Honer, A. (1994). Bastelexistenz. In U. Beck & E. Beck-Gernsheim (Eds.), *Riskante Freiheiten* (pp. 307–315). Frankfurt am Main: Suhrkamp.

Holt, K., Shehata, A., Strömbäck, J., & Ljungberg, E. (2013). Age and the effects of news media attention and social media use on political interest and participation: Do social media function as leveller? *European journal of communication, 28*(1), 19–34. https://doi.org/10.1177/0267323112465369.

Jang, S., & Kim, J. (2018). Third person effects of fake news: Fake news regulation and media literacy interventions. *Computers in Human Behavior, 80*, 295–302. https://doi.org/10.1016/j.chb.2017.11.034.

Jauregui, J., Watsjold, B., Welsh, L., Ilgen, J. S., & Robins, L. (2020). Generational 'othering': the myth of the Millennial learner. *Medical education, 54*(1), 60–65. https://doi.org/10.1111/medu.13795.

Jones-Jang, S. M., Mortensen, T., & Liu, J. (2019). Does media literacy help identification of fake news? Information literacy helps, but other literacies don't. *American Behavioral Scientist*. https://doi.org/10.1177/0002764219869406.

Journell, W. (2019). *Unpacking Fake News. An Educator's Guide to Navigating the Media with Students*. Columbia: Teachers College Press.

Kaptelinin, V., & Nardi, B. (2006). *Acting with technology: Activity theory and interaction design*. Cambridge, MA: MIT press.

Knox, J. (2019). What does the 'postdigital' mean for education? Three critical perspectives on the digital, with implications for educational research and practice. *Postdigital Science and Education, 1*(2), 357–370. https://doi.org/10.1007/s42438-019-00045-y.

Latour, B. (1987). *Science in Action: How to Follow Scientists and Engineers through Societies*. Cambridge, MA: Harvard University Press.

Latour, B. (1992). Where are the missing masses? The sociology of a few mundane artifacts. In W. E. Bijker & J. Law (Eds.), *Shaping Technology/Building Society: Studies in Sociotechnical Change*. Cambridge, MA: MIT Press.

Latour, B. (1999). On recalling ANT. *The sociological review, 47*(1), 15–25. https://doi.org/10.1111/j.1467-954X.1999.tb03480.x.

Law, J. (1987). Technology and heterogeneous engineering: The case of Portuguese expansion. In W. E. Bijker, T. P. Hughes, & T. Pinch (Eds.), *The social construction of technological systems: New directions in the sociology and history of technology*. Cambridge, MA: MIT Press.

Lazer, D., Baum, M., Benkler, Y., Berinsky, A., Greenhill, K., Menczer, F., Metzger, M. J., Nyhan, B., Pennycook, G., Rothschild, D., Schudson, M., Sloman, S. A., Sunstein, C. R., Thorson, E. A., Watts, D. J., & Zittrain, J. L. (2018). The science of fake news. *Science, 359*, 1094–1096.

Liao, V., & Fu, W. (2013). Beyond the filter bubble: interactive effects of perceived threat and topic involvement on selective exposure to information. In *Proceedings of the SIGCHI Conference on Human Factors in Computing Systems(CHI '13)* (pp. 2359–2368). New York, Association for Computing Machinery. https://doi.org/10.1145/2470654.2481326.

Lindau, A. (2010). *Verhandelte Vielfalt. Die Konstruktion von Diversity in Organisationen*. Wiesbaden: Springer.

Livingstone, S., Van Couvering, E., Thumin, N., Coiro, J., Knobel, M., Lankshear, C., & Leu, D. (2008). Converging traditions of research on media and information literacies. In J. Coiro, M. Knobel, C. Lankshear, & D. Leu (Eds.), *Handbook of research on new literacies* (pp. 103–132). New York: Lawrence Erlbaum.

Masschelein, J. (2010). E-ducating the gaze: the idea of a poor pedagogy. *Ethics and education, 5*(1), 43–53. https://doi.org/10.1080/17449641003590621.

McDougall, J., Zezulkova, M., van Driel, B., & Sternadel, D. (2018). Teaching media literacy in Europe: evidence of effective school practices in primary and secondary education. NESET

II report. Luxembourg: Publications Office of the European Union. https://nesetweb.eu/en/resources/library/teaching-media-literacy-in-europe-evidence-of-effective-school-practices-in-primary-and-secondary-education/. Accessed 1 October 2020.

O'Hara, K., & Stevens, D. (2015). Echo chambers and online radicalism: Assessing the Internet's complicity in violent extremism. *Policy &Internet, 7*(4), 401–422. https://doi.org/10.1002/poi3.88.

Otrel-Cass, K. (2019). Epilogue: Of Scales, Spaces, Meshworks, and Maps of Connections. In K. Otrel-Cass (Ed.), *Hyperconnectivity and Digital Reality* (pp. 145–153). Cham: Springer. https://doi.org/10.1007/978-3-030-24143-8_9.

Pariser, E. (2011). *The filter bubble: How the new personalized web is changing what we read and how we think*. London: Penguin Press.

Pegrum, M. (2010). I link, therefore I am: network literacy as a core digital literacy. *E-Learning and Digital Media, 7*(4), 346–354. https://doi.org/10.2304/elea.2010.7.4.346.

Pörksen, B. (2018). *Die große Gereiztheit. Wege aus der kollektiven Erregung*. München: Hanser Verlag.

Radziwill, N. M., & Benton, M. C. (2017). Evaluating quality of chatbots and intelligent conversational agents. *arXiv preprint arXiv*, 1704.04579.

Redecker, C. (2017). European framework for the digital competence of educators: DigCompEdu. Seville: The European Commission's science and knowledge service. https://ec.europa.eu/jrc/en/digcompedu. Accessed 1 October 2020.

Scherke, K. (2011). Transnationalität als Herausforderung für die soziologische Migrationsforschung. In G. Marinelli-König & A. Preisinger (Eds.), *Zwischenräume der Migration. Über die Entgrenzung von Kultur und Identitäten* (pp. 79–90). Bielefeld: Transcript Verlag.

Sciannamea, R. (2020). Fake News: Evolution of a rising concept and implications for the education system. Doctoral thesis. Milano: Università degli Studi di Milano-Bicocca.

Sørensen, E. (2009). *Materiality of learning. Technology and knowledge in educational practice*. New York: Cambridge University Press.

Tandoc, E., Lim, Z., & Ling, R. (2018). Defining 'Fake News': A typology of scholarly definitions. *Digital Journalism, 6*(2), 137–153. https://doi.org/10.1080/21670811.2017.1360143.

Williams, S., Fleming, S., & Parslow, P. (2010). *This Is Me-Digital Identity for careers*. Reading, UK: Central Archive at the University of Reading.

Williamson, B., Potter, J., & Eynon, R. (2019). New research problems and agendas in learning, media and technology: the editors' wishlist. *Learning, media and technology, 44*(2), 87–91. https://doi.org/10.1080/17439884.2019.1614953.

Zimmermann, F., & Kohring, M. (2018). Fake News als aktuelle Desinformation. SystematischeBestimmungeinesheterogenenBegriffs. *M&K, 66*(4), 526–541.

Zuboff, S. (2019). *The Age of Surveillance Capitalism: The Fight for a Human Future at the New Frontier of Power*. London: Profile Books Ltd..

Part III
Philosophy, Ethics and Religion

Listening Like a Postdigital Human: The Politics and Knowledge of Noise

Derek R. Ford and Masaya Sasaki

1 Introduction

The postdigital designation continues to be a site of popular and scholarly contestation, which reflects its immanent and historical unruliness. The latter concerns the term's lineage and deployment over time, while the former concerns the reality it names. Like all history, the history of digital technologies is not linear or predictable, but contingent and messy. Florian Cramer (2015) presents a useful exegesis of the term 'postdigital', exploring its literal, colloquial, esthetic, technological, and temporal deployments and meanings. The digital is, literally, anything that is counted, even if such counting entails a modification (reduction, abstraction) of the thing. 'Digital' comes from the 'digits' of the hand. Thus, an 1877 presentation at the American Dental Association referenced 'digital education' in relation 'to differences, within dentistry, in dexterity of the left and right hands' (Fawns 2019: 133). Analogue refers to that which is not—or perhaps cannot—be divided into discernible units, and 'instead consists of one or more signals which vary on a continuous scale, such as a sound wave, a light wave, a magnetic field' (Cramer 2015: 18). There is 'only digital or digitized information: chopped-up numbers, letters, symbols, and any other abstracted units, as opposed to continuous, wave-like signals such as physical sounds and visible light' (23).

The computer, then, is both digital and analogue: 'The electricity in a computer chip is analogue, as its voltage can have arbitrary, undifferentiated values within a specific range' (22). The computer *digitizes* information and data by transforming inputs into discrete units (ones and zeros), a process enabled by both digital and analogue agents. As Petar Jandrić puts it, 'human beings have always been digital' (2019: 172). We have always, that is, accorded data into discrete categories. Even

---

D. R. Ford (✉) · M. Sasaki
Education Studies, DePauw University, Greencastle, IN, USA
e-mail: derekford@depauw.edu; masayasasaki_2021@depauw.edu

© The Author(s), under exclusive license to Springer Nature Switzerland AG 2021
M. Savin-Baden (ed.), *Postdigital Humans*, Postdigital Science and Education,
https://doi.org/10.1007/978-3-030-65592-1_7

the binary code long predates the twentieth century technologies we associate with the digital era, as the arrangement of events, ideas, and senses into systems of two 'has been used in various forms of communication such as smoke signals and drums' (162). We have also, of course, always been analogue, as our bodies and being in the world exceeds and escapes those categories.

Discussions of the postdigital human generally revolve around the nexus between the human and machine, both of which—in addition to the nexus itself—are open to debate. In fact, one of the most productive possibilities of the concept of the postdigital human is precisely that it opens up the human, the machine, and the relations between them to struggle and dispute, which in effect subjects everything they are defined *against*, in addition to the unique properties ascribed to each, to investigation and problematization as well. One of the central categories here has to do with intelligence or knowledge, as can be seen in recent developments in and controversies over different forms of 'artificial intelligence', a term John McCarthy coined in 1955. Interestingly, artificial intelligence was seen as a project of, in McCarthy's words, 'making a machine behave in ways that would be called intelligent if a human were so behaving' (1955: 11). The cursory definition is a mapping of 'human' intelligence into machinery while at the same time not defining human intelligence, thereby implicitly leaving that definition open. Postdigital technologies continue to forefront the struggle to define intelligence, evidenced by the '"AI Effect," whereby as soon as AI can do something, it is no longer considered to require intelligence' (Dyer-Witheford et al. 2019: 9). Intelligence is maintained as an exclusive property of the human through a dynamic antagonism with technological capacities. By highlighting the blurred and sometimes indistinguishable lines between humans and technology, postdigital humans offer the possibility of opening up our conceptions of agency, politics, and community.

The industrial revolution is one of the central eras for understanding the contemporary debates over the human–machine nexus and division. In the first volume of *Capital*, Karl Marx defined the machine as 'a mechanism that, after being set in motion, performs with its tools the same operations that were formerly done by the workman with similar tools' (1967: 352). Machinery was the technological foundation upon which the capitalist mode of production properly came into form. Previously, capital had seized on previous technologies and forms of production, particularly handicraft production. Yet no matter how it transformed handicraft production, it could not come into its own because of the fact that such production rested upon the cognitive, physical, and other intelligences of the human worker. As capital is a mode of production in which labor is subordinated to and controlled by capital, the latter had to wrest such intelligence from the former. Machinery is the ongoing product of this transformation, as can be seen in the AI Effect, which acknowledges that AI technologies are the objectifications of intelligence into machinery.

In the *Grundrisse* manuscripts, written between 1857 and 1858 but not published until the early twentieth century (and not translated into English until the late twentieth century), Marx wrote about this intellectual transfer in a few pages collectively known as the 'Fragment on Machines'. Here, Marx anticipates his theorization of machinery in *Capital*, noting that as capital subjects labor processes to its logic, it produces 'the *machine*, or rather, an *automatic system of machinery*... set in motion by an automaton, a moving power that moves itself; this automaton consisting of numerous mechanical and intellectual organs, so that the workers themselves are cast merely as its conscious linkages' (1973: 692). The unfinished result is that 'the accumulation of knowledge and of skill... is thus absorbed into capital, as opposed to labour, and hence appears as an attribute of capital' (694). While the role of the 'Fragment on Machines' in Marx's theory of value, the falling rate of profit, and so on, continues to generate significant debates, what is significant for this chapter is the interplay between the subjectivity of the worker and the machine. Marx's conception of machinery ultimately rests on a hyphen between the machine and the human, which signals the dispersion of intelligence between and amongst them.

The key point here is that this ongoing and dynamic interplay continuously raises the question as to what constitutes knowledge and intelligence and the extent to which these should be defining attributes of the human. This is a question, for example, that the disability struggle continuously foregrounds because, as Ashley Taylor notes, intellectually disabled people are defined by the presumed absence of 'sufficient reasoning or deliberative capacity to participate in research and decision making that could influence policy decisions' (2018: 7). More generally, if the human is a privileged category accorded to particular subjects who possess certain capacities defined as intelligences (such as rational thought and autonomy), the struggles of all oppressed groups for recognition and self-determination run up against the problem of whether they should struggle to demonstrate their intelligence according to these definitions or challenge, expand, and/or dismantle them.

The concept of the postdigital human, then, can potentially contribute to these struggles in productive ways. This chapter does so by approaching intelligence and knowledge in the postdigital era through the sonic. Although sound has always been a central concern for education, the sonic dimensions of education have only become a more intentional concern of such research in the past few decades. While this work has opened up various important paths, there is a neglected examination of the relationship between sound, listening, intelligence, and knowledge. In fact, in education, sounds are seen as educational precisely because they transmit information from which we can express, interpret, attend to, and generate knowledge by applying our intelligence, thereby creating restrictive definitions of the human and knowledge and reasserting the privileged status of the human.

In this chapter, we mine the postdigital human's potential for opening up agency, politics, and forms of life in liberatory directions by focusing on sound and listening. We do this by revisiting the history of music production and reception in the twentieth century, paying attention to the shifting definitions of noise on the one hand, and information, knowledge and sound on the other. We begin by situating the argument within some debates about postdigital esthetics, which have tended to concentrate on the visual sense and cognitive properties of the human and the machine. We move next to tell a story of technological transformations in sound and noise, before turning to what listening like a postdigital human might entail and how it can open up restrictive and exclusive definitions of agency, politics, and forms of being together.

2 Postdigital Esthetics

In a 2012 panel at 'South by Southwest', James Bridle organized a panel titled 'The New Aesthetic: Seeing like Digital Devices' (2012) highlighted the slow but decisive ways that 'our technologies and devices are learning to see, hear, to place themselves in the world'. As digital devices increasingly see the world, humans in turn increasingly see the world like digital devices. This raised a series of interesting debates about the postdigital world and its esthetics, including the relationship between technology and human, or the hyphen in postdigital-humans, and the very question of the postdigital. This was not a new debate, as Michael Hardt and Antonio Negri, to name just one recent example, noted in *Empire* that 'today we increasingly think like computers' (2000: 291).

For David Golumbia, the 'like' in 'seeing like digital devices' is incorrect, because there is no simile implied by Bridle. In other words, for Bridle it is not about seeing *like* digital devices, but rather that our sight *is* digital. Golumbia maintains that 'digital devices, and machines in general, do not *see* in the way people or even animals do' (2015: 123). They might take in the same data, but seeing remains an act or sense that is inseparable from the body as a whole. At the same time, there are things that only digital devices *can* see. For example, algorithmic processing of data takes place in such a quantity and at such a velocity that it is imperceptible to the human. The only way the human can see this is, according to David M. Berry, through 'the mediation of software', which renders the human 'twice (or more) removed from the inscriptions they wish to examine and read' (2015: 125). Golumbia's worry is that what is visible to the digital is beyond human sight, which is evident in his discussion of high frequency trading (HFT), where stocks are traded in quantities and at speeds beyond the human's ability to grasp.

Even though humans create the algorithms on which HFT runs, the trades still 'literally move faster than the electrical and chemical impulses of neurons can register' (Golumbia 2015: 125). Machines see *other machines* in ways that humans—including those who might wish to regulate HFT—*cannot see*. We can only see the *traces* of their processes and sight, and, as noted above, to do this we need to rely on other machines. Moreover, the algorithms themselves are often rendered opaque to the public through proprietary protections (Paul and Levy 2015). As such, the sight of digital devices is autonomous from the human, and what is visible to the digital is invisible to the human. The most explicitly linear danger here is the automation of the justice system, in which the machine judges or, more precisely, *calculates*. Golumbia was not nostalgic about a pre-digital era per se, but leaves us with the question as to if 'there are spheres wherein human beings must retain not just ultimate but thoroughgoing influence, *even if* the affordances of the technical system might seem to dramatically outpace those of the human one' (2015: 133).

While postdigital writing about the new esthetic is about 'seeing like digital devices'—whatever exactly that might mean and whatever particular technopolitical implications it has about the relationship between 'the human' and 'the digital'—it is interesting to note that the esthetics of sound have not factored much into the postdigital human. This is particularly noteworthy given that the first mention of the postdigital, to my knowledge, appeared in an article about computer music. In 'The Aesthetics of Failure', Kim Cascone coins the term as a result of the fact that 'the revolutionary period of the digital information age has surely passed' (2000: 12), such that digital technologies no longer significantly disrupt life. At the same time, the implications of postdigital sound at the time had not been fully fleshed out relative to the new Internet-based music scene in which digital technologies are both tools for and means of distribution of computer music.

For Cascone, postdigital music comes from the *failures* of digital technologies, and in particular the 'glitches, bugs, application errors, system crashes, clipping, aliasing, distortion, quantization noise, and even the noise floor of computer sound cards' that comprise 'the raw materials composers seek to incorporate into their music' (2000: 13). He traces a lineage within twentieth century artists who turn the background of the industrial revolution into the foreground. In other words, the noise of capitalist production transitioned from the ground to the figure through the Italian Futurists and John Cage. For the Futurists, industrial noise was a source of energy and matter for sonic compositions. For Cage, on the other hand, it was the dichotomy of noise/sound and silence that had to be challenged. What this intimates is a need to examine the relationship between the mode of production and our sonic modes of engagement. Because machines and later digital technologies were so crucial in rearranging both of these independently and interdependently, and because machines and digital technologies are not autonomous from but deeply interconnected with the 'human', any investigation into posthuman and postdigital esthetics has to attend to the transformations as they impact listening practices and the audible surround.

One of the fundamental works investigating the history of these transformations remains R. Murray Schafer's 1977 book, *The Soundscape: Our Sonic Environment and the Tuning of the World*, in which Schafer reviews the historical changes in the sonic environment and our listening practices, focusing in particular on the changes brought about by the industrial and electric revolutions. The book is also a deeply pedagogical one, although the pedagogical logics of the work remain rather implicit and, in many ways, explicitly linked to traditional conceptions of humanism. At the same time, he notes that soundscape studies are made increasingly possible by the expansive transformations in our conceptions and practice of music, including those brought about by digitization. In particular, Schafer attributes the very intelligibility of something like soundscape studies on five transformations: (1) the introduction of percussion instruments, which brought 'nonpitched and arhythmic sounds' into music; (2) aleatory processes where sounds are subjected to chance and contingency; (3) the diffusion of the borders between the orchestra and the urban environment; (4) the practices of '*musique concrete*', which inserts any sound from the environment into a composition via tape; and (5) sound technologies and electronic music that enabled a wider and diverse engagement with sounds (1994: 5). Taken together, these have facilitated our ability to engage the world as a sonic orchestra—one that now includes the sounds and voices of digital technologies. Although the book was written before the advent of the primary devices we associate with the postdigital today, it provides a helpful historical and theoretical orientation to develop dominant and potentially subversive posthuman practices of listening.

One of the most significant transformations germane to posthuman listening is the transition from the country to the town to the megalopolis. The latter comes into being with the industrial and electric revolutions and overturns the variations within and distinctions between the town–country dichotomy of the previous era, which definitively moved from a hi-fi to a lo-fi soundscape. A hi-fi soundscape 'is one possessing a favorable signal-to-noise ratio' (Schafer 1994: 43), which enables one to hear distinct sounds as a result of lower levels of diffused or ambient noise. In a lo-fi soundscape, there is such an overwhelming mass and density of sounds that the ability to discern discrete acoustic signals is made more difficult. There is simply more ambient noise, yet what is interesting is that this ambient noise is increasingly loud and, we would assume, intrusive. Revolutions in economic energy and lighting production have enabled manufacturing to take place nonstop as workers were forced to work according to the same unending dictates. Curiously, however, the noise of machines was largely accepted. Yet this resulted in an interesting development whereby the definitions of noise, sound, and music were expanded and diffused themselves, such that 'by the early twentieth century the sounds of technology became more acceptable to the urban ear, "blending" with the natural rhythms of antiquity' (72).

The electric revolution augmented and intensified this soundscape through two primary mechanisms. First, electric technologies enabled sound to be packaged and stored. Second, they allowed sounds to split from their original source. Schafer terms this later phenomenon 'schizophonia', a combination of *schizo*, a Greek prefix that means 'split, separated' and the Greek word, *phone*, meaning voice. The phonograph enabled both the packaging/storing and the distribution of sounds. Before the phonograph, sounds were tied to their originators, but the phonograph—and later the tape, compact disc, and digital computers—allowed their separation as well as their transformation around the world and their preservation for future listeners. The tape in particular made it possible to digitize sounds in the sense described by Cramer (2015). For while the tape was an analogue technology, it was able to be spliced and separated into discrete (digital) units.

With the electric and industrial revolutions, music merged with the environment. Two revolutionary sonic interventions were crucial, both of which are also cited by Cascone. First, the Italian Futurist, Lugi Russolo, created 'an orchestra of noise-makers, consisting of buzzers, howlers and other gadgets, calculated to introduce modern man to the musical potential of the new world about him'. Russolo brought the background of the world into the foreground, positioning it not as ambient noise but as intentional signals. Cage did something similar but by different means. Rather than conducting with noise, his *4′33′* brought the assumed background of 'silence' into the foreground of the composition. The musical technology of the electric revolution, in particular, intensified the range of sounds and frequencies in an effort to extend the tonal range available toward the inaudible in two directions: beyond audibility (too loud for human listening) and below audibility (too quiet for human listening).

3 Postdigital Listening and (Anti)Colonialism

If Schafer (1977/1994) attends to the shifting soundscapes of capitalism and the new modes of listening and audibility brought about by new modes of production, Michael Denning's study of anti-colonial phonographs during the electric revolution expands our understanding into considerations of nationality, imperialism, and race. Here, the technologies of the electric revolution worked to prefigure, inaugurate, and facilitate struggles against decolonialism. Denning (2015) focuses in particular on the phonograph revolution in vernacular music in the 1920s, mostly between 1925 and the Great Depression. What he calls a 'noise uprising' was located in and between, and facilitated by, the colonial ports. It thus took place in the Americas and Caribbean, Africa, Asia, the Pacific Islands, and elsewhere. While we tend to think of original phonograph records as artifacts from *previous* musical cultures, these were absolutely modern and contemporary. Moreover, they were fundamentally linked not only with Empire and imperialism but also with the emerging anti-imperialist and decolonial movements. He even suggests that they prefigured the political wave of decolonization in the twentieth century. The capitalist mode of production not only abstracted the sonic environment and created a lo-fi atmosphere but also worked to facilitate a counterrevolution of a hi-fi audible soundscape and attendant listening practices that upset the colonial harmonics of the era.

Capitalism, after all, was not just a European or Western development. From its very origins, it was an international and internationalizing system. Thus, in *Capital,* Marx constantly references the fundamental role that colonialism and slavery played not only in the prehistory of capitalism but also in its ongoing transformations. It was not merely that the original capital was acquired through brutal practices of colonialism and slavery, but that capitalism worked back on those systems as it expanded, which in turn propelled capitalism in Europe in new directions and intensified degrees of exploitation.

The vernacular musics 'emerged on the edges and borders of the empires of global capitalism, in the barrios, bidonvilles, barrack-yards, arrabels and favelas of an archipelago of colonial ports', which were 'linked by steamship routes, railway lines, and telegraph cables, moving commodities and people across and between empires' (Denning 2015: 38). In other words, it was not a unidirectional top-down process of creating a new soundscape, but a dialectical engagement that facilitated resistance through new audible configurations and listening practices. The ports were particularly important, as they brought together and merged different peoples and cultures, creating soundscapes that 'reverberated with sounds out of place, discordant noises' (40). In response to the standardization and abstraction of the industrial factory, capitalism also facilitated 'the dissemination of vernacular musics', which 'together... created, not a "world music," but a radically new configuration of world musical space, a new musical world-system' (68). It was not uniform, and its challenge manifested precisely as a 'cacophonous counterpoint', as the 'barbarous accents and incomprehensible noises of these idioms... led to the moral panics of the era' (107).

The vernacular noise entailed two dominant phenomena: noisy timbres and syncopated rhythms. Regarding the first, the music, because it was often the result of errant encounters of different peoples, 'usually combined instruments with distinct and often clashing timbres' which used both Western and Indigenous instruments. Thus, rather than seeing the Western soundscape as imperialistic, we see an anti-colonial reappropriation of instruments and thus a reconfiguration of that soundscape. Denning notes, for example, that Western instruments 'became indigenous instruments', such that it no longer made sense to speak of the guitar as being a non-African musical device. Regarding the second, the music's use of syncopation, 'a more or less technical term for the displacement of accents to the weak or off beat' (188), caused a significant disruption and became not only an esthetic but also a political category.

Moreover, this sonic resistance also reversed the exportation of capital from the center to the periphery, as the phonograph records emanated in diverse pathways. Thus, even though the financial profits often emanated back to the imperial core, at the same time the capitalistic worldwide distribution helped to ignite the inspiring anti-colonial struggles of the mid-twentieth century. It was not the *content* of the message but the very form of it and how their 'very sound disrupted the hierarchical orders and patterns of deference that structured colonial and settler societies', which 'were heard as a violation of the musical order, an active challenge to the social "harmony"' (155) of the capitalist mode of production. The sounds of capitalism and imperialism are not only unconfined to the sounds of weapons and machines but even those sounds do not operate in a deterministic way. As Schafer reminds us, 'no sound has objective meaning' (1994: 137).

It is suggested that, at least in part, it was the anti-colonial noise uprising in tandem with the internal development of the capitalist mode of production that brought about the need for a reconfiguration of sounding technologies and their filtration through digital conceptions of information and communication transmission. As the distinction between noise and sound is not internal to the properties or relations internal to either, both are social conceptions that change in response to political, economic, and social struggles. Thus, the bourgeoisie condemned the noise of the proletarian crowds of the late nineteenth and early twentieth centuries while the progressive movements found inspiration and a new form of collective being by their participation within them.

As information and knowledge grew in importance for capitalism—and hence also for colonialism and imperialism—noise began to be defined as anything that would hinder production or that would limit or disable the effective transmission of inputs to outputs. In our increasingly 'infocentric' society, noise is pitted against information. For Mack Hagood, infocentrism posits an ontology that naturalizes what it produces by figuring that 'life is a battle for control between self-organizing information and the entropy that would dissolve it into noise' (2019: 156). One way, this materialized in digital technologies, was through AT&T's production of long-distance telephones. In order to reduce the noise of long-distance calls to maximize the information relayed, 'the solution reached was to compress messages into a binary code that *eliminated all surplus*, leaving only the elements necessary to decompress the full message at the output end' (156–157).

By the 1980s, when digital technologies began spreading in earnest in the music industry, the ability to convert musical signals into ones and zeros allowed for greater precision, attention to micro-details, and the elimination of background noise. When we hear music that has been digitally recorded, we hear 'no noises accompanying them' (Brøvig-Hanssen and Danielson 2016: 61). The silence of the sounds, then, helped listeners acknowledge the previously unheard noise in musical recordings. Once we utilize these technologies, they train us in listening and hearing, so that we listen for—and as a result, hear—signals and codes rather than noise. To the extent that we listen for and hear noise, we do so in an effort to eliminate it or—what may amount to the same thing—transform it into information.

4 Listening and the Postdigital Human

Faced with the overabundant noises of the lo-fi megalopolis, Schafer wants to enact a pedagogy of clairaudience, which entails *cleaning hearing* or *cleaning the ear*. This entails sensitizing the ear to the lo-fi sounds, so that the ear can effectively digitize the exhaustive babbling of the metropolis. There is nonetheless a glaring paradox in the project, for although Schafer wants us to acknowledge the world as one big orchestral soundscape in which we are all listeners and composers—an orchestra undoubtedly populated with digital technologies—the ultimate module, agent, and model is the 'human ear'. His main objection with the contemporary lo-fi soundscape is that 'human vocal sounds are masked or overwhelmed', which produces 'an inhuman environment' (1994: 207).

In response, we have to reorient ourselves to the soundscape through the model of the human ear, which he states are the best machines for listening. 'The human ear', he writes, 'conveniently filters out deep body sounds such as brainwaves and the movement of the blood in our veins', while 'the human hearing threshold has been set conveniently just beyond a level which would introduce a continuous recital of air molecules crashing together' (Schafer 1994: 207). The human machine is therefore silent not because it is soundless, but because it eliminates the noise of the body and filters out unwanted or undesirable noise. 'The perfect machine', he writes, 'would be the silent machine: all energy used efficiently. The human anatomy, therefore, is the best machine we know and it ought to be our model in terms of engineering perfection' (207). Moreover, although he acknowledges the importance of listening habits and practices, he leaves these unproblematized as he moves to pedagogy and design. For example, his pedagogy is guided by questions such as 'What sounds do we want to preserve, encourage, and multiply?' (205). Yet the answer to these questions will hinge on what and how we can hear and listen, which are in turn bound up with our assumptions of and dispositions toward intelligence, information, and noise. Bringing his concerns and pedagogy to the postdigital era, what exactly is the human ear and the human anatomy? If the contemporary postdigital human listens differently from its previous iterations, what are these differences, and how can these differences inform a pedagogical project aimed in a liberatory direction?

To get at one approximation of this, we can return to the different sonic technologies of the late twentieth century and extend Schafer's insights into the revolutionary transformations in listening brought about by the radio and the cassette. In his study of Islamic soundscapes and the role of cassette sermons in the Islamic Revival, Charles Hirschkind examines the revolutionary transformations in soundscapes inaugurated by the Islamic cassette recordings in Egypt. One break with the proliferation of cassette recording and playing technologies is that they undermined the previously dominant centralized forms of broadcasting and film, a subversion 'indebted in no small way to the weakening of copyright protections in the face of the possibility of infinite duplication afforded by the cassette' (Hirschkind 2006: 53). Indeed, while we might associate the cassette as a pre-digital technology, with Cramer (2015) we can understand that it is a fully digital technology in that it renders the analogue sermon into a discrete and reproducible unit. Moreover, cassettes facilitate postdigital listening by 'floating free of subjects', which means their listening 'is now left to the whims of subjective appropriation' (Hirschkind 2006: 91). They are also free from the authority of the state, which is unable to contain their production, reproduction, and distribution. Indeed, in Egypt, most tapes 'circulate through informal practices of exchange and home duplication' (60). Efforts to distribute Islamic cassette sermons by the state and traditional authorities have largely failed to take hold. While people can listen to cassettes privately, they are also broadcast in and outside cafes, restaurants, taxis, and cars, creating 'what might be called Islamic soundscapes, ways of reconfiguring urban space acoustically through the use of Islamic media forms' (6).

The specificities of the role of listening in Islam are important, and they might hold keys to understanding and reconfiguring posthuman listening in the rest of the world as well. This is a kind of ethical listening that is not organized around the *grasping* or *consumption* of the content but the affective disposition of the listener. As the Quran is sublime in that it cannot be fully interpreted or understood, its force must be felt. Islamic scholarship, he notes, has generally not articulated rules of *speech* but instead ways of *listening*. When a sermon fails, it is because of the listener and not the orator. 'The agency', he notes, 'is largely attributed to the hearer... *Sam*, in other words, is not a spontaneous and passive receptivity but a particular kind of action itself, a listening that is a doing' (Hirschkind 2006: 34).[1] Thus, these

---

[1] *Sam* is one mode of listening in Islamic traditions that entails one's ability to actively listen and hear the words of God.

listening practices might help the 'ear cleaning' project Schafer proposes, but without constructing an artificial binary between the digital and the human. The urban soundscape is not a lo-fi environment to militate against, but rather a rich sonorous site of struggle in which to intervene. For Hirschkind and those he interviewed, their listening was a kind of posthuman listening that was transformed by the digital technology of the cassette and the particular relations it enabled and opened. This is radically different from a form of listening oriented around the attempt to capture as much *information* as possible.

The limitation for listening like a postdigital human here is, of course, the location of agency. As such, a closer approximation to a liberatory sonic pedagogical project might be those that more concretely challenge the limitations that restrictively define the human and agency in general. In terms of the pedagogy of listening, one of the most dangerous practices concerns that naturalization of vocal timbre. Nina Sun Eidsheim introduces this by way of the acousmatic question that the listener is asked: *what* or *who* am I hearing? This question assumes that we can discern an answer, identify a source, and generate knowledge about the source (person) and the sound (voice). Yet the very reason for asking the question is because we cannot formulate an answer; 'we ask the question because voice and vocal identity are *not* situated at a unified locus that can be unilaterally identified' (3). She turns the question around so it is asked of the listener's listening: '*Who am I, who hears this?*' (Eidsheim 2019: 24). Timbre is not a knowable thing but a process. By naming and measuring sounds, we block the infinite potentiality of timbre by insisting on limited concrete actualizations. While timbre is an errant phenomenon that cannot be pinned down, it 'is often used to make truth claims about voice and the person emitting the vocal sound' (5). This means, in turn, not only that (vocal) timbre is seen as a unique and genuine product of an identifiable subject, but also that the pedagogy of timbre—how we come to voice and listen—reproduces systems of oppression, to the extent that 'the practice of essentializing vocal timbre is the unexamined foundation upon which racialized vocal timbre is maintained' (154).

Both in formal and everyday settings, 'we are conditioned to *hear what we listen for* and to assume that what we hear is indisputable' (Eidsheim 2019: 50), so that when 'we subsequently hear them, and because we hear them, we believe the perceived meaning to be verified' (51). This is most evident when there is a gap between what we are listening for and what we hear. One striking example she offers is of Angelina Jordan, a young Norwegian girl, performing Billie Holiday's 'Gloomy Sunday'. The disbelief and shock that strikes the audiences (on the TV show on which Jordan performed, in the audiences where Eidsheim has presented her research and that strikes Eidsheim herself) is the disruption of the belief that the voice is an essential expression of a unique identity. Holiday's voice has been essentialized as the expression of Black suffering and her own particular autobiography; it is heard as an expression of a story of Blackness and her own story of hardships, tragedy, and so on. How could this young girl from Norway then sound so similar?

The disruption is pedagogically powerful but also ambiguous. On the one hand, it can strengthen our commitment to timbre as essence. Here, 'the listener holds an image of an original voice in his or her mind, comparing it with the evidence available as a more or less favorable reproduction with a greater or lesser degree of fidelity' (Eidsheim 2019: 164). In other words, timbre *as timbre* is not heard. On the other hand, the relationship between timbre and essence can be weakened. When we hear 'both the voice of the singer at hand and that voice inflecting the idea of the imitated voice', we should be moved 'to question the very foundation upon which the assumption of vocal essence rests' (165). The pedagogical task, then, is to listen to our listening. For Eidsheim, this pedagogy consists 'of demonstrating that the practical experience of exploring more of the wide range of timbral potential inherent in each voice offers a perspective on any single timbre' (57), so 'that every timbral quality or meaning may be interrogated' (58). Timbre itself, as a limitless potentiality, does not *possess* or communicate any meaning; instead 'any and all meaning is generated outside the form' (184). This does not mean foreclosing the political, but rather holding politics in tension with potential. When we realize that 'a collection of styles and techniques is distinguishable through one name, it may also be distinguishable through another name, and another, and another, and yet another' (193). The infinite potentiality of timbre is manifested *through* each particular actualization, a process that challenges presumptions about the 'essence' of the human.

A postdigital example of this pedagogical process can be found in autotune technologies. Interestingly, autotune was developed to correct or enhance vocal sounds by eliminating divergences from the intended pitches and frequencies of the sounds. In a sense then, they were developed to closedown the possibilities of timbre. However, over time other potentials of autotune were explored in ways that foregrounded the digital intervention in—or interaction with—the voice. Here, the machine's voice merges with that coming from the human: 'When the voice is manipulated and takes on a mechanical or robotic sound, this link to the real "self" of the singer is broken' (Brøvig-Hanssen and Danielsen 2016: 128–129). Since our dominant assumptions link the voice to a human essence—and thus deprive those without voices or whose voices are not heard to the status of agents—the overt autotuning of the voice continues to be controversial. Moreover, the autotuned voice is disturbing. When the voice as an assumed instrument linked to the interiority of the human is blended with the digital in such a way, as Dominic Pettman puts it, we realize that 'there is something profoundly *im*personal about the voice, something alien' (2017: 39). The boundaries between the human and machine are blurred, and the voice of each emerge with their own limitations and potentials.

5 Conclusion

It is possible to hear and listen to their sonic choreography in ways that unsettle assumptions of the clear boundaries between the human and machine and the link between the voice and an interior essence and, as a result, the perceptual biases that ontologically order agency. This is precisely where its liberatory possibility lies, since autotuned voices become generalized throughout so many genres of popular music. It becomes impossible to tell where the machine ends and the human begins and, thus, where to locate the intelligence of the sound. This, in turn, destabilizes our conceptions of sound and the binary between sound and noise. This could represent an insurrection in the current ontological and epistemological regimes that privilege not only 'the human' but particular forms of the human.

References

Berry, D. M. (2015). The Postdigital Constellation. In D. M. Berry & M. Dieter (Eds.), *Postdigital Aesthetics: Art, Computation, and Design* (pp. 44–57). New York: Palgrave Macmillan.
Bridle, J. (2012). The New Aesthetic: Seeing like Digital Devices. South by Southwest. https://schedule.sxsw.com/2012/events/event_IAP11102. Accessed 8 August 2020.
Cascone, K. (2000). The Aesthetics of Failure: 'Post-Digital' Tendencies in Contemporary Computer Music. *Computer Music Journal, 24*(4), 12–18.
Cramer, F. (2015). What is "Post-Digital"? In D. M. Berry & M. Dieter (Eds.), *Postdigital Aesthetics: Art, Computation, and Design* (pp. 12–26). New York: Palgrave Macmillan.
Denning, M. (2015). *Noise Uprising: The Audiopolitics of a World Musical Revolution*. New York: Verso.
Dyer-Witheford, N., Mikkola Kjøsen, A., & Steinhoff, J. (2019). *Inhuman Power: Artificial Intelligence and the Future of Capitalism*. London: Pluto Press.
Eidsheim, N. S. (2019). *The Race of Sound: Listening, Timbre, and Vocality*. Durham: Duke University Press.
Golumbia, D. (2015). Judging like a Machine. In D. M. Berry & M. Dieter (Eds.), *Postdigital Aesthetics: Art, Computation, and Design* (pp. 123–135). New York: Palgrave Macmillan.
Hagood, M. (2019). *Hush: Media and Sonic Self-Control*. Durham: Duke University Press.
Brøvig-Hanssen, R., & Danielsen, A. (2016). *Digital Signatures: The Impact of Digitization on Popular Music Sound*. Cambridge, MA: The MIT press.
Fawns, T. (2019). Postdigital Education in Design and Practice. *Postdigital Science and Education, 1*(1), 132–145. https://doi.org/10.1007/s42438-018-0021-8.
Hardt, M., & Negri, A. (2000). *Empire*. Cambridge, MA: Harvard University Press.
Hirschkind, C. (2006). *The Ethical Soundscape: Cassette Sermons and Islamic Counterpublics*. New York: Columbia University Press.
Jandrić, P. (2019). Digital. In D. R. Ford (Ed.), *Keywords in Radical Philosophy and Education: Common Concepts for Contemporary Movements* (pp. 161–176). Boston: Brill. https://doi.org/10.1163/978900440467_012.
Marx, K. (1967). *Capital: A Critique of Political Economy (Volume 1)*. Trans. S. Moore and E. Aveling. New York: International Publishers.
Marx, K. (1973). *Grundrisse: Foundations of the Critique of Political Economy*. Trans. M. Nicolaus New York: Penguin.
McCarthy, J., Minsky, M. L., Rochester, N., & Shannon, C. E. (1955). A Proposal for the Dartmouth Summer Research Project on Artificial Intelligence. http://jmc.stanford.edu/articles/dartmouth/dartmouth.pdf. Accessed 20 August 2020.
Paul, C., & Levy, M. (2015). Genealogies of the New Aesthetic. In D. M. Berry & M. Dieter (Eds.), *Postdigital Aesthetics: Art, Computation, and Design* (pp. 27–43). New York: Palgrave Macmillan.

Pettman, D. (2017). *Sonic Intimacy: Voice, Species, Technics (or, How to Listen to the World)*. Stanford, CA: Stanford University Press.
Schafer, R. M. (1977/1994). *The Soundscape: Our Sonic Environment and the Tuning of the World*. Vermont: Destiny Books.
Taylor, A. (2018). Knowledge Citizens? Intellectual Disability and the Production of Social Meanings within Educational Research. *Harvard Educational Review, 88*(1), 1–25. https://doi.org/10.17763/1943-5045-88.1.1.

Ethics, Character, and Community: Moral Formation and Modelling the Human

Malcolm Brown

1 Introduction

As discussion of ideas around the 'posthuman' moves from the realm of fantasy to the realm of the conceptually, and perhaps practically, possible, it would be well to be clear from the start what is meant by the 'human' beyond which there is, presumably, a 'post' condition. Being human is certainly to be embodied, and most definitions would include a general capacity for rationality. But the embodied and the rational come together in the moral dimension of the human condition: the capacity to reflect on concepts of right and wrong and the nature of the good. This chapter attempts to explore some of the ways human beings become moral agents and to establish that becoming moral (which I have referred to as moral formation) is not fully conceptualised solely as an aspect of disembodied rationality. Indeed, the fact that moral questions are so fiercely and interminably contested rather suggests that they are intrinsically irreconcilable by the exercise of reason, if reason is taken to be a universal factor accessible in the same way to all humanity.

So, if questions of morals and ethics are essential components in being human, and yet deeply contested among human cultures, it becomes important to ask what kind of moral assumptions might be involved—whether overtly or otherwise—in conceptualising the 'post' element in the posthuman. And if, as I shall argue, the dominant understanding in Western cultures about how humans become moral beings is simultaneously too 'thin' and yet frequently taken to be universal and beyond question, the prospect of the posthuman (in whatever form it might take)

M. Brown (✉)
Church of England, London, UK

Department of Computer Science, University of Bath, Bath, UK

Department of Theology, Religion and Philosophy, University of Winchester, Winchester, UK
e-mail: malcolm.brown@churchofengland.org

entrenching within itself an inadequate account of the moral dimension of being human is deeply worrying. Moral philosophers have, for several decades, been addressing serious flaws in the account of human moral development emerging from the Enlightenment. Yet it is precisely that account which continues, often hubristically, to shape most technological cultures. And our tragedy may be that the pace of change in moral philosophy, whilst even now helping to shape other disciplines and even practical politics, is quite unable to keep up with the pace of technological change. What we *can* do is rapidly outstripping our understanding of what we *may* do if we are to build a deep account of the good for humanity.

2 Conceptualising the Human

When the Labour politician Nye Bevan famously referred to his party rival Hugh Gaitskell as a 'desiccated calculating machine', it was not intended as a compliment. Such a person, he continued, 'must speak in calm and objective accents and talk about a dying child in the same way as he would about the pieces inside an internal combustion engine'[1]. Bevan's aphorism turns on the adjective 'desiccated' in a way that cuts straight to a significant distinction between what is characteristically seen as human and what is not. To be desiccated is to be dry, arid, and rigid—but, more than that, it connotes something that once was moist, succulent, and dynamic, but is no longer. Bevan was, in effect, accusing Gaitskell of abandoning something of his essential humanity and failing to distinguish between matters that are susceptible to cool calculations of value and things which carry a non-calculable worth because they touch on our inherent identity as human. To be fully human is to be not merely cerebral but visceral, and how the cerebral and visceral connect is one of the constant ambiguities and puzzles at the heart of human affairs. The distinguishing ability of humans to calculate and think rationally has tended to characterise discussions of human uniqueness, at least since Descartes. But the moist and messy reality of being human, which instead of distinguishing us from other animals reinforces our shared creatureliness, has never faded from sight, as the metaphorical power of blood, tears, and other aspects of embodiment attests—not least in religious and political imagery.

Whilst it may seem perverse to begin an exploration of the ethics of contemporary (and future) technologies with a reference from over 60 years ago, it seems to me important to locate the moral issues facing us now within a broader historical conspectus. When we talk about what it means to be human, even as the challenges to that concept multiply in unexpected and perplexing ways, it is worth taking a longer view and relating contemporary questions to thought patterns and controversies that have been faced before. My sources, too, are drawn in part from periods before concepts of the posthuman had currency and before the technologies with

---

[1] Bevan was speaking at a Tribune rally in September 1954, responding to Clement Attlee's call for an unemotional response to German re-armament. Gaitskell was to become leader of the Labour Party the following year and is usually understood to have been the butt of Bevan's jibe.

which we are today grappling were conceived. For ideas, being less than brand new does not make them intrinsically irrelevant or uninteresting. For examples to have come from a past era does not automatically mean they have nothing to say to today's questions.

The calculating machine of 1954 was a crude piece of equipment compared to even the most basic computer of today, but although, as in Bevan's case, the comparison is often derogatory, at various periods and in some contexts, it has been positive or morally neutral. George Orwell recalled (from about 1915) a prep school master extolling the human body as superior to any Rolls Royce or Daimler, and the idea of the body as a finely tuned machine long remained unexceptional (1968: 352). It is as if the human cultures that have been most exposed to technological innovation cannot quite work out the relationship of the technology to the self. But the metaphorical association between a person perceived to have abandoned their full humanity and the machine, computer, or calculator persists. It captures, and reinforces, the sense that the bodily, messy, and hard to quantify side of human existence is not an accident nor an aberration, but intrinsic, and that, whilst the capacity for rational thought may be a distinctive human characteristic, it is not adequate to define being human. A person who treats all matters as the subject of rational calculation has shrunk, as if they have been dried out and are no longer fully alive.

Technology is now moving far beyond the concept of computers as calculating machines writ large. If the concepts associated with posthumanism have any chance of realisation, it opens the prospect, not only of humans eviscerating their nature by acting like calculating machines but perhaps also of machines enhancing their nature to become, at least in some respects, as humans. This is not merely in the sense of being super-rational but in embracing a much wider range of human characteristics. It is already commonplace to imagine technologies with emotional intelligence and some form of moral awareness, even though this has not been actualised and perhaps never will be. If people can behave in ways that are subhuman, digital technologies may be taking the opposite journey to demonstrate some of the characteristics that, through most of history, have been unique to humans. As Elaine Graham puts it, '[t]echnologies call into question the ontological purity according to which Western society has defined what is normatively human' (2002). But, taking Bevan's jibe as our imaginative starting point, does the technology make us more like a calculating machine (however sophisticated) or better able to avoid the emotional category error which Bevan identified in the images of the dying child and the internal combustion engine?

3 Being Human and Being Good

If the posthuman combines aspects of the technology with aspects of what is currently thought of as human, perhaps in ways not yet fully defined or understood, is it possible to talk of the outcome as being more, or less, human? This seems like an intuitively sensible question, but one that is surprisingly hard to answer. I started with the thought that human beings can diminish their humanity by the ways they think and act and that one way this can happen is by overemphasising the mechanical, logical, and calculating aspects of human reason. If human enhancement, of whatever sort, is achieved through greater affinity to, and with, technology, will it paradoxically enhance the aspects of our being that exacerbate our always-existing tendency to dehumanise ourselves? To try to address these questions, I want to turn to the ethical question of what it might mean to be a 'good' human being, a good person, a good occupier of a social role. And in framing the question thus, my approach will draw on a contemporary practitioner in moral philosophy, whose work has influenced many disciplines and genres beyond the narrow study of ethics—Alasdair MacIntyre—to help address some of the problematics of postdigital humanity.

This is not the place to go into a lengthy summary of MacIntyre's work or his influence on ethics. His best-known work is *After Virtue*, first published in 1981, and most of his writing since then has developed and elaborated its central thesis (MacIntyre 1985). McMylor, acutely, describes MacIntyre as a 'critic of modernity' (1994) and it is true that MacIntyre's analysis starts with a trenchant critique of the state of moral thought since the Enlightenment. We have, says MacIntyre, become so caught up in the 'Enlightenment Project' of seeking a universal morality derived from human reason that we have failed to see how attenuated our moral condition has become as a result. For morality derives, in his view, not from abstract reasoning by atomised individuals but from the shared lives of people in community, living by traditions communicated in narrative and embodied in practices of virtue. Only by rediscovering ways to live together well, often according to traditions and stories that are quite different from each other, will we be able to defend the moral life against the barbarians who 'are not waiting beyond the frontiers but have already been governing us for some time. And it is our lack of consciousness of this that constitutes part of our predicament' (MacIntyre 1985: 263).

To anticipate my conclusion here, I will argue that there is a core problem, as technology introduces various approaches to combining human and digital attributes together. It is that these developments are taking place at a moment in the history of ethical enquiry when the kind of insights characterised by MacIntyre are exposing the weaknesses—in some cases the vacuity—of liberal modernity and its accompanying dominant narrative of market economics, but that these moral insights are coming too slowly and possibly too late to avoid potential moral disaster if technology entrenches an inadequate moral understanding within the shape and nature of future humanity. In short, we risk an outright victory for the desiccated calculating machine which may be irreversible, and consequently a catastrophic loss of those aspects of being human that liberal modernity fails to value.

4   Concepts and Boundaries of the Human

Before going further, however, it is important to note the difficulties—conceptual and, importantly, political—in the discourses of being human, posthuman, fully human, or deficiently human. Graham speaks of Western definitions of the human having 'ontological purity', but that may only be true at different discreet periods. Rees and Sleigh (2020) note how the conceptual boundaries of what is to be categorised as human have not only varied over time but have been shaped by (often unconscious) biases of different ages. Whether or not Neanderthals were human or a distinct species was, in the nineteenth century, discussed in ways which now appear to have been transparently shaped by the politics of imperialism in its encounters between European white people and the indigenous peoples of the regions they had colonised. Historically, the notion of women as incomplete men also entailed implications about the boundaries of the human that would now be very widely rejected. Rees and Sleigh note, helpfully, that '[h]uman is a category that has been defined by many things, almost all of them what it is *not*' (2020: 67) (authors' italics). Current developments in artificial intelligence—even at the relatively crude level of Alexa and Siri—are blurring the boundaries between the human person and the non-human machine. Children have been heard saying, 'I love you Alexa', and a genuine moral question arises about whether to train children to say 'please' and 'thank you' to Alexa. The case for such politeness is that treating a machine gracelessly may lead to the child failing in basic graciousness toward humans. But the risk of that same politeness is that the ability to differentiate the person from the machine may be lost. As the possibilities of digital and postdigital technology grow, vastly to exceed the existing capacities and interactive limitations of Alexa, that simple moral conundrum suggests that future questions about how to behave around technologies when they invade hitherto uniquely human spaces are likely to be intractable.

5   Ethics, AI, and Real Life

Explorations in the ethics of AI and where it may lead are now commonplace but surprisingly inconclusive. For example a surprising amount of energy has been expended in considering the ethics of the so-called 'trolley problem'. This is the thought experiment in which an out-of-control tram is careering toward a junction. Setting the road one way, it will plough into a mother and baby; set the other, it will kill the driver. Which way should the points be set? There are many elaborations of the problem, but in the world of driverless cars ('autonomous vehicles' in the jargon, although the adjective involves making contested ethical assumptions), there is a real and pressing question about the insurance liabilities if the vehicle is programmed to preserve the life of the occupant. But the 'trolley problem' is not just a hypothetical case. Something very like it will really have happened, and one actual case, long before computers were involved, reveals a lot about how moral judgements are made and how human beings, in practice, consider that kind of ethical dilemma.

In 1957, a freight train, hauled by an old-fashioned steam engine was climbing a steep gradient out of Buxton in Derbyshire. As it neared the summit, the steam pipe to the brake burst in the cab, making access to the controls impossible. The driver stayed with the train as it began hurtling at full power down a long, steep gradient. The signalman at the next junction saw the train approaching and had to decide in a moment whether to turn it into a dead end where it would crash and kill the driver or allow it onto the main line where it could potentially kill hundreds. He chose the latter course of action—the action that many people, confronted with the trolley problem, tend to see as wrong. Yet the Inquiry exonerated him and sympathised with his decision. As the Inspecting Officer noted, the signal box, and the signalman himself, stood directly in the path of the train if it had been turned into the dead end. Self-preservation is 'hard wired' into human beings—as the Inquiry understood (Ministry of Transport 1957). The hypothetical 'player' who pulls the point lever or programmes the driverless car is not an anonymous and contextless other, but a person whose own relation to the context may be significant in its own right.

Yet, self-preservation is not always the dominant human reaction to danger. Some, confronted by a hypothetical case such as the above, are convinced that they would place their own life second to the prospect of extensive loss of others' lives. Some have clearly made just that choice in real situations, although if their decision is recorded it may only be posthumously. The point is that both decisions point equally to the aspect of being human that is felt and emotive, rather than part of the coolly rational calculating machine side of life. There really is no 'correct' moral answer to the problem, only one which is expedient, perhaps in terms of the commercial interests of driverless car makers or their insurers. This human aspect of moral decision-making probably emerges from a person's upbringing and life experience. How, then, might it be pinned down sufficiently to explore whether or not it is susceptible to incorporation in some posthuman development which melds the human and technology?

A first question may be to ask where such impulses come from. When I shared the 1957 version of the trolley problem with groups of students and colleagues (albeit, not chosen in any statistically significant manner), it was interesting that those with a religious—especially a Roman Catholic—upbringing were more likely than others to say that they would have put their own life second to some conception of the interests of unknown others. No causal significance should be placed on this observation, but it remains intuitively suggestive given the stronger conception of the person-in-community that one finds in Catholic Social Teaching compared to most strands of Protestantism or secularism. The point here is twofold: that responses to a profoundly moral dilemma can be diametrically opposed yet equally derived from the non-calculating aspects of being human and that they are likely to be determined largely by the stories and moral traditions assimilated through life.

6 Human Moral Formation: Narratives and Markets

The term that, perhaps, best captures this idea originates in the Christian tradition but is not confined to it. This is the idea of Moral Formation—the processes by which we become good human beings.

Following MacIntyre, it is not the exercise of disembodied reason through which we learn to be moral beings, nor is there a universal morality which is accessible by reason divorced from community and culture. What it means to be a good human person is learned from the stories we hear told which situate us within a community. So, the narratives by which a community describes itself to itself will be expected to have a profound impact on how its people learn what constitutes behaving morally.

Narratives work at the level of cultures and societies as well as smaller communities. In much of the West, especially the UK and US, an especially dominant narrative has been that of the market as the paradigm for relationships and for establishing value across a wide range of human activities. One problem with dominant narratives is precisely that they are treated as paradigmatic rather than contextual. The market narrative has spread well beyond the sphere of unequivocally economic relationships and invaded (which is not, I think, too strong a word) areas of human activity which had not hitherto been seen as susceptible to interpretation through an economic metaphor. The worlds of many institutions, which grew out of the need to embrace an ongoing dialogue about the ethics for which they exist, have been transformed by the dominant market model into organisations supposedly geared to delivering a single and measurable set of objectives (Berry 1999). Hospitals, universities, and schools come to mind, and even some predominantly economic institutions such as banks have found their purposes narrowed until the complex ecosystem balancing profit with service are reduced to the tyranny of the bottom line (Jenkins 1991). It is this market narrative which provides the context for the rolling out of new technologies and within which the boundaries of the human and posthuman are being challenged. Market mentalities matter.

Naturally, a dominant narrative such as the market contains within it an implicit model of the human. Assumptions about cost/benefit maximisation as a primary human motivation underpin the narrative, along with constructs such as the 'rational and informed consumer' which are based on idealisations rather than empirical observations about how human beings behave. It has seemed for 40 or more years that our culture has tacitly accepted the desiccated calculating machine as its preferred understanding of the human person.

The market is a characteristic institution of the Liberal Enlightenment project which is the object of MacIntyre's critique. The inadequacies of liberal individualism and its associated emotivist ethics are becoming more and more apparent, not least in the difficulty of communicating the concept of the common good during the Covid-19 pandemic. So are the failings of the market model in terms of delivering the kind of politics and promise that it has always claimed (the failure to change anything significant in the economic system, let alone address its ideology, following the 2008 crash shows how resilient a failing narrative can be). Yet, this is still the dominant ideological framework in which contemporary questions about the human and posthuman are being translated into innovative technologies. It matters, then, how human priorities are conceived, and how ethical considerations are embodied in the developments that follow. If the traditions which have informed some of the deep responses to human situations are eclipsed by a currently dominant narrative which is enshrined in the way we approach technological innovation and its impact on the human, important aspects of human behaviours and thought could be in deep jeopardy.

MacIntyre characterises the human inadequacy of the market paradigm by addressing Adam Smith's famous contention (which is true enough, but only as far as it goes) that '[i]t is not from the benevolence of the butcher, the brewer or the baker that we expect our dinner but from their regard to their own interest' (Smith 1776: I, ii). As MacIntyre comments:

> If, on entering the butcher's shop as an habitual customer I find him collapsing from a heart attack, and I merely remark, 'Ah! Not in a position to sell me my meat to-day, I see,' and proceed immediately to his competitor's store to complete my purchase, I will have obviously and grossly damaged my whole relationship to him, including my economic relationship, although I will have done nothing contrary to the norms of the market (MacIntyre 1999: 117).

The political philosopher, Raymond Plant, makes a similar point in his analysis of the market ideologies deriving from Hayek and Friedman and promulgated politically in the 1970s by Keith Joseph and (in terms of practical politics) by Margaret Thatcher. Integral to Hayek's version of market theory is the principle that social justice can only arise where there is both agency and intention. An outcome (such as poverty) is only unjust if someone intended it and had the agency to make it the case. If a tree blows down on my house but not yours, it is a matter of bad luck not injustice. Thus, since the workings of a market economy involve neither agency nor intention, being the aggregation of millions of independent and autonomous actions, market outcomes are not a matter of justice—or of morality.

It is easy to see how this position can flow into a particular conception of being a good person. Famine in another continent, for example *demands* no response from me (although I may make a response from altruism) since I neither intended it nor had agency to cause it. Likewise, a benevolent response to those who experience bad luck cannot be a moral requirement upon me. But, as Plant comments, justice is not just a matter of how something came about but of human response. 'If I can save a child from drowning at no comparable cost to myself, any failure to save the child even if its predicament was the result of some impersonal force (perhaps the wind blowing it into the water) would be unjust' (Plant et al. 1989: 79). Plant has captured something important here about how humans regard justice and morality, but the market ideology has attenuated our ability to articulate such ideas and embed them in social structures.

MacIntyre is not dismissing the mechanisms of the market as if they embodied the sum of our social and human failures. He is suggesting, rather, that '[m]arket relationships can only be sustained by being embedded in certain types of local nonmarket relationship, relationships of uncalculated giving and receiving' (MacIntyre 1999: 117). But, if market ideology is still the dominant (or at least a dominant) narrative shaping social relationships, and yet does not offer explanations of how people should behave which satisfy the human desire to act ethically, how will that missing element be incorporated in any new development which impacts upon the way humans, or posthumans, behave? Again, the desiccated calculating machine seems to have the floor to itself and the visceral, feeling, aspects of being human, which do so much to inform ethical conduct, have to fight for a hearing.

The market is, of course, only one aspect of the Liberal Enlightenment Project which MacIntyre is critiquing. He argues, in *After Virtue* (1985), that detaching of ethics from narrative, community, and tradition has impoverished the way we understand what it means to be a good person—that is, the question of character. MacIntyre goes on to argue that we inhabit the character of a good X, Y, or Z when we understand the practices that are intrinsic to those roles. Thus, a good gardener, a good doctor, a good teacher, a good architect will not just deliver the 'external goods' associated with that role (growing flowers, getting children to pass exams, constructing a building) but will grasp, and practice, the role's 'internal goods'. Internal goods are what distinguishes a role well played. Thus, as he argues, the object of a game of chess is to win—that is the external good of the practice of chess—but you can teach a child to win at chess by cheating, which utterly destroys the internal goods associated with the game which are what distinguishes a game played well. For human beings to inhabit a character means pursuing external and internal goods alongside each other. Learning that this is so is part of a person's moral formation as they grow to become, not just a good person but a good exemplar of the roles they adopt and practice.

7 Character Dependency and the Self

How technology can reproduce the notion of character, marked by practices which preserve and promote the internal goods of an activity or role, is conceptually problematic. Partly this is because today's technological developments are taking shape in a moral culture which has preferred to treat internal goods as negligible and to play down concepts of character, in favour of more measurable and less culturally specific approaches to understanding the human. It is [to pick up MacIntyre's starting point in *After Virtue* (1985)] because the very vocabulary of virtue, community, and character has fallen into desuetude that we lack not only the moral vocabulary to describe our context and define our problems but even, much of the time, the awareness that this is a problem. It is hardly surprising, then, that despite widespread uneasiness about any technological developments which introduce unknown factors into our perceptions of ourselves and our bodies, it is much harder to express the roots of that disease (the often inarticulate unease about GM crops is a familiar example). My contention is that a recovery of the language of virtue, community, tradition, character, and so on, as counterweights to the dominant narrative of individualism and markets, might help us articulate aspects of what is essentially human, and thus inform technological developments in which the human and the technological are less and less distinguishable.

MacIntyre also explores another facet of being human which is inadequately articulated in a liberal individualist culture. In provisionally defining humans as dependent, rational animals, he does not jettison the distinctive human characteristic of rationality but refuses to allow the fact of our rational nature to lead inexorably to the trope of the autonomous, reasoning, individual. He asks: 'what difference to moral philosophy would it make, if we were to treat the facts of vulnerability and affliction and the related facts of dependence as central to the human condition?' (1999: 4)

Human autonomy is, paradoxically, only achievable because dependency is a basic characteristic of being human. We can only develop into autonomous, reasoning, beings because our initial dependency as infants has been responded to well by parents and others (MacIntyre 2016: 49). Our autonomous reasoning capacities are also, for most people, enabled to function only because all sorts of minor (and sometimes major—think Stephen Hawking) dependencies are met by other people. Dependency on others immediately highlights the human need for community.

Despite the fact that 'community' is a notoriously slippery word to pin down (Plant 1978), precise definitions are not needed for us to understand that our innate human dependency requires that we belong in some sort of network of human others. This returns us to the MacIntyrean understanding of the centrality of community to ethics; communities being the groups that tell stories and thus develop narratives about what it means to be a good person. We do not come to understand the nature of the good by the exercise of autonomous reason (although to be sure, that reasoning capacity enables us to explore and refine concepts of the good). It is in our moral formation as dependent beings, dependent on a community of others that, by learning to belong, we learn to be good. He memorably challenges the common perception that a moral choice is like being confronted by a fork in the road—shall I turn left or turn right?—where our decision is a rational and binary choice between competing goods. Rather, he says, 'I can only answer the question "What am I to do?" if I can answer the prior question "Of what story or stories do I find myself a part?"' (MacIntyre 1985: 216). It is our embeddedness in community which enables us to be part of a story which enables us to act ethically at all.

Nor are narratives simply things which individuals opt into, or out of. We become persons through participating in stories that are about us, but which are of wider salience and therefore locate us among others—in community. The self is not an autonomously created, or chosen, entity but something both conferred upon us from without and constructed from within. As MacIntyre puts it, the unity of the self, 'resides in the unity of a narrative which links birth to life to death as a narrative beginning to middle to end' (1985: 205). Moreover, 'the story of my life is always embedded in the story of those communities from which I derive my identity' (1985: 221). We are close, here, to an Aristotelian teleology. 'The good life' is not just a set of desired ends but is discovered in the pursuit of our *telos*. In contrast, liberal culture prioritises means, procedures, and rules, to the acute neglect of the *telos*.

Already, the ways in which technologies are entering the field of social care raise serious questions about the boundaries between the human and the digital. Social care in the UK is grossly underfunded and inadequate to meet growing numbers of dependent elderly people. Covid-19 has seriously exacerbated an already-untenable situation with carers often being given no more than 15 min per visit to do a range of personal and domestic support duties. I know from experience that many carers manage to combine that rushed and frantic role with real conversation, humour, and interest which is often the only human contact the client has in the day. But in order to spread the thin human resource still further, AI is already being used to offer conversation—or perhaps the simulacrum of conversation—whilst the human carer spends less time with the client, their duties focussed on the mechanical tasks of wiping bottoms, mopping up ulcers, and doing the dishes: tasks for which robotics have not yet found a cost-effective alternative to human labour (Savage 2020). This is a good example of how the dominant narrative of the market, with cost-benefit at the heart of the rational calculation, seems to marginalise that which is essentially human and elevate the technological or mechanical to usurp important aspects of human relationship. For conversation is not a one-way street or simply an exchange where the benefit is felt by one party alone. Having a conversation is transitive—one has a conversation with someone else, it is not a solitary pleasure. So, what is it that the dependent person is engaging with when they turn (or are forced to turn) to AI as a 'conversation partner'?

In terms of a culture which acknowledges only functional definitions, it can be difficult to differentiate the technological speaker (the bot) from a human interlocutor. There is (depending upon how loose one is with one's definitions) something analogous to a brain in the bot, which allows and promotes interaction. It can produce the semblance of conversation, reacting to verbal, and sometimes non-verbal, stimuli generated by the human it addresses. If all we sought from conversation was a creative reaction to our own thoughts and feelings, it is hard to fault the bot. But what if, however inchoate, our desire is to encounter another person in all their unpredictability and messiness? That is, someone who has a life story embedded in the communities from which they derive their identity. When two human beings converse, however superficially, they are drawing consciously or otherwise on that embeddedness and on their own story. It moulds not just the content but the tone and tenor of their responses. It makes human conversation unpredictable, taking the participants in directions they had not planned, and they may never understand how they got there. Calculation is part of it, to be sure—a conversation partner can be manipulative or use conversation for ulterior ends. But that is precisely why human conversation, which draws on the embedded narratives that have formed a person as a moral being, is so vital to being human.

It may be that for many lonely and deeply dependent persons, an AI-generated pseudo-conversation is better than the silence of an empty house, although the Covid-19 lockdown has led many to realise the inadequacy of digital meeting platforms like Zoom and to crave the encounter with 'persons in three dimensions'. But my point is that, in this instance, technology is being used to replace the aspect of the carer's role which is most essentially human and leaves the human person with those humdrum tasks which require a person to act most like a machine. This is about more than conversation. An important way in which human beings value one another and express their commitment to shared narratives and significant communities is by giving one another time. This reflects the fact that life is finite and time a scarce resource, in the language of economics. So, giving another person open-ended and un-entailed time is an expression of their value to us merely for being a fellow human being rather than for the benefit they can give us. In a different sort of vocabulary, it would be called an act of love.

The promise of technology was once to free people from physical labour to make more room for human interactions—not least, the pleasures of conversation. Now, under the remorseless logic of the desiccated market-oriented calculating machine, precisely the opposite is happening in just the sector of the labour market where large numbers of low-paid people, mainly women, are active. The class and gender aspects of this are interesting and disturbing, but tangential to the key point about how technology, under the dominant narratives of our culture, is being used to collude in dehumanisation rather than enhancing or complementing the essentially human.

8 Technology and Responsibility

The whole question of human dependency raises fascinating questions about the shape which dependency might take in the world of the posthuman. Whilst advanced algorithms can, if not yet 'think' for themselves, at least follow their own internal logic in ways which are not directly guided or determined by human agency, they are nonetheless the creations of humans and (crudely speaking) the quality of what one gets out of them depends on the quality of what is put in. As 'Asimov's Law' puts it, humans, not robots, are responsible agents. Joanna Bryson emphasises that '[r]esponsibility is an attribute assigned to members of our society to maintain our society. Human centring is the only coherent basis for AI ethics' (Bryson 2020). A leading AI ethicist, Bryson echoes MacIntyre in her insistence that the technological cannot adequately be described or understood without an account of the human need for other people. She says, '[h]ouse fires, vaccination, air pollution, water supplies, physical security, physical intimacy all depend on neighbours. So does international security (at a different scale)' (2020). But is Bryson, here, working with an assumption about the distinctiveness of the human as opposed to AI which, over time, may be eroded or vanish into some form of the posthuman?

If the human is technologically modified, it may be a response to dependency in a good sense (think Stephen Hawking again, and the technology that allowed him to communicate at a high level). But where the interface between the human and the technological is not overt, as in some conceptions of how the posthuman may manifest itself, the risk arises of darker versions of human dependency. Just as safeguards are built into business ethics to reveal, wherever possible, hidden financial dependencies that could skew moral (and market!) decision-making, so undeclared dependencies which lie behind posthuman manifestations need to be flushed out. Unacknowledged technological dependencies could conceal motives and interests behind, perhaps, a façade of benevolence. The technology that makes the posthuman possible will be somebody's technology, even if not an individual's, and will be framed, whether overtly or otherwise by their own moral formation before being built into new forms, perhaps resembling the human person.

Where people are, in general, unaware of the particularities of their own moral formation, or assume their morality to be based on the kind of unexceptional reasoning that is supposed to be accessible to all, the prospect of immense moral bias is plain. The moral assumptions of one culture—or one segment of a culture—could be built into the human–technological interface in ways which are more dangerous for being hidden behind cultural biases. The technology will have emerged in a narrative about what technology is and what it can and should do—most probably in our contemporary culture, as I have argued, a market narrative. The responsible agent behind it will be human, even if the 'product' is in some way posthuman. And unless the boundary between the human and the non-human is overt—unless, so to speak, Hawking can be distinguished from his wheelchair—the potential for manipulation and moral ambiguity is immense.

Bryson (2020) is, I believe, correct to say that human centring is the only coherent basis for AI ethics. It must then follow that the permissible level of technological melding with the human will be extremely limited. Much of what is described as the posthuman is, to date, an unrealised set of possibilities, developing products and thought experiments. If ethics is to contribute at all to such developments, it should be to argue that boundaries around the human should not be malleable just because they are not susceptible to precise definitions. If necessary, as Bryson (2020) suggests in the context of AI, national and transnational governmental and legal structures need to be put in place to maintain and police such boundaries. A core purpose of government and law is to maintain proper accountability. If, as Bryson (2020) suggests, the person with legal accountability for a robot should be attributed ('Whose little robot are you?!') then should the boundary between robotics and personhood be transgressed, it follows that the person undertaking the experiment should be attributed and accountable, not the posthuman outcome of their work. Robots are products; people should not be allowed to be made, even partially, into products or commodities.

9 Averting Moral Disaster?

Can any of this scenario be averted whilst allowing the technological advances toward posthumanism to continue? It would surely take a seismic cultural shift in countries such as the US and UK before the significance of community and practice in moral formation was appreciated sufficiently to influence assumptions about the human person and, perhaps just as importantly, the business models that drive technological innovation. The few straws in the wind that suggest such a shift are almost too small to discern.

In the UK, prior to the 2019 General Election, there was a degree of revival in the One Nation Tory tradition within the Conservative Party which went some way toward embracing a kind of MacIntyrean communitarian approach. Here was a major political party reaching back into its history to rediscover insights that dated back to Edmund Burke (Norman 2013). And this embryonic movement was mirrored in the Labour Party by the emergence of the Blue Labour tendency, drawing explicitly on Catholic Social Teaching and with the Labour peer, Maurice Glasman, an academic disciple of MacIntyre, as a leading figure (Geary and Pabst 2015). But the One Nation Tory tradition disappeared from the Parliamentary party before the 2019 Election. Nor has Blue Labour fared much better to date. Yet the simultaneous emergence of political movements, embodying a sort of MacIntyrean analysis and approach, in opposing parties, suggests that the energy to translate academic insights into practical policies remains. But political change at the required depth takes place on a time frame incapable of responding quickly to the pace of technological innovation.

In the academy, the engagement between MacIntyrean virtue ethics and technology is well under way. Shannon Vallor's work is a good example of this. She dismisses the idea that better technical systems can secure human flourishing unless accompanied by 'broader and more intensive cultivation of technomoral virtues such as wisdom, courage and perspective' (Vallor 2016: 216). The current depth of interdisciplinary interest in AI Ethics is another source of provisional optimism. Bath University's Centre for Doctoral Training in Accountable, Responsible and Transparent AI[2], with which I am associated, is an interesting case in point. Established with substantial public funding, and involving numerous partners drawn from among the creators and users of technological innovations, other academics and social institutions, its postgraduate cohort is both international and multidisciplinary. It offers a space for the industry, the academy, and representatives of social institutions to talk openly about ethics. Other ventures around the country will be doing similar things. But, again, it remains an open question whether the pace of academic research in a hugely contested subject like ethics can keep pace with what is becoming technically possible in technological disciplines and in industry.

10 Conclusion

I have tried to show that humans' development as moral beings—their moral formation—is only fully understandable if we move beyond the Enlightenment conviction that the nature of the good and of right conduct can be derived from the exercise of some universal capacity for reason. I have drawn on Alasdair MacIntyre's work to

---

[2] See http://www.bath.ac.uk/centres-for-doctoral-training/ukri-centre-for-doctoral-training-in-accountable-responsible-and-transparent-ai/. Accessed 16 October 2020.

epitomise this argument because he has led the way into a stronger understanding of how community, tradition, narrative, and practice are foundational for human moral formation. I could have used other sources—Charles Taylor or Michael Sandel from philosophy, Stanley Hauerwas or John Milbank from the sphere of theology, or others—each of whom would have made comparable points in different ways. MacIntyre's critique of modernity is, perhaps, the most incisive and helps reveal not only the attenuated framework that most of Western culture now tries to deploy in pursuit of ethical issues but also the way the paradigmatic discourse of the market economy which, claiming that market outcomes are beyond morality, has infiltrated so many areas of life that the moral content of our relationships is obscured (as with Adam Smith's butcher). This broad analysis, from MacIntyre and others, is gaining traction across the academy and even in political life but, to date, only on the outlandish fringes of the commercial and business worlds. The effect of this disparity in the timescale of different kinds of change is that a tragically inadequate account of being human will inform developments in relation to the posthuman, just as the limitations and inadequacies of that modernist account begin to be inescapable in other sectors of society.

The political, legal, and academic structures that might enable technological innovation—or at least its practical application—to be restrained until social moral discourse has caught up, simply do not currently exist. Innovation is treated as, in itself, justification for its enactment. But until such structures can be created, the posthuman should, I suggest, remain in the worlds of fiction and fantasy. The desiccated calculating machine is too prominent in our cultural sense of the human already, without allowing it to breach the boundaries that still, just about, protect our human moral integrity.

References

Berry, A. J. (1999). Accountability and Control in a Cat's Cradle. *Accounting, Auditing & Accountability Journal, 18*(2), 255–297. https://doi.org/10.1108/09513570510588751.

Bryson, J. (2020). Lecture inaugurating the partnership for the Centre for Doctoral Training in Accountable, Responsible and transparent Artificial Intelligence. 28 January, Bath: University of Bath.

Geary, I., & Pabst, A. (2015). *Blue Labour: Forging a New Politics*. London: I. B. Tauris.

Graham, E. (2002). *Representations of the Post/Human: Monsters, Aliens and Others in Popular Culture*. Manchester: Manchester University Press.

Jenkins, R. (1991). *Changing Times, Unchanging Values?* Manchester: The William Temple Foundation.

MacIntyre, A. (1985). *After Virtue: A Study in Moral Theory* (2nd ed.). London: Duckworth.

MacIntyre, A. (1999). *Dependent Rational Animals: Why Human Beings Need the Virtues*. London: Duckworth.

MacIntyre, A. (2016). *Ethics in the Conflicts of Modernity: An Essay on Desire, Practical Reasoning and Narrative*. Cambridge: Cambridge University Press.

McMylor, P. (1994). *Alasdair MacIntyre: Critic of Modernity*. London: Routledge.

Ministry of Transport and Civil Aviation (1957). Report on the Collision which occurred on 9th February 1957 at Chapel-en-le-Frith (South) in the London Midland Region of British

Railways. London: Her Majesty's Stationery Office. https://www.railwaysarchive.co.uk/docsummary.php?docID=290#:~:text=The%20report%20into%20the%20collision,for%20his%20devotion%20to%20duty. Accessed 8 September 2020.

Norman, J. (2013). *Edmund Burke: Philosopher, Politician, Prophet*. London: William Collins.

Orwell, G. (1968). Such, Such Were the Joys. In G. Orwell (Ed.), *The Collected Essays, Journalism and Letters of George Orwell, Vol. IV, 'In Front of Your Nose'* (Vol. 1945—1950). London: Secker and Warburg.

Plant, R. (1978). Community, Concept, Conception and Ideology. *Politics and Society, 8*(1), 79–107. https://doi.org/10.1177/003232927800800103.

Plant, R., et al. (1989). Conservative Capitalism, Theological and Moral Challenges. In A. Harvey (Ed.), *Theology in the City* (pp. 69–97). London: SPCK.

Rees, A., & Sleigh, C. (2020). *Human*. London: Reaktion Books.

Savage, M. (2020). Can artificial intelligence fight elderly loneliness?. BBC, 26 March. https://www.bbc.com/worklife/article/20200325-can-voice-technologies-using-ai-fight-elderly-loneliness. Accessed 8 September 2020.

Smith, A. (1776). *The Wealth of Nations*. https://www.ibiblio.org/ml/libri/s/SmithA_WealthNations_p.pdf. Accessed 7 September 2020.

Vallor, S. (2016). *Technology and the Virtues: A Philosophical Guide to a Future Worth Wanting*. Oxford: Oxford University Press.

The Computer's Hidden Theology and Its Prospects for a Postdigital Humanity

Steve Fuller

1 Introduction: In Search of a Post-classical Understanding of the Computer

Historians tend to understand the emergence of the computer's centrality to virtually all forms of organized inquiry after the end of the Second World War as corresponding to the breakdown of the political economy of 'classical science', notwithstanding Michael Polanyi's and Karl Popper's best efforts to defend it for the rest of the twentieth century. The main normative principle of 'classical science' in this sense is that the path to truth is paved by free inquiry, which in turn requires a regime in which 'errors' can be committed with impunity (Fuller 2000: Chap. 5). Classical science presumed that the various costs of doing research—from financial to personal—could be borne privately, or at least without placing any substantial burden on the wider society. This allowed errors to be interpreted positively as learning experiences, not negatively as a disqualification from engaging in further research. In such a world, the computer was an option not a necessity.

The classical attitude works only if society is neither materially endangered nor economically ruined by the failure of a particular research project. In the 1960s, at the peak of the Cold War's 'Big Science' policy orientation, Derek de Solla Price

---

This is a substantially enhanced version of a paper originally publihsed in Russian as Fuller, S. (2019). Судьба человечества в перспективе алгоритмического деизма (The Fate of Humanity under Computational Deism). In A. Argamakova & E. Maslanova (Eds.), *Социальные и цифровые исследования науки: коллективная монография* (Social and Digital Studies of Science: A Collective Monograph) (pp. 10–22). Library of the Journal *Библиотека журнала* (*Epistemology & Philosophy of Science*). Special thanks to the Russian translator, Alexandra Argamakova, for her tireless efforts.

S. Fuller (✉)
Department of Sociology, University of Warwick, Warwick, UK
e-mail: S.W.Fuller@warwick.ac.uk

© The Author(s), under exclusive license to Springer Nature Switzerland AG 2021
M. Savin-Baden (ed.), *Postdigital Humans*, Postdigital Science and Education,
https://doi.org/10.1007/978-3-030-65592-1_9

(1963) memorably dubbed the classical vision, 'Little Science'. He saw it as based on the idea that society does not expect too much of larger value to come from science but is pleasantly surprised when it does. All of this changed in the era of Big Science, when organized inquiry across the disciplines was scaled up to resemble an industrial enterprise. The idea of scaling up science was not itself new. Indeed, when science has been on a wartime footing, the state was its principal funder and agenda setter, and scientists were mobilized with an eye to meeting certain explicit targets. But after each war, scientists typically returned to their relatively modest university and corporate labs. However, the quick start of the Cold War after the end of the Second War prevented such redeployment. On the contrary, all the major scientific powers remained in a state of 'permanent emergency' for nearly a half-century. And it was from this unprecedented scaled up research environment that the computer became the dominant instrument and, arguably, object of science.

A good way to understand the ascendancy of the computer in this context is as internalizing the externalities of Big Science. Historian of science Peter Galison (1997) has noted the role of the Monte Carlo—a random number generator designed to simulate complex stochastic processes—in providing the lingua franca for coordinating the work of the large interdisciplinary teams involved in generating knowledge of nuclear physics during the Cold War. But shortly after the Cold War ended, *Scientific American* writer John Horgan (1996) went one better, publishing a provocative book entitled *The End of Science*, arguing that the mounting costs of scientific research meant that computer modelling would become the lingua franca for evaluating knowledge claims in *all* fields. Hypotheses that have become too expensive to test empirically under normal laboratory conditions would be tested in silico by simulation. Horgan predicted that this shift would give epistemological centre stage to aesthetic criteria of the sort common to mathematics and literature.

Horgan was writing when states were rapidly downsizing their funding of physics-based research after the end of the Cold War. But it also coincided with the increasing use of computer models—including customized software—in the ascendant biological sciences, from pharmaceuticals to genetics and evolutionary theory. Although Horgan rightly recognized that this development had profound implications for what 'scientific validation' might mean in the future, he was clear that economics was driving the change. However, in what follows, I will argue that this change also plays out deeper philosophical and even theological currents about the relationship between humans and their creations that have persisted throughout the entire history of organized inquiry in the West.

2 Taking Artificial Intelligence as Seriously as Human Intelligence

Former world chess champion Garry Kasparov (2017) has repurposed an old proverb to capture the problem of ethics in artificial intelligence (AI): 'If you don't like what you see in the mirror, don't blame the mirror'. In other words, AI is only as moral as the people programming it. And Kasparov's saying appears wise against the backdrop of current AI research, the market demand for which reproduces, for example the gender discrimination that modern human history has struggled to overcome. Thus, the two biggest markets for AI manufacturing are, on the one hand, service and companionship (typically 'female') and, on the other, drone warriors (typically 'male'). Indeed, it is unlikely that Saudi Arabia's celebrated granting of citizenship to the Hanson Robotics gynoid Sophia in 2017 would have happened, had it been created as a male. That Saudi Arabia limits the freedom of movement of female *Homo sapiens* was no doubt instrumental in the standard that it used to determine whether a female robot might count as a citizen. Unsurprisingly, then, psychoanalytically oriented Marxists have had a field day with AI, as they observe the obvious ways in which AI research amounts to a kind of 'return of the repressed'. In other words, all of the supposedly banished prejudices and injustices in our 'liberal democratic' society manage to get resurrected in a potentially more virulent fashion in our most 'progressive' technologies.

The above critique makes superficial sense, but it fails to take seriously AI's potential autonomy from its original programmers. Imagine that Kasparov had been talking about parents' relationship to their children. In that case, parents would be forever blamed for the children's failures. Yet, many if not most of those 'failures' would have been the result of the children improvising on what their parents taught them either directly or indirectly (i.e. in terms of what the parents explicitly prohibited and tacitly allowed). In short, even though parents 'program' their children in some strong sense, that programming underdetermines the children's responses to particular situations, which is the level at which moral judgements are normally made. Indeed, one of the aims of a self-programming computer, which is normally seen as the gold standard of artificial intelligence research, is that we come to see computers as exercising a sense of discretion that is distinctly their own, resulting in decisions that programmers typically cannot predict.

To be sure, we are only at the start of an important discussion about how to hold such autonomous intelligent machines accountable for their actions. While most ethicists still prefer to hold the human machine designers and/or their clients to account, this becomes increasingly difficult to maintain, as machines are recognized for their 'creativity'—indeed, to such an extent that humans cannot distinguish computer-based works of art, literature, or science from those of their fellow *Homo sapiens*. And if such machines are potentially eligible for intellectual property rights for their original works, perhaps they are equally eligible for punishment for their crimes. After all, both creativity and criminality are, sociologically speaking, 'deviant behaviours' that deliberately challenge existing standards of conduct. The difference is that creativity is permitted and even valorised, while criminality is prohibited and even condemned. (Jean-Paul Sartre 1952/2012's assessment of Jean Genet's life is a great place to begin problematizing this asymmetry.) The question here is what would constitute an appropriate level of punishment for a computer sufficiently creative that it could commit a crime. Some lawyers argue that the algorithm enabling the criminal behaviour should be decommissioned altogether, which in human terms is comparable to saying that we should sterilize everyone who shares some relevant genomic pattern with the criminal. While some 'negative eugenicists' in the past have advocated versions of such policies, they are nowadays seen as needlessly harsh.

From the start of my career, at the dawn of postmodernism, I have believed that the 'impossibly high' cognitive and ethical standards that have been promoted by modern philosophy imply *not* that those standards are wrong as such but rather that beings other than 'humans'—as ordinarily understood—might be better placed to act in accordance with them. In that case, the interesting question becomes how we would interact with such creatures, which may be of our own creation, as in the case of AI. Over a quarter-century ago, I developed this point as an implication of the 'naturalism' that was popular in analytic philosophy at the time (Fuller 1993: Chap. 3). I argued that if philosophers develop exorbitant normative standards—say, utilitarian ethics or Bayesian epistemology—they should then search for the sorts of entities that are capable of realizing them. It turns out, 'naturalistically' speaking, that ordinary humans are not especially good, even though humans were the ones who came up with the standards. At this point, we reach a normative impasse: we need to either fix the standards or fix the humans.

The typical 'postmodern' line is to argue that the standards are at fault. This has led philosophers to dismiss normative standards such as utilitarianism and Bayesianism as requiring a 'godlike' view of the consequences of decisions taken, and perhaps even of the information needed for taking those decisions. Yet, at the same time, there remains this project called 'artificial intelligence', which explicitly aims to create non-human entities that might satisfy such standards. My own view is that we should take both of these points quite seriously and even literally. In short, yes, our modernist normative preoccupations have been about achieving a divine horizon and, yes, we have begun to take efforts to enable entities, including ones not confined to our ape-like bodies, to do just that. Therefore, we should envisage a substrate-neutral or 'morphologically free' version of an intelligence test—the ultimate Turing Test that could spot intelligence in human, animals, and machines, as well as their various associations as 'extended minds', 'corporations', or 'superorganisms'. Indeed, this is a project now being pursued by José Hernandez-Orallo (2017) of the Technical University of Valencia under the rubric 'the measure of all minds'.

In that case, seen from a suitably normative standpoint, the seemingly aberrant behaviour of an android or even a human-based cyborg might be understood as teaching ordinary *Homo sapiens* a lesson. This point highlights a blind spot in the analysis of Nick Bostrom (2014) and others who nowadays predict the end of humanity at the hands of 'superintelligent' computers. They fail to see that we might effectively acquiesce to the superiority of such machines without a fight—in other words, without ever perceiving an existential threat because the terms of engagement will have substantially changed along the way. Such an acquiescence scenario seems hard to imagine now for three main reasons: (1) Artificial intelligence research is not sufficiently advanced at a technical level. (2) The number of 'cyborgs'—that is, humans who have been significantly enhanced by computer-based means—remains relatively small. (3) The privileged value attached to being 'human' remains relatively intact, notwithstanding the best efforts of animal rights and climate change activists.

Only as long as all three conditions remain in place does Bostrom's dystopic scenario make sense. In that respect, it is an illusion generated by historical myopia, which results when present trends are imagined to continue into the indefinite future. But if we imagine 'humanity' to be a journey of collective self-discovery, in which AI plays a defining role, then we need to apply a spatial metaphor to time and hence take the idea of 'historical perspective' rather literally. This means that situations that look very dangerous now may appear that way only because we imagine that what we see in the distance will appear the same once we get there. Yet, what appears horrible from a distance may seem fine once we arrive, and conversely what appears attractive or even innocuous from a distance may be lethal upon arrival. Similarly, once we see the consequences, what appeared awful at the time it happened may in retrospect not have been so bad and perhaps even beneficial—and what seemed good at the time may in retrospect have sown the seeds of disaster ahead. I would urge that this is the spirit in which we should regard today's insistence that we jealously guard our 'humanity' from the supposedly 'de-humanizing' tendencies of artificial intelligence and related cyber-encroachments (cf. Fuller 2019a: Chap. 2). In what follows, I tease out two rather opposed theological currents that have informed the development of computers and their relationship to the human condition for the past two centuries. For reasons that will become clear, I call the first phase *Computational Theism* and the second *Computational Deism*. Both are deeply implicated in various positions in both the philosophy of science and the philosophy of mind.

3 Computational Theism: The Computer as the Image of Its Human Creator

The first phase was already evident in Charles Babbage's plans for the first digital computer, or 'difference engine', in the 1820s. At that time, it was widely believed that the clearest way to demonstrate that one understands the nature of something is to create a machine that does what the original does. At one level, this was simply an extension of Francis Bacon's understanding of experiments as a vehicle to knowledge, which nowadays is associated with the use of computer simulations across all of science. The underlying idea was that mechanical models could manufacture 'realistic' effects, as part of a general tendency for the artifice of the laboratory to replace observation in the natural world. In the case of the computer, the processes of rational thought were being modelled on the machine. In Babbage's day, these processes were still understood in quasi-psychological terms, even though the computer encoded thought in a primitive version of what we now call 'symbolic logic'. And so, just as Babbage's contemporary, James Clerk Maxwell believed he understood how matter moved in the physical world because he could construct a mechanical model of the aether that confirmed the known laws of physics and Babbage believed he understood how thoughts moved in the mental world because he could construct a 'difference engine' that generated outcomes that corresponded to what George Boole subsequently called in his 1854 classic, *The Laws of Thought*.

In Computational Theism, the computer is designed to show mastery of processes that are understood to occur naturally in the mind, at least under ideal conditions, which may exceed normal human capacity. As we shall shortly see, looming here is the prospect that the machine might so exceed human capacity as to approximate divine powers. In any case, a central tenet of Computational Theism is that knowing the identity of both the machine's creator and of the created algorithm is integral to establishing the machine's validity. This helps to explain the stepwise proof procedure that in the twentieth century came to be associated with 'linear programming'. Nowadays we think of this in terms of 'transparency', but theology is also involved—in particular, the creator's capacity to name something into existence. In this respect, computers were effectively 'second creations', analogous to what God did when he created humans by literally dictating his image in clay.

This point explains two countervailing features of the sort of advanced machines associated with artificial intelligence: on the one hand, they bear the creator's signature in their programming code; on the other, they are capable of executing their programme in ways that exceed the creator's expectations, for better or worse. Moreover, the phrase 'second creation' recalls that the figures originally associated with this way of thinking about the role of mechanical models in science—including Babbage, Boole and Maxwell—were also conversant in natural theology. Put bluntly, these people regarded progress in the modelling of natural processes—in some cases, even improving those processes (e.g. calculators replacing humans in mathematical tasks)—as steps towards humanity recovering its godlike powers prior to Adam's fall. This was very much in line with the general thinking behind the Christian dissenters who were largely responsible for the nineteenth century's 'Industrial Revolution', which placed a premium on technologies designed to enhance or even replace human labour as part of the general conquest of our fallen animal nature.

An interestingly ambivalent take on this theological motivation appears in Norbert Wiener's (1964) final work, *God and Golem, Inc.* Here the father of cybernetics imagined the computer as the high-tech successor of the 'golem', the Biblically blasphemous attempt by humanity to reproduce divine creation by building a simulacrum of itself from clay, the main ingredient of which happens to be silicon. Wiener realized that the modern project of artificial intelligence was closer to what the Bible had in mind about humans arrogating divine powers than either Mary Shelley's *Frankenstein* or even Karel Čapek's *R.U.R.* (which coined the word 'robot'), two works that are premised on research that resembles more today's cryonics, stem cell research, and carbon-based synthetic life. Indeed, one reason why the Bible tends to be 'iconoclastic' in the strict sense of opposing any form of 'idolisation' (Think Second Commandment) is that its authors did not know the difference between silicon and carbon. Thus, they thought there was a real possibility that humans could create life just as God did—and perhaps some humans already had, namely, those cultures of the Middle East who worshipped graven images. In this respect, Biblical iconoclasm should perhaps be understood in the same spirit as *eugenics*, except with human *creativity* (in silico) and *procreativity* (in carbo) potentially covered under the same normative regime. But that is a discussion for another day.

Interestingly, chief among those who objected to the construction of mechanical models as the royal road to scientific understanding was Pierre Duhem, a devout Catholic whose philosophical 'instrumentalism' was designed to short-circuit the blasphemous tendencies that worried Wiener by denigrating the epistemic status of such models. For Duhem (1908/1954), when scientists treat their models as the basis for deep 'metaphysical' explanations, they are effectively trying to replace faith in God with the illusion of human mastery in an attempt to second-guess God's judgement. Duhem's own 'Fideist' position was carried forward into both religious and scientific thought in the twentieth century, a period when language itself was regarded as among the potential tools that humans possess for 'world-construction' (*Weltbild*). Here one needs to see the rise of 'apophatic' theology, which stresses the ineffable character of God, as complementing the logical positivist denigration of metaphysical discourse as using words to say things about which nothing sensible can be said—at least in terms of achieving common consent over meaning. Tellingly, both theologian Karl Barth and positivist Rudolf Carnap—the respective exemplars of these two approaches—shared a common Lutheran background. The two sides of this coin were provocatively brought together in 1921, in Wittgenstein's *Tractatus Logico-Philosophicus*. Duhemian instrumentalism continued to be articulated toward the end of the twentieth century—in both religious and scientific registers— in the final 'Gentle Polemics' section of Bas van Fraassen's *The Scientific Image* (van Fraassen 1980: Chap. 7).

4 Computational Deism: The Computer as the Instantiation of an Impersonal *Logos*

This brief excursus into theology brings us to the second phase of the computer's role in scientific inquiry. It too is unlikely to have satisfied Duhem and his instrumentalist followers. In fact, it might have upset them even more, since it involves granting the computer an even stronger metaphysical status—a kind of 'super-realism'. Think of the issue this way. Whatever their other differences, Babbage and Wiener could agree that the computer testifies to humanity's godlike mastery over nature—including the nature of our own minds. The human creator is therefore clearly central to the computer's significance, just as the divine creator is central to natural creation. Indeed, some historians and philosophers of science nowadays invoke the phrase 'maker's knowledge' to capture what is seen as an extension of Francis Bacon's original vision of the scientific method as a privileged means for humanity to recover from the Fall. Duhem would understand this entire line of thought as a heretical take on the Christian understanding of humanity having been created 'in the image and likeness of God' (*Imago Dei*). In contrast, now imagine a radically Platonist understanding of the computer, which ends up denying not only the role of human agency in its creation but also the need to attribute any kind of creativity to God in nature. This is the second phase in a nutshell.

Here the computer is defined not as a simulation mediated by some higher order intelligence—be it human or divine—but as a *direct instantiation* of the *logos*, understood as an abstract universal logic whose existence transcends time and space. In practice, the computer's execution of a suitably programmed algorithm amounts to the playing out of one or more laws of nature, which are a subset of this logic. It follows that the humans who designed the algorithm did not *invent* it, but rather *discovered*—or perhaps *confirmed*—a particular expression of the *logos*, the existence of which does not require a human presence, even in terms of humans potentially benefitting from its results. This is probably the view of the computer that Frege and Gödel would have adopted, and it is explicitly endorsed by the MIT cosmologist Max Tegmark (2017) in his recent book, *Life 3.0*.

However, if algorithms were normally understood this way, they could not be covered as 'inventions' under patent law. As it stands, an algorithm counts as intellectual property when it is taken to be the execution of a unique programme by a specific range of machines, the outcomes of which are of human benefit. This is even less 'metaphysical' than how Babbage and Wiener thought about computers. And because we have become accustomed to think of algorithms as patentable in this sense, it is worth making explicit what the second, 'super-realist' understanding of the computer implies from a moral standpoint. It means that if a 'superintelligent' machine of the sort imagined by Nick Bostrom ends up annihilating humanity, it will not be due to some evil or even negligent algorithm designer. To be sure, that was exactly the prospect that worried Wiener and his fellow Cold War pioneers in artificial intelligence research. But this does not concern our 'super-realist', for whom our doom will have resulted from our own failure to protect and/or defend ourselves from a particular concrete outworking of the *logos*.

This way of casting matters should be familiar from the rather harsh statistically based naturalized version of Deism pursued by, among others, Thomas Malthus and Ronald Fisher in the guise of what we would now call a 'universal theory of natural selection'. Writing more than a century apart, Malthus and Fisher each proposed a timeless mathematical law governing this process. They wrote, respectively, before and after Charles Darwin presented a qualitative 'natural history' version of natural selection that persuaded many that the principle is as much a universal law as any proposed in physics. In recent years, Daniel Dennett (1995) has popularised this strong *logos* version of natural selection as 'Darwin's Dangerous Idea', whereby natural selection is presented as the 'universal solvent', a phrase he borrowed from William James to characterize the ultimate testing ground of all ideas and beings. The most super-realist version of James' vision is Lee Smolin's (1997) 'cosmological natural selection' hypothesis, which proposes that the 'birth' of our universe was effectively the 'survival' of matter after having passing through a black hole in space-time.

A practical scientific consequence of this line of thought is that 'evidence' for the outworking of natural selection in biology today is not restricted to the field (e.g.

prehistoric fossils) or extended only as far as the laboratory (e.g. experimentally generated mutations). In addition, computer programmes may instantiate natural selection, offering both retrodictions and predictions of various dimensions of the evolutionary process, including the morphology of individual organisms, the size and distribution of populations, as well as the contours of adaptive landscapes. In effect, what intellectual property lawyers would regard as no more than a 'proof of concept'—a formal demonstration that a specific thing would likely result if a certain procedure were followed—is treated by today's evolutionary theorists as evidentially equivalent to whatever might be discovered in either the field or the lab, at least if the content of papers published in *Nature* and *Science* is taken as our standard. Computers have facilitated this evidential elision by their unprecedented capacity for articulating alternative visions of the world, as reflected in the coinage, 'virtual reality'. Thus, many of today's evolutionary biologists spend their time constructing computer models of causal pathways by which what is known from the field and the lab could have been generated. The models effectively manufacture new evidence that is then taken to speak for what would otherwise be an unknowable past.

Perhaps the most famous software platform used for this purpose is Avida, originally developed in the 1990s to study what was then called the 'evolution of self-replicating systems' under a variety of parametric constraints. Nowadays, these things are called 'digital organisms', many of which ordinary computer users would recognize as 'viruses'. Avida came to prominence in 2005 during the *Kitzmiller* vs. *Dover Area School District* trial, in which 'intelligent design theory' (a form of scientific creationism) was proposed to be taught in high school science as an alternative to Darwin's theory of natural selection. Put in most general terms, intelligent design theorists argue that many organisms appear to be purpose-made—that is, their parts would never have come into being and then integrated as they have been unless they were made for a purpose. In the trial, Avida was invoked—conclusively, as far as the presiding judge was concerned—as demonstrating that there are various causal pathways by which stable organisms might have resulted in evolutionary time, many of which would not have required some guiding intelligence (Fuller 2008: 190–191).

Of course, we are still no wiser as to whether or not a superior intelligence did create the organisms that have actually existed. All we have learned from Avida is that it is possible that such a deity did not do it. This is a far cry from Michael Scriven's (1959) famous *Science* article, written for the centenary of Darwin's *Origin of Species,* which argued that Darwin's own scientific practice had confounded positivist methodology by showing that one could explain the past without being able to predict the future. Scriven held that Darwin's scientific revolution was not simply about the insights provided by his own theory but also the sort of data on which he relied, which were mainly those of natural history and current plant and animal breeding practices. From Scriven's standpoint, today's computer-based 'pan-selectionism' does violence to Darwin's own distinctive way of doing science.

In effect, the computer has lifted 'natural selection' from a first-order to a second-order concept. Natural selection is no longer simply a theory about the actual world but a worldview governing the operation of all possible worlds. Thus, the computer becomes the 'mind of God' in everything but name. Put another way, in the 2005 trial, the basic fact that neither the Avida software nor the computer hardware running it were self-organizing—they required intelligent human designers—did not figure in judge's reasoning about the probity of intelligent design theory as an alternative to Darwin's intelligence-blind version of natural selection. What prevailed instead was an intuition underwritten by Kuhn's (1970) hegemonic view of scientific paradigms—namely, that the dominant *Weltbild* projected by the paradigm controls the entire field of possible play in a science, until further notice, and regardless of how it was generated.

I earlier mentioned Deism in the context of this 'super-realist' view of the computer because within the Abrahamic religions, Deism provides the most convenient route to a fully Platonist view of natural order, one in which the *logos* reigns supreme. The underlying principle first came to the fore in Islam through the twelfth century works of the Andalusian jurist Ibn Rushd (aka Averroes), which were regarded as heretical in his native Islam. But once translated into Latin, this principle became the portal through which Aquinas and others in late medieval Christendom came to understand the Greek intellectual heritage that they shared with the Muslims.

Ibn Rushd's challenging suggestion was that God, understood as the Supreme Being, created the best possible world—one so perfect that the world can be understood as if the deity had never existed. Put another way, God's perfection implies that he could create the world only once—and that it would have to be this world—after which it operates as an autonomous system without any need for the deity to intervene. To expect further interventions would be to cast doubt on God's capacity to create the best possible world at all. Fast forward more than 500 years, and we find Leibniz advancing the same view against Newton's followers, who seemed to allow divine miracles as a vehicle for enabling Newton's mathematical laws to work properly. Leibniz simply thought that Newton himself had not quite penetrated the 'Mind of God' and thus was projecting his own ignorance onto the deity. What Newton presented as opportunities for God to remind us of his existence, Leibniz interpreted as Newton covering up his own mathematical shortcomings by making God seem like a clockmaker who needs to rewind his invention as it periodically ran down.

Let us grant that Leibniz vulgarized Newton's position for rhetorical effect, given that Newton himself was well disposed to the idea that regardless of how regular nature appears to humans, at every moment God could have done otherwise. Nevertheless, Leibniz succeeded—perhaps *malgré lui*—in demonstrating that the perfection of the divine creator's handiwork renders redundant any need to know the deity's identity. The blasphemy implied here, which was also present in Ibn Rushd, should be obvious: Knowledge of nature replaces faith in God wholesale, so that science triumphs over religion. This blasphemy is nowadays a secular commonplace, supposedly backed by Ockham's Razor. Accordingly, one should remain agnostic if not outright sceptical about whatever 'lawgiver' might be behind the 'laws of nature' because the laws themselves remain true regardless of their ultimate source. In that respect, the laws are 'self-instantiating'.

It is against this emerging post-theological sensibility that what philosophers now call 'Cartesian scepticism' has loomed so large in the modern era. There was still a lingering desire to know the divine creator, usually for moral reasons, which led to fears that, say, one might not be able to distinguish between a clockwork order designed by a good and an evil deity. What David Chalmers and Nick Bostrom have popularized in recent times as the 'simulation hypothesis' fully secularizes this point by envisaging an existential decision not between a good and bad deity but between no simulator and a simulator as being responsible for the world we experience. In this context, no simulator is presumed to be the better option, or at least the one that conforms to our natural intuitions of living in a relatively benign world. Indeed, quite *unlike* the first phase of the computer's scientific history, 'simulation' is understood pejoratively here. This reflects the triumph of Leibniz's Deism over both Babbage's Theism and Duhem's Fideism. The best God need not be the God who governs least, but rather the God who leaves the fewest fingerprints that he has governed at all. One can perhaps understand how the 'invisible hand' emerged as an idealized organizational principle for human affairs in the same eighteenth-century environment that bred Deism.

5 Conclusion: The Path Back to the Political Economy of the Computer and the Postdigital Future

At various points, I have asked the reader to forgive me theological excursions as we probed the computer's increasing centrality to scientific inquiry and the human condition more generally. The payoff of this indulgence is to show that the increasingly God-free, or 'atheistic', attitude to the laws of nature fostered in the modern period by Deism is now being reproduced in the increasingly human-free ('ananthropic'?) world that computer-based technologies allow. A good indicator is the diminishing political-economic significance of the labour theory of value that had united Aquinas, Locke, and Marx in their faith in the uniqueness of human creativity. Even Marx, who welcomed the role of technology in alleviating the drudgery of work, nevertheless believed that it released humans to engage in forms of labour that more clearly highlighted the distinctiveness of their species being. And even though capitalism has long formally disavowed the labour theory of value, the theory's spirit lives on in the mystique attached to 'innovation', understood as a productivity-enhancing 'god of the gaps' (aka the 'Solow residual') that forever keeps the economy dynamic (Fuller 2020).

But notwithstanding capitalism's residual 'brand loyalty' to the 'human', we end where we begin: A shift in political economy that points to a deeper reorientation of humanity's distinctiveness. I refer to the looming threat of 'technological unemployment' to sectors of the economy that stray well away from manual labour into those forms of 'intellectual labour', including art and science, that even Marx thought in principle could not be replaced by machines (Fuller 2019b). However, in the emerging world of Computational Deism, humans and computers are increasingly seen as alternative platforms for the delivery of 'functionalities' whose value transcends the platforms' material differences. It is with this prospect in mind that the 'cyborg' starts to appear as an attractive 'blended' middle way for sustaining humanity.

However, from a strictly postdigital standpoint, the focus needs to shift to the contrasting role of the *logos* in Computational Theism and Computational Deism. For the former, programming a computer is an upgraded version of the Biblical breathing of the *logos* into clay to create life; for the latter, programming simply realizes a universal *logos* that could have been brought about by a variety of programmers. A good way to think about this distinction is in terms of Roman Jakobson's (1971) influential contrast between the 'metonymic' and 'metaphoric' poles of language processing, respectively. In the metonymic mode, the programmer remains connected to the programmed entity by authorizing the legitimacy of its outputs, even if it exceeds the expectations or desires of the programmer. Just as everything is fine if God approves of what humans do, the same applies to humans vis-à-vis computers. In this context, Bostrom's fear of 'superintelligent' computers is a latter-day version of the Adamic Fall, in which everything turns out to be far from fine.

Computational Theism's metonymic mentality is most compelling when imagining a 'mainframe' computer that is physically separate from its programmer and whose overall numbers are relatively few. The relation here is crypto-parental. The guiding intuition is that the computer might mature into adulthood, for better or worse—as in Kant's definition of 'Enlightenment'. However, the standalone computer's independent agency or 'autonomy' has been gradually dissolved with the advent of distributed computer networks, corresponding to the personal computer and, more recently, the smartphone. That brings us into the metaphoric space inhabited by Computational Deism, in which the line of descent from created to creator becomes less clear. After all, any number of programmers could be responsible for the implementation of a particular computer programme. Under those circumstances, the search for the original programmer—a reversion to the metonymic mode—becomes rife with anxiety. This anxiety has been historically expressed as Cartesian scepticism, but it is nowadays regularly manifested in terms of hackers, bots, and other 'rogue agents' who can produce effects at least superficially similar to those produced by 'reliable sources'. The ambivalence surrounding the phrase 'virtual reality' epitomizes these concerns.

In conclusion, perhaps the simplest and the most useful way to think about the shift in attitude from Computational Theism to Computational Deism is as a by-product of the increase in the population of independently embodied computers, which then start to compete with their human creators and users along a variety of dimensions, from intellectual performance to sheer energy consumption. This point has interesting, albeit counterintuitive sociological implications. Sociology's default understanding of societal evolution, most closely associated with Emile Durkheim, plots a trajectory from what he called 'mechanical' to 'organic' solidarity, which roughly corresponds to the transition from a simple to a complex form of social organization. In the former, the society's members are basically interchangeable, whereas in the latter each member performs a specialized function. Ecologists, drawing on parallels between human and animal societies, have recast this transition in terms of a shift from 'categoric' to 'corporate' group structure, which in turn mirrors Jakobson's 'metaphoric' and 'metonymic' poles, respectively (Hawley 1950: Chap. 12). However, in a postdigital ecology populated by human and artificial intelligences on an increasingly equal footing, the relevant trajectory may well be reversed, such that the machines become rivals, if not replacements, of the humans rather than complements. This prospect is adumbrated by the difference in sensibility between Computational Theism and Computational Deism. It is a world in which the Turing Test comes to set a new standard of equality and fairness (Fuller 2012: Chap. 2; Fuller 2019a: Chap. 2). Once again, the cyborg looks an attractive middle way through.

References

Bostrom, N. (2014). *Superintelligence*. Oxford: Oxford University Press.
Dennett, D. (1995). *Darwin's Dangerous Idea*. London: Allen Lane.
Duhem, P. (1908/1954). *The Aim and Structure of Physical Theory*. Princeton: Princeton University Press.
Fuller, S. (1993). *Philosophy of Science and Its Discontents* (2nd ed.). New York: Guilford Press.
Fuller, S. (2000). *The Governance of Science*. Milton Keynes, UK: Open University Press.
Fuller, S. (2008). *Dissent over Descent*. Cambridge, UK: Icon Books.
Fuller, S. (2012). *Preparing for Life in Humanity 2.0*. Palgrave: London.
Fuller, S. (2019a). *Nietzschean Meditations: Untimely Thoughts at the Dawn of the Transhuman Era*. Bern, SZ: Schwabe.
Fuller, S. (2019b). Technological Unemployment as a Test of the Added Value of Being Human. In M. A. Peters, P. Jandrić, & A. J. Means (Eds.), *Education and Technological Unemployment* (pp. 115–128). Singapore: Springer. https://doi.org/10.1007/978-981-13-6225-5_8.
Fuller, S. (2020). Knowledge Socialism Purged of Marx: The Return of Organized Capitalism. In M.A. Peters, T. Besley, P. Jandrić, & X. Zhu (Eds.) (2020). *Knowledge Socialism. The Rise of Peer Production: Collegiality, Collaboration, and Collective Intelligence* (pp. 114-143). Singapore: Springer. https://doi.org/10.1007/978-981-13-8126-3_7.
Galison, P. (1997). *Image and Logic*. Chicago, IL: University of Chicago Press.
Hawley, A. (1950). *Human Ecology: A Theory of Community Structure*. New York: The Ronald Press Company.
Hernandez-Orallo, J. (2017). *The Measure of All Minds*. Cambridge, UK: Cambridge University Press.
Horgan, J. (1996). *The End of Science*. New York: Broadway Books.
Jakobson, R. (1971). The metaphoric and metonymic poles. In R. Jakobson & M. Halle (Eds.), *Fundamentals of Language* (Vol. 2, pp. 90–96). The Hague: Mouton.
Kasparov, G. (2017). *Deep Thinking: Where Machine Intelligence Ends and Human Creativity Begins*. London: John Murray.
Kuhn, T. (1970). *The Structure of Scientific Revolutions* (2nd ed.). Chicago, IL: University of Chicago Press.
Price, D. (1963). *Little Science, Big Science*. London: Penguin Books.

Sartre, J.-P. (1952/2012). *Saint Genet*. Minneapolis, MN: University of Minnesota Press.
Scriven, M. (1959). Explanation and prediction in evolutionary theory. *Science, 130*, 477–482.
Smolin, L. (1997). *The Life of the Cosmos*. Oxford, UK: Oxford University Press.
Tegmark, M. (2017). *Life 3.0*. New York: Alfred Knopf.
Van Fraassen, B. (1980). *The Scientific Image*. Oxford, UK: Oxford University Press.
Wiener, N. (1964). *God and Golem, Inc*. Cambridge, MA: MIT Press.

Postdigital Humans: Algorithmic Imagination?

John Reader

1 Introduction

This chapter will undertake a theological exploration into postdigital humans arguing that responding to 'the other' (in need) is central to religious practice. Drawing on the work of Catherine Keller (2018), I suggest that a sense of the interconnectedness of life is essential to our responses to both the environmental and the digital on two levels. First, the relationships built up by 'the slow work of time' and second, the instinctive (pre-autonomous) responses and interventions called upon by an immediate encounter. The focus of the chapter is on the latter as I examine the extent to which the use of algorithms in a postdigital development of the human may pre-empt or destroy what is required for those encounters.

To clarify what is meant by the pre-autonomous, autonomy suggests a thoughtful and measured response assuming the capacity to stand back from any situation and reason one's way through to a decision, probably with a high degree of reflexivity and self-awareness. By proposing the term 'pre-autonomous', one is acknowledging that there are moments of human contact which precede such a reflexive process, when an instant response is called for by something as simple as eye contact or an immediate feeling that one needs to engage. Within philosophy, this is encountered in the work of Levinas, followed by Derrida, who argue that even reason contains such a moment, or 'acquiescing to the testimony of the other' in terms of instinctive trust and response (Levinas 1998; Derrida 1997; Reader 2005). This chapter seeks to address whether or not this form of imagination—placing oneself in the position of the other and eliciting a response—is possible in the postdigital and posthuman which rely upon algorithms determined by a process of logic and calculation. The second section of the chapter draws on the work of Stiegler (2016),

---

J. Reader (✉)
William Temple Foundation and School of Education, University of Worcester, Worcester, UK

© The Author(s), under exclusive license to Springer Nature Switzerland AG 2021
M. Savin-Baden (ed.), *Postdigital Humans*, Postdigital Science and Education,
https://doi.org/10.1007/978-3-030-65592-1_10

who argues that the speed at which the digital functions pre-empts the processes of critical thought and theoretical knowledge, and so will extend this argument to the type of pastoral response as above. This is in the light of the possible enhancements of the human in the future as detailed among others by Michio Kaku (2018). If this is what the postdigital might become, what are the implications for the exercise of imaginative empathy central to a religious practice? The understanding of time itself will emerge as central to the discussions.

The theological (and philosophical) counterpoint to this will focus on the issue of calculation; reduction of 'others' to statistics and objectifying others by so doing. Hence, the issue of imagination and whether or not this aspect of what it is to be or become human can be built into the postdigital human and what this would look like. Stiegler is optimistic that this might be possible. What is certainly required is a theological and philosophical critique of the deployment of calculation at speed in the use of algorithms, in both the development of postdigital humans and in gaining a deeper appreciation of how responses to 'the other' might function in practice.

2 Postdigital Humans

It is becoming clear that the postdigital is already here, in the sense that developments of the digital are now embedded in the mainstream of human activity to the point where they are no longer either controversial or even the focus of attention. Although the prefix 'post' has its limitations, it is possibly the most effective means of articulating the changes that have already taken place, for instance in the field of biology and gene reconfiguration. As Foucault used to say about power, the postdigital is like the air that we breathe rather than an external component that is grafted onto existing forms of life (Foucault 1980). Hence discussion about the posthuman needs to take into account that this is present reality, and not a projection into a distant future. The boundaries are blurred, messy, and complex, and the challenge is to keep track of developments which are already well underway (Reader 2005).

It would seem that there are two main strands of thought related to the posthuman. One is of continuing enhancements of humans that do not fundamentally alter what it is to be human; and the other involves more significant changes that may produce an almost unrecognizable shift in the nature of humanity itself. These can be illustrated by an examination of the work of the American physicist and futurologist Michio Kaku (2018). In the first category, Kaku refers to the work of John Donoghue, who has developed technology that enables the body to restore certain functions that have been lost or damaged (Kaku 2018: 207). This involves the insertion of a chip into a person's brain, connected to a portable computer, that then enables control of their exoskeleton. Patients are able to control the motion of an exoskeleton in order to carry out simple tasks such as operating household appliances, controlling a wheelchair, or surfing the web. This is possible because the computer can recognize certain brain patterns associated with specific body movements, and electric impulses can then be converted into appropriate actions. Such techniques are immensely helpful to people who have lost certain bodily functions whether as a result of illness or war wounds. Kaku also mentions the possibility of strengthening the human body biologically through what has been dubbed 'the Schwarzenegger gene' which could help those suffering from degenerative muscle diseases (Kaku 2018: 208).

Further enhancements include cochlear implants, artificial retinas, and a device that detects ultraviolet radiation which can cause skin cancer. There is the possibility that these types of development might begin to shade into more significant changes though. 'Already, it is possible to create a chip that can pick up our brainwaves, decipher some of them, and then transmit this information to the internet' (Kaku 2018: 210). The example of the late Stephen Hawking, who had a chip placed in his glasses that could pick up his brainwaves and send them to a laptop, comes to mind. The question is how much further this might be taken, and Kaku suggests it is a short step to telekinesis, or even to connecting the brain directly to a robot that could then execute human mental commands. In the future, interacting with machines through thought may become the norm. Seen as a process of enhancement, this is supposedly nothing new, since humans have been engaged in these activities from the beginning, but have these now reached a stage where our understanding of ourselves is fundamentally challenged?

Kaku goes on to explore the possibilities represented by what is known as transhumanism. Given that our bodies have developed fairly randomly over time and contain many limitations or imperfections, some now argue that it would be legitimate to deploy technology to create improvements in the basic structure. 'They relish the idea that we can perfect humanity. To them the human race was a byproduct of evolution, so our bodies are a consequence of random haphazard mutations. Why not use technology to systematically improve on these quirks?' (Kaku 2018: 217) The vexed and controversial sphere of genetic engineering is entered at this point, but recent progress in biotechnology has moved in this direction and is a further step along the spectrum of technological enhancement already underway? The boundaries between the human and the nonhuman as machine or advanced technological assemblage have become increasingly blurred and what it is to be or become human is itself brought into question. If this sounds like science fiction, one needs to read *To Be a Machine: Adventures among Cyborgs, Utopians, Hackers, and the Futurists Solving the Modest Problems of Death* by Mark O'Connell (2017) to get a sense of the more radical experiments in developing a different 'humanity' that are already taking place. The subtitle of the book offers enough of a taste of those engaging in such activities without going into further details. Transhumanism is seen by some as an ethical imperative. If improvements can be created, we are morally bound to move in that direction. This is a case of the technology in the hands of those who argue for human control of nature itself running ahead of more familiar or traditional ethical ideas. Yet there is a logic at work here that needs to be addressed and then questioned. This relationship between logic and imagination is central to the argument of the chapter.

3 Responding to 'the Other'

The classic biblical account of how people are to respond to others in need comes in the parable of the Good Samaritan (St Luke: 10. 25–37). The young man questions Jesus when told that we are to love God and then our neighbours as ourselves by responding, 'and who is my neighbour?' It is of course the unlikely figure of the Samaritan, shunned by Jews, who breaks his journey, goes across to the injured traveller, binds up his wounds, takes him to an inn, and pays for his accommodation. By contrast, the religious characters in the story who one might have expected to take similar action, pass by on the other side. One interpretation of this is that the Samaritan acted out of pastoral impulse and took the right action regardless of personal danger or cost (pre-autonomous therefore). The others, however, may well have made a decision on the basis of calculation. The risks to themselves were too great, and they could not sully themselves with another's blood, whatever the circumstances. Does one respond on impulse or resort to calculation before taking, or not taking, action?

This story from 2000 years ago continues to resonate. On the scene of a motorway crash a few years ago, a medic who was in another vehicle had to decide whether to admit their profession and intervene in order to help, despite guidance that their insurance would not cover them in such circumstances (Reader 2005). Rational calculation could produce the conclusion that it was best to remain distant and anonymous, whereas an immediate pastoral response would lead to an intervention. Exactly what thought process is at work here, if it is such? Now that robots are being deployed to offer practical care to human recipients instead of human carers, we have entered the posthuman era and there is the question of how to understand and characterize such responses. What sort of care is this and does it have the same impact upon the recipient as care provided by a human? Might it even be better in some ways, more objective, reliable, and efficient? Is something of the human to human relationship lost in this exchange? What is the role of empathy, for instance? The argument of this chapter is that it is the exercise of the imagination which often makes the difference. Can one imagine what it is like to be in that other person's position? One might call this empathy, but the point is the same. If that was me on the roadside, would I want or expect a stranger to put themselves at risk by attending to my wounds irrespective of potential dangers to themselves? Is there not something fundamental here about what it is to be human? My 'neighbour' is anyone in need, as simple as that. As soon as calculation enters the equation, a very different dynamic and potential outcome is in play. Does digital technology as currently designed and deployed become a factor as we move towards a posthuman and post-digital future?

On the issue of speed in this era of the posthuman (and beyond), it is worth noting some predictions from Bostrom (2017) and then Hanson (2018) in order to understand the challenges to be faced. Bostrom explains speed superintelligence as a system that can do all that a human intelligence can do but much faster. An example of this would be a whole brain emulation running on fast hardware (Bostrom

2017: 64). An emulation operating at a speed of 10,000 times that of a biological brain would be able to read a book in a few seconds and write a doctoral thesis in an afternoon. Events in the external world would appear to unfold in slow motion. Such a speed superintelligence would work more efficiently with digital objects, living in a virtual reality and dealing in the information economy. 'The speed of light becomes an increasingly important constraint as minds get faster, since faster minds face greater opportunity costs in the use of their time for travelling or communicating over long distances' (Bostrom 2017: 65). This may seem far-fetched but given the pace and scope of the developments already noted, these possibilities need to be recognized. How would a mind operating at these advanced speeds respond to 'the other' let alone incorporate what we term imagination?

Hanson makes this even clearer. Human brain neuron fibres send signals at speeds ranging from 0.5 to 120 metres per second. Signal speeds in electronic circuit boards operate typically at half the speed of light. 'If signals in em brains move at electronic speeds, that would be between 1 and 300 million times faster than neuron signals' (Hanson 2018: 79). Proportionally smaller brains could cope with proportionally larger speed ups. If there were an algorithm that could compute a neuron firing in 10,000 of the fastest known circuit cycles, then an emulation based on this would run a million times faster than the human brain. The numbers involved become exponential, but, if there is the prospect of human and nonhuman technological assemblages continuing to develop along these lines, then there is a serious issue of what this might mean for other current normal functionings of humans, and what would happen to capacities such as empathy or imagination. Would these remain part of what a postdigital posthuman might become, and, if not, what would become of the pastoral (and indeed political) responses to 'the other' that are so essential to both private and public relationships?

4 A Contemporary Theological Interpretation

One can begin to recognize that a simple return to biblical narratives has its limitations especially now that the boundaries of the human are themselves increasingly blurred. A theology that can take this into account offers a more appropriate approach to the issue of pastoral response. The developing interconnectedness between the human and technology has been addressed by the work of Catherine Keller in order to illustrate this (Keller 2018). Working largely in a US context, she has brought together a deep knowledge of Christian mystical theology and contemporary philosophy in attempting to respond to the environmental crisis both theoretically and practically. As part of this project, she draws upon process philosophy (and process theology), specifically the writing of Whitehead from earlier in the twentieth century.

The controversial aspect of this is that God is no longer seen as external to the world, either creating or manipulating from afar as some sort of old-fashioned sovereign or even contemporary capitalist mogul, but is always already part of the process of creation itself. As Keller says, the metaphysics of substance is abandoned to be replaced by 'the creative process in which anything actual exists only as an interdependent activity of becoming' (Keller 2018: 138). Divine agency does not control the outcome of any becoming, even its own. We are all in this together, God included. The advantage of this is that Whitehead presents a cosmology of 'rhythmically intertwined becomings' (Keller 2018: 139). Complex though this might sound, it enables an understanding of each element in the universe both developing in its own right but also as connected to all others in dynamic and constructive ways. There is thus an obvious link to quantum physics and ideas of the new materialisms which are nonreductive and profoundly interactive. It allows for other possibilities and a greater freedom for creative activity. It is argued then that this approach is better able to take into account the relationships between the human and the nonhuman, particularly as now experienced in the postdigital and posthuman context. Rather than humans exercising external control over a separate technology, it is the dynamic and ever-changing assemblages or combinations of the human in relationship with the technology and itself developing differently as a result, which become the appropriate focus of attention.

It is what follows from this though that is of most significance for our concerns. In a section entitled 'amorous awakening' (Keller 2018: 154–158), Keller draws out the implications of this approach for how we are to relate to 'the other'. She refers to the Pauline version of what is known as the love commandment as derived from the parable of the Good Samaritan (Galatians: 5.14). The point is that the idea of one's neighbour is now to be extended well beyond that of immediate proximity (the Samaritans were indeed neighbours in that sense) and understood to refer to even the nonhuman, although Keller intends this to mean creation as environment.

> No sovereign subject survives this radical entanglement. Such amorous agonism on behalf of the vulnerable brooks no reduction to moralism, purism or identitarianism. Rather it offers a biblical amplification of an intersectional ethics for a time of unveiled white supremacism, Islamaphobia, climate denialism. (Keller 2018: 155).

Keller is writing against the background of US politics. This interpretation is then extended further through the notion of radical hospitality which requires us to welcome 'the other' regardless of colour, creed, class, or gender. 'The one who loves the other, the other as the very embodiment of difference, is the one who fulfils the law' (Keller 2018: 156). We find ourselves all entangled with one another. For Keller, this has implications for how Christians are to engage in public life, whatever our differences and divisions. In the context of the postdigital and posthuman, it suggests that this amorous awakening should be extended through this exercise of what we might call pastoral imagination, to the new and developing forms of life that are the assemblages of the human and technology. The question then is whether and how this is possible given that the technology at present relies upon the use of algorithms, calculation, and commercially determined processes. Yet responding to 'the other' in all forms is at the heart of the Christian ethical imperative.

5 Stiegler on the Digital and Imagination

In his major work of 2016, Stiegler suggests that computer systems produce what he terms an automatic performativity that channels, diverts, and short-circuits individual and collective protentions by outstripping and overtaking the noetic (i.e. spiritual and intellectual) capacities of individuals, and at the same time by short-circuiting the collective production of circuits of individual and collective development. To explain this unfamiliar terminology: primary protention is the anticipation of the immediate coming moment whereas secondary protention is the anticipation or expectation based on past experience. Protention generally is thus also imagination through which we recollect and recognize what has happened in the past and project it into the future. Tertiary protention refers to the fact that in our everyday lives technology becomes a significant function of the imagination. For instance a Google search will recommend a certain product based on previous choices, through the use of algorithms. Therefore, tertiary protention depends upon tertiary retention since the traces of earlier searches and orientations depend on an algorithmic process.

Every form of noesis is thereby overtaken through this encitement of protentions operating by remote control. Those protentions are continuously being redefined and are always already being erased by new protentions that are even more disintegrated. This is an obstacle to dreaming, wanting, reflecting, and deciding, that is, the collective realization of dreams, and it forms the basis of algorithmic governmentality inasmuch as it is the power of fully computational 24/7 capitalism (Stiegler 2016: 138). This is a process of formation not simply involving individuals but a collective process based on what Stiegler calls the pre-individual funds available in a particular culture or society. This is not the same as the conscious process of becoming more self-aware and defining oneself as an individual but of a locating within a wider context; Stiegler argues that it is wider context that this can be short-circuited. The primary, secondary, and then tertiary protentions, which reflect the processes of engagement with external influences through memory, discourse with others, and then the impact of mechanical or more recently digital means of communication, are now themselves being intervened with in such a way that the process of collective development is being pre-empted and short-circuited. Thus, the spaces and opportunities for what Stiegler calls intermittences, the dreams, desires, and reflections are denied the chance to develop. What occurs instead is an automatization of the human, brought about by encounter with the digital, as determined by the forces of capitalism functioning in a much faster and all-consuming culture. The argument is that the digital itself as employed and deployed by digital capitalism is likely to disrupt and even potentially destroy the spaces for consideration of its impact upon relationships and society more generally.

Stiegler then refers to the USA's 2008 subprime-led financial crisis and the speed at which the financial services now function; credit default swaps and high-frequency trading are good examples of this. The data industry moves at such a pace that it deprives us of the possibility and opportunity to interpret our retentions and protentions, both psychic and collective (Stiegler 2016: 139). Against this,

'Leviathan' Stiegler wants to examine how the digital itself, as pharmakon, can be developed and employed to counteract these damaging impacts. Currently, primary protentions are tied to the object of lived experience, through habit, reasoning, or knowledge accumulated through the objects of perception. These then become secondary protentions through the means by which we remember and communicate and interpret those memories. However, then in the case of the tertiary protentions which are digitally reticulated, the near-light speed at which they function prevent proper time and space for interpretation and reflection. The average speed of a nervous impulse circulating between the brain and the hand is around 50 metres per second, whereas reticulated digital tertiary retentions can circulate at 200 million metres per second on fibre-optic networks (Stiegler 2016: 140).

If it is a question of re-establishing a genuine process of collective and individual development with reticulated digital tertiary retentions, and of establishing a digital age of psychic and collective individuation, this requires systems that are built and implemented and that are dedicated to the individual and collective interpretation of traces, including the use of new automated systems (Stiegler 2016: 141). What we need to examine is how this relates, if at all, to what I call the pre-autonomous, that almost instinctive and spontaneous pastoral response which occurs before any sort of calculation? Stiegler considers that a slowing down can be achieved within digital technology and that there is no need for it to be denied or abandoned.

That being the case investigations of individuation, imagination, reason, and the pre-autonomous form a prerequisite for the collective, pastoral, and political dimensions of the debate. Since it is at these levels that the digital are aimed and already have damaging impacts, it is vital that there is a deeper understanding of and discussion about the speeds at which these new configurations of the human and nonhuman can function. A critical aspect of this will be understandings of time itself.

6 Reason as Either Imagination or Calculation

It can be argued that through the development of technology one particular strand of reason has achieved dominance—that of technical-practical reason—through its applicability in the fields of science, technology, and also the business world. In a much later configuration identified by thinkers such as Habermas (1984), this becomes what is called instrumental reason, thought applied in order to reason through problems in a linear fashion in order to achieve specific objectives. Those objectives are not themselves to be judged according to any ethical criteria, so reasoning is simply a means to an end, hence instrumental.

Malabou (2016) argues that employing Kant's idea of epigenesis to developments in neuroscience shows that reason itself is always subject to a process of evolution. Rather than searching for an original meaning against which one can evaluate current interpretations, it is more appropriate to examine and propose alternative versions which emerge as a result of encounters with contemporary issues and ideas. In which case, the question becomes that of what such versions might be and whether they can be usefully employed in the spheres of science and technology. Is there nothing more than instrumental or technical-practical reason at work?

In the first edition of Kant's *Critique of Pure Reason* (1929), he suggests that the imagination plays the role of a middle term between the understanding and intuition. Indeed it produces 'the pure look' that makes any objective encounter possible a priori. Thinking and objectivity agree with each other in the start from this scene. Imagination opens the horizon prior to the encounter so this becomes a matter of understanding that time itself is at stake in this discussion. In other words, there is what I termed in *Blurred Encounters* (Reader 2005) that pre-autonomous moment or encounter which precedes what then develops into deeper relationship or analysis of a particular situation. Reason can only begin once that encounter has taken place and that is something which is neither planned nor controlled—the very first glance or moment of eye contact between two people which then sparks off a relationship. In the case of the Good Samaritan, it is that direct encounter which then leads to the subsequent appropriate pastoral response.

Derrida, whose work can also figure in this, talks about reason as 'acquiescing to the testimony of the other' and also as hospitality, both of which suggest that there has to be a willingness and openness to receive the other as they are, before any further encounter can take place or develop (Derrida 1997). These ideas are powerful and suggestive and in contrast to the mechanical and controlled interpretations of reason that dominate current thinking. However, is it the case that digital technology now pre-empts that moment of encounter, or the exercise of the imagination as Kant and Malabou would describe it? There is indeed such a suggestion. Digital technology operates on the basis of logic, so instead of imagination playing the role of mediating or presenting that initial moment or look, this will now be communicated via a system where a more means-end instrumental process is in play. Does this mean that the more human dimension which relies upon our individual capacity to perceive, interpret, and then respond is no longer part of the equation? Stiegler argues that the speed at which digital technology functions can pre-empt the process of critical thought and questioning, so this would be an equivalent concern when it comes to those initial pre-autonomous encounters. Is the very action of hospitality, welcoming, or being open to the other itself now determined by a more mechanical or logic-driven process?

Perhaps there is not yet enough evidence to be able to answer this definitively, but one can recognize that there are concerns that imagination, intuition, and perhaps the more subjective dimensions of what we might call reason or rationality are compromised when encounters are mediated solely through that technology. We know that the use of algorithms in marketing presents us with predictions about our wants and desires based on past actions. The future comes at us in the present based on calculations of what we have done in the past, and this might indeed pre-empt any effort we would be inclined to make to consider different options. Time itself is being reconfigured by these mechanisms.

This is now uncharted territory ethically and philosophically and raises again the question of how reason might be evolving in the light of contemporary technological developments. Religious traditions appear to offer a different experience of time in that they operate on the basis of repetition through liturgy and the encounter with buildings, for instance. They can also provide opportunities for times of reflection and meditation, and general slowing down of time which could allow for critical thought, although it is less clear whether they offer anything in the field of the imagination in the initial encounter. Traditional explanations of moments of conversion or epiphanies might be candidates for this, but they seem somewhat remote from encounters mediated by the digital. Is it possible that the digital can be more than simply an operation of logic, but could also present those looks or moments that convey an experience which is associated with welcoming the other as hospitality?

7 Stiegler and Heidegger: The Role of Time in Imagination

With Stiegler we see technics as time in the form of retentions. A hypothesis is that imagination itself is no longer the imagination of the subject but rather shifts from subjects to algorithms and digital objects. Technology is engaging us in our thinking processes in terms of the logical capacities and operations of machines. The obstacle to thinking about protention and algorithm lies in an opposition between imagination (time) and mechanism (formal logic). We tend to believe in the human as the only subject which imagines so although machines produce a range of choices, it is only humans that decide.

In Heidegger (1997), the transcendental imagination is the synthesis of time: it is the faculty that brings the pure intuition of time into order. In Kant, it is through the operation of time that experience is made possible. For Heidegger, time constitutes the finitude of *Dasein* as well as the transcendence of its being—its rootedness in time alone is what enables the transcendental power of the imagination in general to be the root of transcendence. In the *Critique of Pure Reason*, Kant gives three orders of synthesis. First is apprehension; the process by which data come into the mind is passively stored as manifolds; second is reproduction or recollection in imagination as the image is now formed through the power of imagination; third is recognition in relation to a concept which is the recognition of the sameness of the concept's unity.

Apprehension already discloses the being-with and recollection already discloses the already-in, while recognition also means projection into the future because recognition is already ahead of the past and the present. Heidegger reverses the order of the syntheses and identifies the transcendental imagination with his understanding of *Vorstruktur*, so there is a circle of syntheses—therefore having, foresight, pre-grasping, and anticipation are always already in operation. This is the same as his hermeneutical circle where the future is always already present as 'we have it in mind' or 'we are watching out for what is ahead'. One can also draw parallels with the concept of the pre-autonomous as representing a process that is always already in operation prior to any more formal or reflexive reasoning.

In this reinterpretation, the 'I think' is no longer a mere logical subject; it is time grounded in intuition, transcendental imagination, and understanding; therefore, logic cannot be taken as the ground, instead the ground must be time *qua* transcendental imagination. So the rationalists' approach which takes objects as bearers of attributes and treats the unity of subject and predicate as bearing the structure of propositions has to be reassessed, because the understanding of the object does not originate from thought but from time—the object is not merely determined by categories but rather relies heavily on the creative capacity of the intuition and the productivity of the transcendental imagination. So, Heidegger criticizes formal logic as a detemporalization.

Time is the primacy of human existence and the understanding of logos that characterizes the human being must be understood from temporality, and not from logic. Traditional logic or metaphysics, according to Heidegger, must be reassessed through this process of ignorance or forgetfulness. Logical knowledge traverses human experience by creating a short circuit—an analogy is the replacement of the analogue with the digital in modern technology, so that time consuming processes based on mechanical rules can be replaced by logic gates and all impurities be reduced to a minimum. Logical knowledge, as the foundation of modern science and technology, is itself technological. Logic is viewed as the founding discipline of human understanding, and the brain is considered as a device that executes logical principles. AI and indeed the computational mind is one that is deprived of time and care because it is based on purely logical operations. This could be seen both as the end of metaphysics and also a threat to any immediate pastoral response.

Stiegler criticizes Heidegger for not recognizing a fourth synthesis; the memory support that now comes through technics, the technical system itself, organizes memory. It is through technics—but not in its pure form—that logic returns to its place as the foundation of metaphysics. Then what role is left for the imagination? Technics offers a storage function, and the emergence of the visual domain allows for a different kind of inspection, a reordering, and refining of meanings. Writings are technical objects that deal with single streams of data whereas digitization allows the logical synthesis of large amounts of data and knowledge exceeding our imagination. This new sensibility is not passive but comes with a purpose and a force and indeed its own characteristics of temporality—one that needs to be understood through recursivity.

An algorithm is a logical operation by which to figure out different relations, and recursion is an algorithmic technique where a function, in order to accomplish a task, calls itself to accomplish parts of the task (this is not the same as looping!). The human mind can make sense of the recursive function but cannot keep up with it or keep track of it. Google's page rank is a recursive function, and the page ranks are recursively calculated to maintain that they are in time, never obsolete. A recursive function calls itself as many times as possible until a terminal state is reached. Recursion reaches deep down into the question of time. With algorithms, a new synthesis of relations is created, and recursion allows recognition and recollection to happen outside the three syntheses. This is more than a simple human tool feedback loop, but an example of structural coupling. When both humans and machines are understood from the fundamental perspective of relations, it produces a new faculty, tertiary protention (building upon Stiegler's tertiary retention).

An example would be freshly made coffee waiting for you when you enter the house as the machine has predicted this is what you will want on your return. So, a sort of imaginative force operating from an exterior world. Through the analysis of data, or speculation, a possible future has been identified that is always already ahead but that we have not yet projected. This could be understood through one of Heidegger's concepts which is that of 'making present' or bringing something forth into the 'now'. This is not the same as recollection, but a pre-thematic experience of things enabled by the already there in which I am situated: it is an outward movement to the world as temporal ecstasy. In contrast to the present at hand, making present also involves the imagination, it is a bodying forth or movement towards. To make something present is to produce the relations involved and hence to orient. Space is only one of the relations involved in orientation. The primary function of digital technologies is not merely to represent objects but to materialize and accumulate relations, and without these relations there is no transparency of action.

8 Conclusion

The question of technological convergence, first through networks, second through the intervention of imagination, announced the end of the human as holding the central position among objects and being at the centre of knowledge. Humans now have to adapt to the rhythm of the technical system not only physiologically and materially but also cognitively (making present). We are approaching a state of symbiosis with machines where the transcendental imagination becomes a passive force of synthesis because the recognition process can be short circuited: the future is always the present.

What needs to be taken into account is that the idea of time as simply linear, passing from A to B to C is only one interpretation, and that within the philosophical sources being deployed in this chapter there are other possibilities. For Deleuze, for instance there is both virtual time and intensive time. Within the former, there is a progression from determinable but undetermined differential elements to determined or realized actualities as certain events come to pass. Until this happens, other possibilities remain the case. The Good Samaritan might or might not have responded to the traveller, but, having done so, a determinate present is then the case. In the intensive register by contrast, there are thresholds or critical points, which in theology is known as *Kairos* or the right time. Was the pastoral response an example of that person knowing 'the right moment to act'? Then, finally, there is time as measurable and extensive, chronos or calendar time as chronological. It is this understanding of time that may play a decisive role in digital technology functioning through logic rather than imagination, if it is the case that calculation determines whether or not there will be a response (Protevi 2013: 191).

In addition, in *Cinema 2* Deleuze (1989: 80) engages in a sustained and complex discussion of Bergson on the subject of time. Drawing upon Bergson he says that every moment of our life presents two aspects, the actual and the virtual, both perception and recollection. We should have no more difficulty in admitting the virtual existence of pure recollections in time than we do for the actual existence of non-perceived objects in space. Time has to split itself in two as both present and past, one launching then towards the future and the other back into the past. There is a hidden ground of time or two distinct flows: the presents which pass and the pasts that are preserved. So, our understanding of time is central to how we describe our being in the world, and past and present have to be seen as co-present and effective in how we project into the future. If this is true for the technology of cinema, may it not also hold when it comes to digital technology despite the speeds at which it may be able to function? Within each portion of time, there are always other possibilities, including that of the immediate pastoral response, and it would be deterministic to assume that this is automatically factored out by the technologies.

It may be that the theoretical aspect of this is yet to be fully explored and articulated. The examples at the start of this chapter show how the technology could be designed and developed to enhance the well-being of individuals whose lives are disrupted by illness or accident, and it can be argued that there appears to be the possibility of alternative futures building upon the digital. There is perhaps a different experience of time itself as the space in which both imagination can still be a factor, and these advances can be employed in positive and constructive ways, even though this has to be counterbalanced by the manipulative forces of marketing and consumerism. If the Kingdom of God—to use faith terms for a moment—is both present and yet not present, then perhaps here is one possible way into this debate. If through the immediate pastoral response to the other, even if this is mediated by the digital, there is both that which is present and that which is not yet present, the presence of a radical hospitality can potentially become manifest. If time is understood as split between the actual and the virtual in every single moment, then other possibilities are encountered which can retain the possibility of the pre-autonomous pastoral response.

Keller, at the conclusion of *Cloud of the Impossible* (Keller 2015: 313), suggests that attending to the forward surge or arrow of time pointing onwards nuances and complicates our understanding rather than diminishing such alternative interpretations of time. 'At its multiple scales, variant rhythms of nonseparability, waves, currents and vortices, fold and unfold the irreversible and nonlinear space-time of our becoming. The ocean of creativity and fire of apocalypse no longer sit at opposite ends of a time line'. A process theology perspective offers a path into the digital that leaves open the possibility of imagination, although one that requires active pursuit and response. Since speeds belong to chronological time as calculated and controlled, other understandings of time bring that into question and suggest they do not have the final word.

References

Bostrom, N. (2017). *Superintelligence: Paths, Dangers, Strategies*. Oxford, UK: Oxford University Press.
Deleuze, G. (1989). *Cinema 2*. London, UK: Continuum International Publishing Group.
Derrida, J. (1997). *Adieu to Emmanuel Levinas*. Stanford, CA: Stanford University Press.
Foucault, M. (1980). *Power/Knowledge. Selected Interviews & Other Writings 1972-1977*. New York: Harvester Press.
Habermas, J. (1984). *The Theory of Communicative Action. Volume 1. Reason and the Rationalization of Society*. London, UK: Heinemann Educational Books Ltd..
Hanson, R. (2018). *The Age of EM: Work, Love, and Life when Robots rule the Earth*. Oxford, UK: Oxford University Press.
Heidegger, M. (1997). *Kant and the Problem of Metaphysics*. Indianapolis, IN: Indiana University Press.
Kaku, M. (2018). *The Future of Humanity: Terraforming Mars, Interstellar Travel, Immortality and Our Destiny Beyond Earth*. London: Penguin Books.
Kant, I. (1929). *Critique of Pure Reason*. Hampshire, UK: MacMillan Press Ltd..
Keller, C. (2015). *Cloud of the Impossible: Negative Theology and Planetary Entanglement*. New York: Columbia University Press.
Keller, C. (2018). *Political Theology for the Earth: Our Planetary Emergency and the Struggle for a New Public*. New York: Columbia University Press.
Levinas, E. (1998). *Otherwise Than Being: Or Beyond Essence*. Pittsburgh, PA: Duquesne University Press.
Malabou, C. (2016). *Before Tomorrow*. Cambridge, UK: Polity Press.
O'Connell, M. (2017). *To Be a Machine Adventures Among Cyborgs, Utopians, Hackers, and the Futurists Solving the Modest Problem of Death*. London, UK: Granta Publications.
Protevi, J. (2013). *Life, War, Death: Deleuze and the Sciences*. Minneapolis, MN: University of Minnesota Press. USA.
Reader, J. (2005). *Blurred Encounters: A Reasoned Practice of Faith*. Vale of Glamorgan, UK: Aureus Publishing.
Stiegler, B. (2016). *Automatic Society: Volume 1: The Future of Work*. Cambridge, UK: Polity Press.

Transcendent Conformity: The Question of Agency for Postdigital Humans

Alexander Thomas

1 Introduction

The dynamic co-evolution of humans and technology is increasingly undermining stable and long-held notions of the human condition and the conceptual boundaries which have demarcated human beings as individuals. The disintegration of ontological boundaries brought about by digital, genetic, and cybernetic developments require an ongoing normative investigation into the structures, interests, and consequences of this process of technogenesis. Two competing schools of thought that engage with the loss of essentialism and stability of the human are transhumanism and critical posthumanism. Critical posthumanism provokes profound critical and ethical consideration of the implications of the unmooring, whereas transhumanism tends to claim a clear and advantageous direction of travel. This chapter will contend that the transhumanist conception of the capacity for human agency to direct this process, especially at an individual level, is naïve. Critical posthumanism valuably emphasises our embeddedness in an environmental context: the nature and pace of the co-evolution of humans and technology does not exist in a vacuum. The broader social, cultural, political, and economic contexts are vital to engaging with the ethical, epistemological, and ontological implications. Cognizance of the dynamics of advanced capitalism, the dominant mode of societal organisation, should therefore underpin any such analysis. Transcendent conformity is a notion intended to highlight the competitive and controlling logics of advanced capitalism rendering concepts of 'enhancement', 'uplift', and 'transcendence' in its thrall and limited to its narrowly defined aims.

A. Thomas (✉)
University of East London, London, UK
e-mail: a.thomas@uel.ac.uk

The chapter will introduce the transhumanist concept of morphological freedom before undermining the efficacy of its framing by introducing a complexity-based posthumanist notion of agency. It will then consider how human embeddedness in a wider complex ecology of techno-capitalist relations undermines simplistic notions of individual self-determination, before analysing how the rendering of humans into data constitutes a further blow to claims of self-actualisation espoused within the transhumanist paradigm.

2   Transhumanism and Posthumanism

Transhumanism and critical posthumanism are both developing discourses with varied lineages and numerous schisms. As Francesca Ferrando states, transhumanists and posthumanists 'share a common perception of the human as a non-fixed and mutable condition, but they generally do not share the same roots and perspectives' (2013: 2). Transhumanism largely has its roots in Enlightenment humanist rationalism (Bostrom 2005; Hughes 2010) whereas posthumanism has a number of more recent genealogies. Cary Wolfe (2010) identifies the roots of its primary genealogy in the 1960s with Foucault's claim that 'man is an invention of recent date. And one perhaps nearing its end' (1966/2002: 387). This sets posthumanism in direct contrast to transhumanism, as the target of Foucault's 'end of man' concept is the rational humanist ideal that transhumanism identifies as its source. Max More defines transhumanism as 'a class of philosophies that seeks the continued evolution of human life beyond its current human form as a result of science and technology' (2013: 1). Transhumanism is thus a form of hyper-humanism—the idea that humankind will transcend into an enhanced or uplifted successor species through employing its reason. Critical posthumanism is clearly a countervailing force to such a notion:

> Posthuman critical theory unfolds at the intersection between post-humanism on the one hand and post-anthropocentricism on the other. The former proposes the philosophical critique of the Western Humanist ideal of 'Man' as the allegedly universal measure of all things, whereas the latter rests on the rejection of species hierarchy and human exceptionalism. (Braidotti and Hlavajova 2018: 339)

Critical posthumanists tend to reject hierarchical conceptualisations, eschewing the idea of humans at the apex of Earthly species, bringing into question the very concept of 'uplift' and 'enhancement' that is so vital to the transhumanist creed. Transhumanist thinker David Pearce states '[i]f we want to live in paradise, we will have to engineer it ourselves. If we want eternal life, then we'll need to rewrite our bug-ridden genetic code and become god-like' (IEET 2020). Transhumanism places its faith in the application of human reason to develop the instrumentalist capacities of science and technology in a linear progress towards 'paradise'. Posthumanism questions human reason, problematises linear notions of progress, and would dispute any singular utopian vision. If transhumanism is the belief in instrumental progress leading teleologically to a desired end, posthumanism is the 'questioning both of the inevitability of a successor species and of there being any consensus surrounding the effects of technologies on the future of humanity' (Graham 2002: 11): it is the ethical investigation of 'perpetual becoming' (Miah 2008: 23).

3 Morphological Freedom

One of the ideas put forward within transhumanist discourse that is intended to champion human agency in the context of technogenesis is 'morphological freedom'. Anders Sandberg, a prominent transhumanist thinker, defines it as 'an extension of one's right to one's body, not just self-ownership but also the right to modify oneself according to one's desires' (2013: 56). He conceptualises technologies as methods for increasing diversity through self-actualisation: 'new tools for expressing individuality and uniqueness...We express ourselves through what we transform ourselves into' (Sandberg 2013: 59). These proposals are made in relation to the prospect of humans having access to technologies that may offer radical enhancement of mental and physical capacities. The converging development of the NBIC suite of technologies (nanotechnology, biotechnology, information technology, and cognitive science) is the primary basis for this potentiality. Morphological freedom is designed to emphasise an individual's right to utilise these methods of enhancement. Sandberg conceives of:

> a subject that is also the object of its own change. Humans are ends in themselves, but that does not rule out the use of oneself as a tool to achieve oneself. In fact, one of the best ways of preventing humans of being used as means rather than ends is to give them the freedom to change and grow. (Sandberg 2013: 63)

Such a notion is contingent upon a conceptualisation of the Enlightenment liberal human employing their individual rationality, free from influence, to enable forms of self-determination. It is worth drawing attention here to a tendency in transhumanist thought for avoiding analysis of social context. As transhumanism is often identified as a future state or possibility, the social dynamics at the time of its realisation are undefined. The systemic dynamics at play are simply removed. The focus becomes the liberally conceived individual who has all the possibilities afforded by radical technological leaps forward, and none of the limitations rendered by wider systemic factors such as a social context. This naive conceptualisation is implicit in the proposals of morphological freedom. Critical posthumanism counters such a notion by emphasising the continuity of organisms and their environment (e.g. Hayles 1999). As Shaw (2018: 41) notes, whilst identifying the importance of 'second order' cybernetics to the development of posthuman theory, '[l]ife...exists in a network of constant exchange'. Processual relationality that undermines distinct delineation of entities, including humans, is thus vital to the critical posthumanist framework.

4 Posthuman Agency

Central to the contention of critical posthumanism is that the liberal human subject is a myth. As Jaime del Val (2020) potently frames it, humanism's 'human, as an autonomous and superior rational entity, is a chimera that never existed: a colonial, speciest, classist, sexist, racist, heteropatriarcal, phallogocentric project of compulsory abledness'. These prejudicial elements reveal the inefficacy of its supremacist faith in its own power of reason. Critical posthumanism seeks to establish that human reason is embedded in a wider ecology of influences, material, and ideational, that compromise independence and self-determination. Related schools of thought have also taken aim at the humanist conception of reason, including New Materialism which reacts to the emphasis on discourse and language over material embodiment, or the perceived primacy of culture over nature. Karen Barad complains: 'Language matters. Culture matters. There is an important sense in which the only thing that does not seem to matter anymore is matter' (2003: 801). By focusing primarily on material processes, simple individualist notions of agency become untenable, as the individual dissolves into the wider material unfolding of which it is a part. Questions of discourse and culture do not precede but emerge from the material world which is fundamentally interconnected. As Jane Bennett explains, 'an actant never really acts alone...[i]ts efficacy or agency always depends on the collaboration, cooperation, or interactive interference of many bodies and forces' (2010: 21). Bruno Latour's actor-network-theory (ANT) (Latour and Woolgar 1986) takes a similar approach, identifying agency as a quality of networked, material being. The strategy behind this stance is to undermine human rationalist exceptionalism and its related domination of nature.

The reductionism inherent in this position comes at a cost. As Erika Cudworth and Steve Hobden argue, '[t]he flat, non-hierarchical networks of ANT cannot deal with power because it cannot make distinctions between nature and society, or for that matter, between humans, other animals, plants and objects. In theorising power, we need such distinctions' (2013: 16–7). Likewise, there is a risk of paradox in positions which aim at undermining the value of discourse whilst decidedly engaging in it. As Aleksandra Alacaraz states, '[d]iscursivity, normativity, agency, and ethics should be transformed and not denied; we cannot develop an ethics without moral agents' (2019: 103). Rather than compromise ethical thinking altogether by eradicating the moral agent, it 'may be somehow loosely and relatively described, not in strict either/or categories, but in the and/and sort' (Alcaraz 2019: 103). This is key to an effective posthumanist conception of agency, as Cudworth and Hobden demonstrate in calling for an account 'that problematises rather than rejects outright, dualist ontologies...a situated and differentiated notion of agency that understands the ability of creatures and things to "make a difference in the world" as a question of situated relations rather than intrinsic capacity alone' (2013: 18). Just as Cudworth and Hobden (2013) draw on complexity thinking to circumnavigate the intractable system-agency question, it can be usefully employed to move us beyond the trap of the reductionist materialist versus idealist dichotomy, which arguably undermines the efficacy of New Materialism and ANT.

Katherine Hayles (2017) undertakes important work in offering a way of conceptualising agency that is neither blunted by a flat ontology that struggles to account for power differentials nor threatens to fall back into the exceptionalist paradigm of the primacy of conscious human reason. By emphasising their capacity for decision-making and interpretation of meaning, cognising agents can be distinguished from underlying material processes. Nevertheless, by focusing primarily on *nonconscious* cognition, consciousness is denied the privileged role as the sole rational agent in control of all decision-making. She emphasises 'recent discoveries in neuroscience confirming the existence of nonconscious cognitive processes inaccessible to conscious introspection but nevertheless essential for consciousness to function' (2017: 2). Hayles' framing also highlights the increasing number of technical non-conscious cognizers that mediate our experience. Our cognising capabilities are thus embedded in wider 'cognitive assemblages' which enable the consideration of how the co-evolutions of humans and technology are engendering new dynamics. This concept of cognitive assemblages counters the transhumanist tendency to think through technogenesis in humanist, individualist terms. As she states, 'the embodied subject is embedded and immersed in environments that function as distributed cognitive systems…human subjects are no longer contained—or even defined—by the boundaries of their skins' (Hayles 2017: 2). These distributed cognitive systems form part of a 'planetary cognitive ecology' (2017: 3), indicating that cognitive assemblages are interconnected—nested, porous, overlapping systems which align with a complexity theory framework.

Whilst Hayles does not dismiss the existence or cognising capacity of consciousness, she is aware of its role in the myopia which produces the notion of the 'human self [a]s the primary actor, and technologies mere prostheses added on later' (Hayles 2017: 106). Here she cites Damasio's insight that 'consciousness … constrains the world of the imagination to be first and foremost about the individual, about an individual organism, about the self in the broad sense of the term' (in Hayles 2017: 106). Consciousness, by its singular perspectival nature, biases an onto-epistemology towards an overly independent sense of self, often accompanied by an inflated sense of importance. This is an affliction that bedevils much transhumanist thought and can be recognised in the naïve framing of morphological freedom. Alternative and profoundly important philosophical implications can be drawn from this decentring of consciousness:

> assumptions taken for granted in traditional Western cultures are undermined and even negated when the primacy of higher consciousness becomes questionable, including its association with authenticity, its ability to give (human) life meaning, its identification with rational actor economic theory, its entwinement with the development of sophisticated technologies, and the perceived superiority it bestows on humans. (Hayles 2017: 87)

Our embeddedness within natural and technological systems fundamentally undermines any sense of independence from this complex ecology in which we are bound. Hayles (2017) draws attention to the complex systemic interconnection of transport systems, water and sanitation facilities, electric grids, banking systems, and agricultural and medical production—all of which depend on computational systems undertaking cognitive tasks as a dependency for most human cognition. Indeed, the collapse of these systems would likely result in carnage and mass death. The fallacy of the liberal human becomes increasingly evident, and therefore, as we design these systems, we design ourselves as they become fundamental to our survival. The transhumanist obsession with identifying the individual human body as the locus of transhumanist progress is seriously limited. The arbitrariness of identifying the conscious aspect of human reason as, not only the centre but also the totality of agential functioning, becomes clear. With it the idea that human consciousness is capable of some kind of independent self-definition and actualisation, unencumbered by its interconnection with multiple other agential entities, becomes manifestly untenable.

5 Technosystem

Hayles' global complex ecology can be fruitfully conjoined with Andrew Feenberg's notion of the 'technosystem' (2017) and his critical constructivist analysis. Feenberg defines the technosystem as 'the field of technically rational disciplines and operations associated with markets, administrations, and technologies' (Feenberg 2017: x). The interconnectedness of these three systems is evident as markets and administrations cannot be conceived of without technologies and likewise technological development is mediated by market and administrative processes. The technosystem can be understood as a cognitive assemblage: a macro-actor on a grand scale. Its workings mediate the agency of the multiple nested systems of which it is comprised. Feenberg (2017) does not explicitly relate his analysis to complexity thinking nor does he engage with the radical aims of transhumanism. However, a complexity framework enables us to conceptually move between 'systems' that can be nominally identified as they exhibit elements of internal consistency that render them recognisable as systems. All systems are ultimately interconnected, and so any identification is nominal and has the potential to break down or alter over time. The relevance of this to Feenberg's conception is evident when he recognises that the 'technosystem resembles a palimpsest: multiple layers of influence coming from different regions of society and responding to different, even opposed, logics inscribe a shared object or institution' (2017: 26). Furthermore, an understanding of modernity as characterised by an all-pervasive technical rationality that functions as an important mediator of the decision-making of cognizers, both conscious and non-conscious, is profoundly relevant to the process of technogenesis. It is one of the most pertinent factors of the fitness landscape which constrains the possibilities of 'morphological freedom' for individuals.

Integral to Feenberg's notion of the technosystem is that it functions as the grounding of modernity and draws upon a technical, 'scientific', and instrumental rationality:

> The new scientific a priori has three essential features—formalization, quantification, and instrumentalization. Science does not address experience in its immediacy but transforms everything it encounters into quantities subject to formal laws. Things have no essence but are composed of functional units awaiting transformation and recombination. This stance eliminates purpose and hence also potentiality from the world. This is the basis of the value-neutrality of science, its indifference to the good and the beautiful in the interests of the true. (Feenberg 2017: 125)

This points to a duality: the truth of science versus the potential for alternative values derived from our human (or posthuman) experience. It is not that experience necessarily contradicts science or represents the untrue. Rather, '[v]alues…correspond to realities science may not yet understand, indeed may never understand, but which are surely real' (Feenberg 2017: 14). Science cannot explain effectively much of what appears to matter to humans, and it certainly cannot be relied upon to determine exactly how humans should live. Despite this, science often claims a privileged position in the hierarchy of reason due to its apparent value-neutrality as 'an absolute spectator on existence' (Feenberg 2017: 12). However, the central failing of this world view is that the 'modern ideal of knowledge is subsumption under formal rules, but instrumental rationality can provide no criteria for the appropriate choice of this rule' (Feenberg 2017: 130). The truths unveiled by science bring about a continuous technical progress leading to ever more potent means, but do not in themselves effectively determine moral ends.

Both Hayles and Feenberg recognise human values as a necessary component which are increasingly under threat from the complex global cognitive ecology. When Feenberg states his concern about the 'threat to human agency posed by the technosystem' (2017: 38), he is asking whether humans are sufficiently empowered to resist instrumentalising rationality. In line with Lukács' notion of reification, the technosystem 'imposes a rational culture that privileges technical manipulation over all other relations to reality. It narrows human understanding and lives to conform with the requirements of the economic system' (Feenberg 2017: 42). Meanwhile Hayles argues that humans are:

> able to envision and evaluate ethical and moral consequences in the context of human sociality and world horizons…we need a framework in which human cognition is recognized for its uniquely valuable potential, without insisting that human cognition is the whole of cognition or that it is unaffected by the technical cognizers that interpenetrate it. (2017: 136)

It is an incredibly complex feat to actualise the successful and intentional implementation of alternative values in social reality when mediated through the increasingly potent instrumentalising force of the technical paradigm. Both would also acknowledge that human values cannot be universally agreed and are always contextually bound. However, a first step is to recognise the instrumental underpinnings of capitalist aims, its purported ethical neutrality ['Markets don't wag fingers' (Sandel 2009: 14)], and how this exacerbates those instrumentalising tendencies of technological development. The agency of humans to promote alternative views of what technogenesis should constitute is compromised by the ubiquitous instrumentalism of modernity.

6 Competition, War, and Profit

Competitive dynamics manifest themselves very naturally within scientific, instrumental rationality. The proposed objectivity of this form of reason, along with its quantifying techniques and formalising methods, tends to identify or create hierarchies and transparent, positivist judgements. The dynamism of instrumental rationality is reliant on such competition. It is fundamental to producing its evident forms of progress. The liberal humanist framing underestimates the relevance of these competitive social dynamics by emphasising the choice of the individual and downplaying their contextually bound positioning. However, a highly competitive social environment does not lend itself to pluralistic ways of being, instead demanding efficient behaviour as determined by the requirements of socio-economic and related forms of competition. As Lukács elucidated with his analysis of reification, the relationship to oneself becomes 'thing like': we are what is expected or needed of us in specific circumstances.

Given certain economic and social competitive structures, the decision not to participate in technological enhancements could potentially render someone socially and economically moribund (perhaps evolutionarily so). Everyone (who has access) is effectively forced to participate, to keep up. Given the concepts of enhancement, uplift and transcendence are redolent of liberation, the implication here is indicative rather of an imprisoning imperative on action. We have to transcend in order to conform (and survive). There may be a drive to conform to various manifestations of enhancement in perpetuity, which only makes us more efficient at carrying out the activities demanded of us by the instrumental systemic logics in which we are enmeshed. The end point may be an entirely non-human, though very efficient, technological entity derived from humanity that does not necessarily serve a purpose that a modern-day human would value in any way. Instrumentalism and perceived systemic utility become the architect of enhancement.

In their transhumanist tract, *The Proactionary Imperative*, Fuller and Lipinska advocate 'a kind of participatory eugenics' (2014: 128) which they name hedgenetics (a neologism based on hedge funds and genetics). They suggest, 'proactionaries would re-invent the welfare state as a vehicle for fostering securitised risk taking' and 'the proactionary state would operate like a venture capitalist writ large' (2014: 42). By minimising the tolerance of the fitness landscape for pluralistic ways of being, they encourage maximum utility towards the process of transhumanism. The welfare state is designed to encourage people to undertake huge risks in order to enable mass experimentation pushing scientific knowledge forward. Society at large is effectively conceived of as a laboratory, and humans (or at least the existing unenhanced humans of 'Humanity 1.0') are the instrumentalised objects of investigation. There is no focus here on the experiential quality of peoples' lives, which are to be sacrificed for the rights of god-like future humans ('Humanity 2.0'). This is an extreme transhumanist vision—but it emphasises experiential versus instrumentalist-based notions of technogenesis. When individuals are embedded in an unforgiving fitness landscape where they are forced to take extreme risks, they will, as they effectively have no choice.

Maximising instrumentalism is essentially the sole value of this vision. Fuller and Lipinska frame it as serving God by becoming God—but such a God would be defined only by their omnipotence, as no other intrinsic value is evident.

By recognising our embeddedness within complex processual systems and thus our fundamental relationality, posthumanist agency offers a more nuanced and realistic framing of the limitations of the human capacity for self-determination. It also encourages us to look at systems beyond the human level. Two areas of the technosystem which are worth deep consideration are profit and war, as instrumental progress in these areas is perhaps deemed to have more utility than any other. As Chris Hables-Gray explains:

> Science and technology in the twenty-first Century are mainly shaped by market (profit) and military priorities. The sooner new discoveries and inventions can be utilised, the greater their advantage, so incredible resources are poured into those new areas of research that promise maximum returns financially and in military utility. (Hables-Gray 2012: 33)

Indeed, the technologies which transhumanists tend to identify as proffering hope for significant human enhancement potentiality often first manifest themselves in these military and market contexts. This point is made succinctly by Ben Goetzel (2019) when he considers the current purposes of AI: it is mainly used for selling, spying, killing, and gambling. Hayles (2017) too identifies aspects of profit and war-making as exemplars or test cases for thinking through distributed agency in cognitive assemblages. She considers at length the development of autonomous weapons and high frequency trading (HFT).

Hayles (2017) rightly sees HFTs as constituting a new form of vampiric capitalism that is speculative in nature and contributes nothing to the real economy. She provides a thorough and insightful analysis of HFTs in the context of cognitive assemblages, and two particular aspects are worth highlighting here. The first is the fact that the cognitive capacities of the computational paradigm offer certain instrumental benefits over human cognition. Notable amongst these is speed. Hayles explains, 'HFT has introduced a temporal gap between human and technical cognition that creates a realm of autonomy for technical agency' (2017: 142). This shifts certain tasks into the computational realm, which may previously have had human oversight. The ultrafast machine ecology of HFTs has led to an increasing number of ultrafast black swan events. This is attributed to the limited strategies of algorithms having to compete at sufficient speed for the purposes of chasing profits. Algorithms attempting to outperform each other produce swarm-like behaviours: 'their interactions resemble the kinds of moves and counter-moves typical of propaganda (psyops) warfare: feints, dodges, misinformation, and camouflage' (Hayles 2017: 163). The impacts are manifold: 'The predominance of dueling algorithms has created a machine-machine ecology…creating regions of technical autonomy that can and do lead to catastrophic failures' (Hayles 2017: 142–143). This highlights the second point, that machine ontology can create a fragile ecology as it can lead to instrumentalisation towards excessively narrow goals. In this case, the already pathological narrowness of the profit motive is exacerbated. The durability and sustainability of the complex ecology of the financial system may be undermined by this one small aspect of technical superiority. It should be noted that it is the supposed 'enhancement' that machines offer in this realm that makes them integral to the assemblage, and yet the outcomes seem only to bring downsides for most of humanity.

The creation of a machine–machine ecology could have even more significant implications in the context of war. Given the potential of autonomous weapons to become destabilising in their plenitude and devastating effect, it is unsurprising that there has been wide-ranging demand that development of this technology is curtailed. In a letter signed by numerous high-profile figures, its signatories state, '[t]he key question for humanity today is whether to start a global AI arms race or to prevent it from starting. If any major military power pushes ahead with AI weapon development, a global armaments race is virtually inevitable' (in Walsh 2017: 174). An arms race is considered inevitable in this scenario because of something fundamental to the development of technologies which helps explain theories espousing the autonomy of technological progress and the enframing of the technological mindset. The instrumental power yielded by this technology shifts the fitness landscape so that those who do not have access to this power are strategically incapacitated. Those who have the capacity to do so are thus almost forced to keep up. This is a high risk, high reward situation and competitive logics tend to result in a race to the bottom in terms of instrumental capabilities at the expense of other potential values.

John Gray's prognosis of the implications of technological development in the quest for immortal life highlights the intractability of the problem of developing radical technologies with potential for human enhancement: they have other applications. Gray states:

> The end-result of scientific enquiry is to return humankind to its own intractable existence…Instead of enabling death to be overcome, it produces ever more powerful technologies of mass destruction. None of this is the fault of science…The growth of knowledge enlarges what humans can do. It cannot retrieve them from being what they are. (Gray 2011: 235)

His notion that humans are, by nature, normatively deficient represents a dubious essentialism. The competitive logics of our current social systems exacerbate the normative challenges we face. Warfare is an instructive case as it simultaneously exemplifies our moral failings as a social species on a grand scale and offers concrete and easily imagined disasters as a consequence of our increasing instrumental powers. The hyper-instrumentalization of war and profit-making through an increasingly potent machine–machine ecology again undermines the possibilities for alternative values effectively influencing technogenesis.

7 Posthuman Data

Just as human agency is compromised by the demands of the superstructure of the 'technosystem', it is compromised by systems at a more granular level. Life is broken down into its constituent parts driven by contemporary capitalism's trajectory towards formalising, quantifying, and controlling as much as possible. Braidotti recognises a post-anthropocentricism inherent to this process:

> advanced capitalism both invests and profits from the scientific and economic control and the commodification of all that lives. This context produces a paradoxical and rather opportunistic form of post-anthropocentricism on the part of market forces which happily trade on Life itself. (Braidotti: 2013: 59)

The result is a translation of bio-into-info. This is part of a broader process in which data forms the ultimate commodity. By abstracting people into data, they are transcoded from individuals (human subjects with bodies and theoretical rights) to dividuals (following Deleuze), that is, the 'subject digitized' (Franklin in Cheney-Lippold 2017: 172). The relational ontology of posthumanism that recognises our interconnection as 'materially embedded subjects-in-process circulating within webs of relation with forces, entities and encounters' (Braidotti and Hlavajova 2018: 8), here turns into something much more sinister:

> Because a single piece of data means nothing on its own, the fetishized autonomy of the liberal subject would starve without the other. Patterns are made from a population, not one person. How algorithms interpret us necessarily connects us to the lives of others. This sentiment, in all its humanistic beauty, is also regulating. It controls life on the basis of what 'we' do. (Cheney-Lippold 2017: 199)

The transmogrification of human subjects into data as a formative process in the creation of a new social reality, and the parallel loss of agency this entails, fundamentally emphasises the posthuman condition.

Herbechter (2013: 15) understands posthumanism as 'benevolent or "strategic" misanthropy'. The quantification of life as capital constitutes a nightmarish form of posthuman existence: 'Sensors quantify, alienate, and extract conceptions of self, reducing life as seen by capital to what can be recorded and exchanged as digital data...the sum total of data produced by an individual marks them into an abstracted bucket' (Thatcher et al. 2017: 17). This is not a promising monster or the rebellious cyborg, rejecting conformity, but rather a literal information flow: a capital-defined abstracted entity that is at once processual, reductive, and manipulable, 'a digital commodity that may be continually bought and sold in order to call forth an orderly, predictable stream of consumption' (Thatcher et al. 2017: 17). Through this reorientation, life is established as an ever-intensifying process of data extraction and heuristic interpretation leading to a recreation of the social world directed towards wealth extraction. It is an entirely amoral and instrumental orientation. It is also self-perpetuating. Much as the despoiling of nature through techno-capitalist social relations is increasingly evident, enabling capital to direct the process of technogenesis will leave most human life despoiled by that process too. Thus, whilst critical posthumanism offers a rich and perceptive critique of transhumanism, it also offers discursive concepts which can be co-opted for strategic and, in this case, malevolent misanthropy.

8 Surveillance Capitalism

Shoshana Zuboff (2017) relates the tale of how the instrumentalist mindset and the reductive quest for profit developed into the logics of 'surveillance capitalism'. She cites B.F. Skinner's radical behaviourism as a conceptual precursor to the process. Skinner defines behaviour as 'what an organism is doing—or more accurately what it is observed by another organism to be doing' (in Zuboff 2017: 366). His attempt at establishing an objective science of human behaviour thus requires a shifting of the frame from the internal workings of consciousness to the outer traces of behaviour. There is also a significant power shift—the observed is objectified and by their very being creates information; the observer selects aspects of this, their 'operant behaviour', which becomes data. The data is the source of new knowledge: the science of radical behaviourism, which itself produces the knowledge of how to control people and societies. Skinner calls for the 'minimum of interaction between subject and scientist' (in Zuboff 2017: 370); indeed the less the subject is aware of the process, the purer the data, the closer the scientist comes to laboratory conditions. This brings to mind Foucault's panopticon in which an individual 'is seen, but he does not see; he is the object of information, never a subject in communication' (in Kaplan 2009: 264). Surveillance capitalism constitutes a commensurate process as '[i]nstrumentarian power bends the new digital apparatus—continuous, autonomous, omnipresent, sensate, computational, actuating, networked, internet-enabled…The result is a panvasive means of behavioural modification' (Zuboff 2017: 375). The quest of analysing behavioural data to create knowledge products of control is the ultimate goal of this process.

Transhumanist aims also share the desire for control, certainty, and limitlessness, and thus find a co-conspirator in the market. The extraction imperative, which drives the demand for ever more expansive and granular data through competition for surveillance revenues, is central to improving the quality of prediction products. The demand for predictability moves ever closer to a demand for certainty, and the surest way to attain this is to 'intervene at its source and shape it' (Zuboff 2017: 200). This is where the imperative to control becomes explicit. Thus, we see the development of tools which Zuboff labels 'economies of scope', namely those which provide a depth dimension to knowledge surveillance, that capitalists are then able to gain access to, which are 'aimed at your personality, moods, and emotions, your lies and vulnerabilities. Every level of intimacy would have to be automatically captured and flattened into a tidal flow of data points for the factory conveyor belts that proceed toward manufactured certainty' (Zuboff 2017: 199). This intimate knowledge still needs to be coupled with tools that exploit it, Zuboff's 'economies of action'. As she explains,

> In order to achieve these economies, machine processes are configured to intervene in the state of play in the real world and real people and things. These interventions are designed to enhance certainty by doing things: they nudge, tune, hurt, manipulate, and modify behaviour in specific directions by executing actions as subtle as inserting a specific phrase into your Facebook newsfeed, timing the appearance of a buy button on your phone, or shutting down your car engine when an insurance payment is late. (Zuboff 2017: 200)

Whilst nudging and manipulation fall short of control, the trajectory is clear. The potency of prediction products increases exponentially, fuelled by an ever-expanding array of data sources. This is provided not only by the tools that aid in a culture of 'quantifying the self' such as fitness monitors but also increasingly by the wider environment through the internet of things.

Surveillance capitalism is not just about condensing information into data, but turning that data into tools which construct the social world. This relies upon the control of individuals in a way that undermines their ability to have a political and agential voice in shaping the new social reality that is constructed. Absolute knowledge aims at absolute certainty, but the certainty is simply 'societal optimisation for the sake of market objectives' (Zuboff 2017: 399). The asymmetry of knowledge is a prerequisite for the concentration of power that underpins the logic of surveillance capitalism: 'ubiquitous computing is not just a knowing machine; it is an actuating machine designed to produce more certainty *about us* and *for them*' (Zuboff 2017: 201). The unprecedented inequality of access to the division of learning 'drifts into pathology and injustice' (Zuboff 2017: 185). Such pathology represents an 'audacious, implacable web' (Zuboff 2017: 338–339), due to the increasing ubiquity of tools of data extraction. The very production of the kind of knowledge required for a social world governed by algorithm is premised on the sources of that knowledge being unaware of what is extracted from them, and excluded from the possibility of accessing and learning from that knowledge—a deeply ossified social structure. It is a privileged and demarcated realm that is directed towards the eventual automation of human desires and actions. This is a form of technogenesis that entirely undermines the concept of morphological freedom.

9 Heuristics, Colonialism, and Totalitarianism

The process by which data is created is fundamentally heuristic. As Cheney-Lippold points out, raw data is an oxymoron. The production of data, at its genesis, is encased in a web of pre-existing meanings, in which data 'are not given; they are made' (2017: 54). David M. Berry argues that 'for computer scientists it is the translation of the continuum into the discrete that marks the condition of possibility for computationality' (in Cheney-Lippold 2017: 48). Usefulness is predicated on the basis of capitalist relations, and interests are necessarily pitted against each other: 'What these algorithms do "unlock" is the ability to make your life useful on terms productive for algorithms' authors' (Cheney-Lippold 2017: 253). But the abstraction of data, the perceived efficacy of algorithms, cover up complex ethical questions of social relations. As Theodore Porter states, 'numbers turn people into objects to be manipulated' (in Cheney-Lippold 2017: 53). The manipulation of numbers appears far less controversial than the manipulation of people. But if 'we are data', they can amount to the same thing.

> Any measurable type is necessarily incomplete, much like any attempt to represent the world in abstraction. Accordingly, a measurable type's aim is instead directed towards operability and efficiency, not representative exactness…This reindexing of categorical meaning away from the human centred complexities of narrative, context, and history and towards measurable datafied elements within a closed set…casts the measurable type as a discursively contained, and empirically defineable, vessel of meaning. (Cheney-Lippold 2017: 48)

Data seems to have a rarified air. In the tradition of positivism, it denies its own social construction and assumes a sense of scientific neutrality that belies the interest-based and technically delimited way in which it reindexes 'categorical meaning'. This gets to the heart of the heuristic/instrumental relation: on the one hand, it is not directly representational and, on the other, it is itself productive. The inextricability of instrumental rationality from the implicit values it embeds in the social world is evident.

Thatcher et al. (2017), and Couldry and Mejias (2019a, b) have employed the term 'data colonialism' in analysing these practices: 'Data colonialism combines the predatory extractive practices of historical colonialism with the abstract quantification methods of computing' (Couldry and Mejias 2019a: 336). The asymmetry of power relations between those who provide data and the corporate institutions that collect and own the data is reflective of prior capitalist methods of primitive accumulation (Thatcher et al. 2017) and privatisation and colonisation of space and time. Heidegger warned that technology's enframing turns nature into a 'standing reserve' and that humans too would also be consumed in this process. The colonial nature of extracting this new manifestation of value from human behaviour in the form of data is bolstered by the supporting logics of advanced capitalism which entails a 'corporeal corkscrewing inwards' (Beller in Thatcher et al. 2017: 10). Zuboff's rhetoric captures the pathological vampirism: 'forget the cliché that if it's free, "You are the product". You are not the product; you are the abandoned carcass. The product derives from the surplus that is ripped from your life' (2017: 377). This extraction, or ripping, must be normalised and rationalised to enable the colonial practice it represents.

Chris Anderson's belief that big data would bring about an end to theory is symptomatic of a mindset which no longer asks the question, why. He states: 'Forget taxonomy, ontology, and psychology. Who knows why people do what they do? The point is they do it, and we can track and measure it with unprecedented fidelity. With enough data, the numbers speak for themselves. The big target here isn't advertising, though. It's science' (Anderson 2008). Anderson is suggesting that big data will give us answers for everything as long as we ask the meaning of nothing. The utopia of certainty is a fantastical realm where divisions, different viewpoints, clashes of interest, political debates are all dispatched from reality. In other words where the human social world is no longer sullied by the contestable, perspectival, messy experience of the human. There is no need for 'theory' in this fantasy, because everything is *known*, though nothing may be understood. In order to create such a totalising state, it is not only the human that must be colonised but also the wider environment too. Fuller and Lipinska's reference to black sky thinking is apt to bring such a vision to an apotheosis. They state, 'replacing the natural with the artificial is so key to proactionary strategy...some proactionaries speak nowadays of "black sky thinking" that would have us concede—at least as a serious possibility if not a likelihood—the long-term environmental degradation of the Earth' (2014: 99–100). If it is to become fully malleable and tame, the Earth too must go through the process of heuristic interpretation and adaption to the demands of certainty. In the same way as capitalism has a growth fetish, dataism has an extraction fetish. These two processes complement or perhaps more accurately exacerbate each other.

Capitalism conceptualises limitlessness as a logical presupposition for its proposed endless growth, whereas dataism has totality in mind. In order to reach Anderson's proposed 'n = all world' (in Cheney-Lippold 2017: 147) whereby there is no longer space for theory, everything must be datafied. However, as Zuboff notes,

> On the trail of totality, surveillance capitalists enlarge the scope from the virtual to the real world. The reality business renders all people, things, and processes as computational objects in an endless queue of equivalents without equality...the pursuit of totality necessarily leads to the annexation of society, social relations, and key societal processes as a fresh terrain for rendition, calculation, modification, and prediction. (Zuboff 2017: 399)

The phrase 'equivalents without equality' is something of a refrain for Zuboff. It draws attention to the asymmetry of these social relations, where most people constitute the resource from which value is extracted. But also implicit in this is the heuristic, interest-laden process by which reality is reconstituted into computational objects. What it seeks to create is *a* totality—a reality entirely mediated, controlled, and defined by the interpretation of data; but the data itself can never reflect the totality of the physical world, or the complexity of human social reality. The process is self-referential and endless, there is 'no limit to the appropriation, since what is appropriated is what is increasingly constructed to be ready for appropriation' (Couldry and Mejias 2019a: 344–345). Instrumentalism is at the heart of such a construction. Action takes precedence over meaning. A homeostatic world without theory is one in which there is no politics. If interests digress then they can be reconstituted to cohere. Along with theory, ethics is expelled from this notional imaginary. There is no need to ask 'why' when 'what' is guaranteed. As Zuboff argues, humans suffer the havoc reaped by 'the remote and abstracted contempt of impenetrably complex systems and the interests that author them, carrying individuals on a fast-moving current to the fulfilment of others' ends' (2017: 376–377). In this system, humans have come to share the same destiny as the rest of nature under capitalist relations: a resource, abstracted and banal.

The Cambridge Analytica scandal suggests there is already a potency to the dark arts of political manipulation using data, but the efficacy is disputed. Such is the novelty and nature of this and similar scandals that little is truly known about their actual effect. The complex socio-political environment, the global pandemic, the apparent disintegration of the neoliberal consensus, economic instability, the geopolitical machinations from the fading power of the US to the rising power of China, the undermining of trust between major powers and the return of nationalism, and the technical undermining of 'facts' caused by deep fakes, filter bubbles, and feedback loops in the new media landscape all create a pervasive sense of uncertainty. Nevertheless, the uncertainty is in part due to the nascent and experimental attempts of the digital realm to interpret, influence, and control humans.

10 Conclusion

As the technical achievements improve, bolstered by the acquisition of 'ever-more-predictive sources of behavioural surplus: our voices, personalities, and emotions' (Zuboff 2017: 8), we may well see confluence rise, concentrations of power and an increasing regulation of authoritarian certainty. Whether in its early agitated state, or mature soporific one, the move towards totality, driven by power, profit, and the urge to control constitutes a new enclosing of the technical world upon human freedom. In focusing on the individual, and advocating for instrumental progress over all other values, transhumanism represents a continuation and intensification of advanced capitalist logics that undergird the subversion of human agency and enclosing of other potential forms of technogenesis. Marcuse claimed that, 'when technics becomes the universal form of material production it circumscribes an entire culture; it projects a historical totality—a world' (in Feenberg 2017: 42). This expresses the convergence of human and technical reality into one entity through the total domination by the latter.

References

Alcaraz, A. (2019). *Cyborg Persons or Selves*. Szczecin: Wydziale Malarstwa.
Anderson, C. (2008). The End of Theory: The Data Deluge Makes the Scientific Method Obsolete. Wired, 23 June. https://www.wired.com/2008/06/pb-theory/. Accessed 20 August 2020.
Barad, K. (2003). Posthumanist Performativity: Towards an Understanding of How Matter Comes to Matter. *Signs: Journal of Women in Culture and Society, 28*(3), 801–831. https://doi.org/10.1086/345321.
Bennett, J. (2010). *Vibrant Matter: A Political Ecology of Things*. Durham: Duke University Press.
Bostrom, N. (2005). A history of transhumanist thought. *Journal of Evolution and Technology, 14*(1), 1–25.
Braidotti, R. (2013). *The Posthuman*. Cambridge, UK: Polity Press.
Braidotti, R., & Hlavajova, M. (Eds.). (2018). *Posthuman Glossary*. London: Bloomsbury.
Cheney-Lippold, J. (2017). *We Are Data*. New York: New York University Press.
Couldry, N., & Mejias, U. (2019a). Data colonialism: rethinking big data's relation to the contemporary subject. *Television and New Media, 20*(4), 336–349. https://doi.org/10.1177/1527476418796632.
Couldry, N., & Mejias, U. (2019b). *The Costs of Connection: How Data is Colonizing Human Life and Appropriating It for Capitalism*. Palo Alto, CA: Stanford University Press.
Cudworth, E., & Hobden, S. (2013). Of Parts and Wholes: International Relations beyond the Human. *Millennium: Journal of International Studies, 41*(3), 430–450. https://doi.org/10.1177/0305829813485875.

Del Val, J. (2020). Metahumanist Manifesto: its genealogy, evolution and relevance 10 years after. https://metabody.eu/wp-content/uploads/2020/07/METAHUMANIST-MANIFESTO-INTRODUCTION-Jaime-del-Val-1-1-1-final-web.pdf. Accessed 20 August 2020.

Feenberg, A. (2017). *Technosystem*. Cambridge, MA: Harvard University Press.

Ferrando, F. (2013). Posthumanism, Transhumanism, Antihumanism, Metahumanism, and New Materialisms. *Existenz, 8*(2), 26–32.

Foucault, M. (1966/2002). *The Order of Things: An Archaeology of the Human Science*. London: Routledge.

Fuller, S., & Lipinska, V. (2014). *The Proactionary Imperative, A Foundation for Transhumanism*. Basingstoke: Palgrave Macmillan.

Goetzel, B. (2019). Human Level AI [YouTube video]. https://youtu.be/IWgPKw1n1DQ. Accessed 20 August 2020.

Graham, E. L. (2002). *Representations of the Post/Human*. New Brunswick: Rutgers University Press.

Gray, J. (2011). *The Immortality Commission*. London: Granta Books.

Hables-Gray, C. (2012). Cyborging the Posthuman: Participatory Evolution. In K. Lippert-Rasmussen, M. R. Thomsen, & J. Wamberg (Eds.), *The Posthuman Condition: Ethics, Aesthetics and Politics of Biotechnological Challenges* (pp. 25–37). Aarhus: Aarhus University Press.

Hayles, K. (1999). *How We Became Posthuman*. Chicago, IL: University of Chicago Press.

Hayles, K. (2017). *Unthought, The Power of the Cognitive Unconscious*. Chicago, IL: University of Chicago Press.

Herbrechter, S. (2013). *Posthumanism*. London: Bloomsbury.

Hughes, J. (2010). Contradictions from the enlightenment roots of transhumanism. *Journal of Medicine and Philosophy, 35*(6), 622–640. https://doi.org/10.1093/jmp/jhq049.

IEET (2020). Origins and theory of the world transhumanist association. https://ieet.org/index.php/IEET2/more/bostrom20071226. Accessed 20 August 2020.

Kaplan, D. (Ed.). (2009). *Readings in the Philosophy of Technology*. Plymouth: Rowman & Littlefield.

Latour, B., & Woolgar, S. (1986). *Laboratory Life, The Construction of Scientific Facts*. Princeton, NJ: Princeton University Press.

Miah, A. (2008). A critical history of posthumanism. In B. Gordijn & R. Chadwick (Eds.), *Medical Enhancement and Posthumanity* (pp. 71–94). Dordrecht: Springer. https://doi.org/10.1007/978-1-4020-8852-0_6.

More, M. (2013). The Philosophy of Transhumanism. In M. More & N. Vita-More (Eds.), *The Transhumanist Reader: Classical and Contemporary Essays on the Science, Technology, and Philosophy of the Human Future* (pp. 1–11). Chichester: Wiley-Blackwell.

Sandberg, A. (2013). Morphological Freedom – Why We Not Just Want It, but Need It. In M. More & N. Vita-More (Eds.), *The Transhumanist Reader: Classical and Contemporary Essays on the Science, Technology, and Philosophy of the Human Future* (pp. 56–64). Chichester: Wiley-Blackwell.

Sandel, M. (2009). *What Money Can't Buy: The Moral Limits of Markets*. London: Penguin.

Shaw, D. (2018). *Posthuman Urbanism*. London: Rowman & Littlefield.

Thatcher, J., O'Sullivan, D., & Mahmoudi, D. (2017). Data Colonialism Through Accumulation by Dispossession: New Metaphors for Daily Data. *Environment and Planning D: Society and Space, 34*(6), 990–1006. https://doi.org/10.1177/0263775816633195.

Walsh, T. (2017). *Android Dreams*. London: Hurst & Company.

Wolfe, C. (2010). *What Is Posthumanism?* Minneapolis, MN: University of Minnesota Press.

Zuboff, S. (2017). *Surveillance Capitalism*. London: Profile.

Index

A
Actor–network theory (ANT), 4, 94, 99, 101, 172
Agency, 132, 136
Alexa, 129
Algorithmic governmentality, 161
Algorithmic imagination
    calculation, 162–164
    contemporary technological developments, 163
    degree of reflexivity, 155
    development of technology, 162
    digital, 155, 158, 161–163, 166
    distinct flows, 167
    empathy, 159
    environmental, 155
    fields, 162
    human brain, 159
    human dimension, 163
    implications, 156
    information economy, 159
    interpretation, 158–160, 167
    intervention, 166
    mechanical and controlled interpretations, 163
    motorway, 158
    neuroscience, 162
    opportunities, 164
    postdigital, 155–157
    posthuman, 155
    recognition process, 166
    religious characters, 158
    role of time, 164–166
    science and technology, 163
    self-awareness, 155
    signal speeds, 159
    technical system, 166
    thinking and objectivity, 163
AlgorithmWatch (2019), 8
Altruism, 132
American Dental Association, 111
Aristotle, 134
Artificial intelligence (AI), 82, 112, 142–145
    and augmented intelligence, 6
    challenges, 6
    deep AI, 5
    embodied AI, 6
    enactive AI, 6
    in marketing, 5
    marketing AI, 6
    and neurology, 20
    and postdigital humans, 6
    pragmatic AI, 6
    research, 6
    as robots/thinking machines, 5
Artificial intelligences, 3
Asimov's Law, 136
Attention, 156
Augmented intelligence, 6
Automated decision-making (ADM), 8
Automatic facial recognition (AFR), 8, 83
Automation, 82
Autonomous intelligent machines, 143
Autonomous weapons, 177, 178
Autonomous, autonomy, 129, 132, 134
Autonomy, 155
Avida (computer programme), 149, 150

B

Babbage, C., 145–147, 151
Bath, University of, 138
Bayesian epistemology, 144
Behaviour, 26, 27
Bergson, H., 167
Bevan, N., 126, 127
Big Brother Watch, 8
Big Science, 141, 142
Bio-informational capitalism, 7, 11
Biologization, 9
Body, the, 127
Boole, G., 146
Bostrom, N., 144, 145, 148, 152, 158, 159
Braidotti, R., 170, 179
Brain emulation, 158
Bryson, J., 136, 137
Burke, E., 138
Buxton, D., 130

C

Cages, 73–78, 80–83
Calculability, 72, 74, 81, 84
Calculating machine, 126–128, 130, 131, 133, 136, 139
Carbon, 22
Catholic social teaching, 130, 138
Character, 125–139
Chatbot, 35–39, 45, 49
Chatbot-style life coach, 49
Chinese Room experiment, 27
Chronos, 166
Co-evolution, 169, 173
Cognitive assemblages, 173, 174, 177
Cold War, 141, 142, 148
Colonialism, 181–184
Communism, 5
Community, 125–139
Competition, 176–178
Complexity, 172–174, 182, 183
Computational deism
    autonomous system, 150
    biology, 148
    Cartesian scepticism, 151
    computer programmes, 149
    digital organisms, 149
    direct instantiation, 148
    evolution of self-replicating systems, 149
    human agency, 148
    human creator, 147
    intellectual property, 149
    intelligent design theory, 149, 150
    inventions, 148
    metaphysical, 148
    natural selection, 148, 149
    plant and animal breeding practices, 149
    scientific inquiry, 147
    scientific method, 147
    self-instantiating, 151
    simulation hypothesis, 151
    superintelligent machine, 148
    super-realism, 147
    super-realist, 148, 150
    virtual reality, 149
Computational Theism, 145–147
Computer-related digitalization, 22
Computers, 21, 23
Computing, 71–73, 75, 82–84
Consciousness, 17, 173, 174, 180
    and behaviour, 17, 22, 23
    cognitive abilities and functions, 25
    easy problem, 25, 27
    hard problem, 26, 27
    humanity, 25
    natural limits, 26
    subjective and the objective, 26
    turing test, 27
Consumer, 131
Consumer consumption, 83
Control, 72, 74, 75, 81, 84
Conversation, 135, 136
Covid-19, 7, 21, 48, 72, 73, 76–84, 131, 135
Criminal behaviour, 143
Critical information management, 96, 97
Critical pedagogy, 20, 21, 29
Critical philosophy, 20
Critical posthumanism, 17, 20, 169–172, 179
Cultural-historical activity theory (CHAT), 94
Cyber capitalism, 11
Cyborg, 23, 29, 144, 152

D

Darwin, C., 148–150
Data, 72, 74, 75, 77, 78, 83, 84, 182
Decision-making, 173
Deepfakes, 93
Deleuze, G., 166, 167
Dependent, dependency, 133–136
Derrida, J., 155, 163
Dialogue, 131
Dickpics, 102
Difference engine, 145
Digital afterlife, 10, 11
Digital competences, 89, 90

Index 189

Digital computer, 145
Digital economy, 82
Digital ecosystems, 59
Digital footprints, 91
Digital humanities, 71, 81–83
Digital identity, 91–94
Digital immortality, 10
Digital on death, 11
Digital organisms, 149
Digital presence, 91
Digital transparency, 61
Distributed cognitive systems, 173
Duhem, P., 147

E
Echo chamber, 91–93
Economic and social competitive structures, 176
Economic value, 53, 60
Economics, 128, 131, 132, 136
Ecosystems, 22
Efficiency, 72, 74, 81, 84
Enlightenment Project, 128
Enlightenment, the, 126, 128, 138
Environmental crisis, 159
Epigenesis, 162
Epistemology, 20
Ethics, 12
   intimacy, 3, 11, 12
   machine morality, 12
   postdigital humans, 11
   robotic, 12
Eugene Goostman (computer program), 27
European Commission (2018), 103
Evaluation, 35, 37
Evolutionary development, 28
Extrinsic motivation, 40, 46, 47

F
FaceOff, 8
Face-to-face interviews, 37
Fake news, 89
Feenberg, A., 174, 175, 184
Ferrando, F., 170
Fideism, 151
Filter bubbles, 90, 92, 93
Financial system, 177
Focus groups, 37–39, 45, 46
Foucault, M., 156
Friedman, M., 132

G
Gaitskell, H., 126
General Data Protection Regulation (GDPR), 8
General intellect, 66–67
Genes, 24, 26
Genetic engineering, 157
Glasman, M., 138
God's point of view, 26
Good Samaritan, 158, 160, 163, 166
Good, the, 125, 126, 134, 138
Goods, internal, externa, 133
Government, 137
Graham, E., 127, 129

H
Habermas, J., 162
Hanson, J., 158, 159
Hauerwas, S., 139
Hawking, S., 134, 136, 137, 157
Hayek, F., 132
Hayles, N.K., 171, 173–175, 177
Heidegger, M., 164–166
Heuristics, 181–184
High frequency trading (HFT), 114, 177
Higher education (HE)
   anti-human university, 63, 64
   anxiety machines, 55
   authoritarian reproduction, 59–61
   collective, 54, 57, 66
   communities of practice and networks, 54
   competitive and marketised environment, 56
   composting, 55, 63, 64
   conversation, 54, 55
   cybernetic, 63, 64, 66
   data-managed work, 54
   digital, 54, 61–63
   digital tools, 54
   economic value, 53
   engagement, 55
   finance capital and epidemiology, 53
   financial and epidemiological crises, 54
   flows of data, 54
   humane values, 53
   institution, 55
   marketised/marketable outcomes, 53
   narratives, 53
   national and international, 55
   physical and emotional circumstances, 55
   political decision, 53

Higher education (HE) (*cont.*)
  political economics, 55
  postdigital, 65–67
  pressure vessels, 55
  rollback, 53
  shadow of value
    acceleration, 57
    conduct of daily life, 57
    digital and technocratic management, 58
    digital life, 56
    digital technologies, 58
    economic value and services, 56
    flexploitation, 56
    forms of production, 56
    general intellect of society, 57
    institution emerges, 56
    labour processes, 57
    labour-power, 57
    machinery and large-scale industry, 56
    mental conceptions of the world, 57
    mode of production, 57
    multiple crises, 58
    policy-focus, 58
    political economic context, 58
    production process, 57
    self-exploiting and entrepreneurial, 58
    social relations, 56, 58
    surpluses, 58
    technology, 58
  social reproduction, 53
  society, 54
Historical computers, 23
Homo sapiens, 20, 22, 24, 25, 28, 29, 143, 144
Hospitality, 160, 163, 167
Human behaviour, 182
Human beings and technologies, 19
Human energy, 65
Human inside systems, 61
Human intelligence, 142–145
Human moral formation, 131–133
Human race, 22
Humane values, 53, 58
Humanism, 4, 5, 115
Humanities, 4, 5, 17, 71, 73, 75, 81–84
Humans, 71–84
Humans and machines
  ADM, 8
  AlgorithmWatch, 8
  Big Brother Watch, 8
  bio-informational capitalism, 9
  digital afterlife creation, 10
  during Covid-19 pandemic, 7
  education, 7
  experience, 7
  face recognition and verification, 8
  FaceOff, 8
  free smart digital assistants, 10
  myth/possibility, 9
  super-intelligence, 9
  technological singularity, 9
  virtual assistants, 10
  Whole brain emulation, 9
Humans and technology, 5
Hyper-instrumentalization, 178
Hypothesis, 164

I
Ibn Rushd (Averroes), 150
Identity management, 99, 100, 103
Imago Dei ('image of God'), 147
Imperialism, 129
Individuation, 162
Industrial Revolution, 146
Information Communication Technologies (ICTs), 90
Information literacy, 90
Information literacy for education, 93, 94
Information management, 103, 105
Injustice, 132
Instrumental rationality, 182
Instrumental systemic logics, 176
Instrumentalism, 147, 177
Integration, 59
Intellectual property rights, 143
Intelligence, Artificial, 129
Intelligence, emotional, 127
Intelligent design theory, 149
Intention, 132
Interface, 38, 40, 42, 47–49
Interguard, 83
Internet of Things (IoT), 83
Interviews, 37, 38, 44–46
Intimacy ethics, 3, 11, 12
Intrinsic motivation, 46
Irrationality, 74, 76, 81

J
Jakobson, R., 152, 153
Joseph, K., 132

K
Kairos, 166
Kaku, M., 156, 157
Kant, I., 162–164
Keller, C., 155, 159, 160, 167

Index

L
Labour Party, Blue Labour, 138
Labour processes, 66
Lateral surveillance, 13
Law, legal, 137
Leibniz, Gottfried von, 150
Levinas, E., 155
Liberalism, 5
Life, 17, 23, 24
Linear programming, 146
Lived experience, 54, 63–65
Lockdown, 76–81
Logical knowledge, 165
Logical operation, 165
Logos, 148, 152

M
Machine learning, 3, 5, 11, 12
Machine morality, 12
Machine–machine ecology, 178
MacIntyre, A., 128, 131–134, 136, 138, 139
Malabou, C., 162, 163
Market, the, 131–133, 135, 139
Mass intellectuality, 66, 67
Materiality of Learning, 94
Maxwell, J.C., 145, 146
McDonaldisation, 72–76, 79–84
McDonaldised society
    cages, 74, 75
    computer science, 71
    consumer consumption, 73
    Covid-19 pandemic, 72, 73
    dehumanisation, 72
    digital developments, 72
    digital humanities, 71, 81–83
    digital progress, 72
    digital technologies, 74
    discourse, 72
    efficiency, 72, 74
    equal, 84
    fast-food restaurant, 74
    Higher Education, 74
    homogeneity, 72, 84
    human activities, 72
    human and non-human, 71
    human companion, 72
    objective, 72–74, 79, 82, 84
    organisational practices, 72
    physical contexts, 74
    policy language, 73
    postdigital analysis, 84
    postdigital context, 75–78
    postdigital humans, 71, 72, 81–83
    postdigital participation, 73
    postdigital positionality, 73
    pre-digital/semi-digital, 84
    process, 74
    quality of experience, 74
    quantitative perspectives, 84
    self-description, 73
    self-determination, 73
    subjective, 72, 73, 79, 84
    techlap/techlash
        'cages of self-isolation, 81
        computer processing, 79
        consumer consumption category, 79
        coronavirus, 80
        corporate players, 78
        democracy, 78
        digital technologies, 78
        education, 78
        fleeing populations, 79
        implications, 78
        lockdown, 79
        objective evaluation, 79
        physical loss, 81
        postdigital human, 80
        public education, 78
        racial disparities, 80
        social distancing logos, 81
        social media, 81
        statistics disparities, 80
        virus, 80
McMylor, P., 128
Mechanical models, 147
Milbank, J., 139
Modernity, 128, 139
Moral agent, moral agency, 125
Moral formation, 125–139
More, M., 170
Morphological freedom, 171
Motivation, 35, 40, 43–46

N
Narratives, 128, 131–137, 139
Natural evolution, 29
Naturalistic dualism, 26
Neanderthals, 129
Necropolitics, 60
New aesthetics, 114
New Materialism, 172, 173
Newton, I., 150
Noise, 113, 115, 116, 118, 119, 123
Non-conscious cognition, 173
Novice users, 35, 40

O

Objective, 72–74, 79, 82, 84
Operant behaviour, 180
Opinion management, 98, 99, 103
Orwell, G., 127
Oxymoron, 181

P

Pandemic, 72, 73, 76–80, 84
Pastoral care, 156, 158, 160, 163, 166
Peer–to–peer monitoring, 13
Philosophical inquiry, 26
Philosophy, 17, 20, 27, 28
Philosophy, moral, 126, 128, 134
Physical sounds, 111
Planetary cognitive ecology, 173
Plant, R., 132
Platform University, 65
Political economy, 62, 151
Positionality, 73, 79, 83
Post-digital, 71–84, 128
    in artistic practice, 19
    description, 4
    emergence of technoscience systems, 4
    relationship of users, 36
    ungraspability, 4
    as a vector, 4
    VLC, 40, 45, 48
Postdigital age, 21
Postdigital context, 75–78
Postdigital era, 19, 21
Postdigital human
    AI, 112
    (anti)colonialism, 117–119
    autobiography, 121
    'Beyond Digital' (1998), 18
    cleaning hearing, 119
    cleaning the ear, 119
    cognitive properties, 113
    communication, 112
    computer music, 115
    'controlling' and 'building' technologies, 18
    definitions, 21
    digital and analogue, 111
    digital devices, 114
    digital education, 111
    digital technologies, 18, 111, 119
    economic energy, 116
    electric and industrial revolutions, 116
    electric revolution, 116
    Fragment on Machines, 113
    grasping/consumption, 120
    hearing, 119
    HFT, 114
    human machine, 119
    human–machine nexus and division, 112
    industrial and electric revolutions, 115
    industrial revolution, 112, 115
    influence policy decisions, 113
    intellectual transfer, 112
    intelligence, 112, 113, 120
    knowledge, 112, 113, 115, 121
    light wave, 111
    lighting production, 116
    limitation, 121
    listening, 117–119
    listening habits and practices, 119
    machinery, 112
    music production and reception, 113
    numerous mechanical and intellectual organs, 113
    pedagogical process, 122
    pedagogical task, 122
    pedagogy, 120
    pre-digital technology, 120
    recognition and self-determination, 113
    sonic compositions, 115
    sonic dimensions, 113
    sound, 111, 113, 115, 116, 118, 119, 121, 123
    soundscape, 119
    technopolitical implications, 115
    transformations, 115, 120
    urban soundscape, 121
    velocity, 114
    visual sense, 113
    voice, 116, 121–123
Postdigital humanity
    AI, 142–145
    anxiety, 152
    Big Science, 142
    classical attitude works, 141
    classical science, 141
    Computational Theism, 145–147
    computer-based technologies, 151
    computer models, 142
    ecology, 153
    enlightenment, 152
    functionalities, 152
    human condition, 151
    human intelligence, 142–145
    innovation, 151
    intellectual labour, 152
    labour theory of value, 151

learning experiences, 141
logos, 152
nuclear physics, 142
permanent emergency, 142
physics-based research, 142
political economy, 141, 151
role of technology, 151
scientific inquiry, 151
scientific validation, 142
smartphone, 152
sociological implications, 152
superintelligent computers, 152
technological unemployment, 151
Postdigital humans, 156, 157
   artificial intelligences, 3
   autonomous combat robots/AIs, 12
   challenge, 14
   concerns, 11
   development and use, 7
   digital media, 7
   enhancement of humans, 6
   ethics, 11, 12
   evolution, 5
   fair trade goods, 12
   intimacy ethics, 12
   lateral surveillance, 13
   machine learning, 12
   Project Cyborg, 6
   surveillance, 12
   technological growth, 7
   use of AI, 6
   virtual humans, 12
   VLC (*see* Virtual life coach (VLC))
Postdigital interval, 13
Postdigital life, 24
Postdigital non-carbon-based humans, 28
Postdigital project, 19
Postdigital thinking, 18–21
Postdigital truths
   critical information literacy, 103
   digital competence, 90, 101, 102
   digital environments, 104
   digital identity, 91–94
   educational context, 103
   fake news, 89, 102
   Flora, 102
   human actors, 101, 102
   identity management, 103
   information literacy competence, 102, 104
   information management, 103
   managing compromised online spaces, 90, 91
   Maria, 102
   network competences, 104
   online environments, 104
   opinion management, 103
   platforms and information sources, 102
   political intentionality, 104
   social media, 103, 104
   socio-material methodology, 94, 95
Posthuman agency, 172–174
Posthuman challenge
   AI, 129, 130
   being good, 127, 128
   being human, 125, 127, 128
   boundaries, 129
   cerebral and visceral, 126
   character dependency, 133–136
   concepts, 129
   contemporary technologies, 126
   equipment, 127
   ethics, 125, 129, 130
   human characteristics, 127
   human uniqueness, 126
   markets, 131–133
   moral disaster, 137, 138
   morals, 125
   narratives, 131–133
   practices, 128, 130, 133, 139
   real life, 129, 130
   responsibility, 136, 137
   self, 133–136
   technological innovation, 127
   technology, 127, 136, 137
Posthumanism, 4, 19, 20, 170, 171
Posthumanist theory, 4
Posthumanist thinking, 19, 23
Postmodern, 144
Power relations, 182
Pre-autonomous, 155, 158, 162–164, 167
Predictability, 72, 74, 76, 81, 84
Privacy, 78, 83
Process philosophy, 159
Profit, 176–178
Project Cyborg, 6
Protein genes, 24
Protention, 161, 162, 164, 166
Protestantism, 130

Q
Qualitative enquiry, 35
Qualitative research, 39, 40, 45, 46

R

Radical behaviourism, 180
Radical postdisciplinarity, 21, 29
Rational, rationality, 125–127, 130, 131, 134, 135
Rationality, 73–75, 80–82, 84
Reason, 155, 162–164
Recursion, 165
Recursive function, 165
Rees, A., 129
Responsibility, 136, 137
Right, 125, 130, 134, 138
Robotic ethics, 12
Robots, 24

S

Sandberg, A., 171
Sandel, M., 139
Scriven, M., 149
Search 2.0, 12
Security, 73, 79, 82, 83
Self-designed evolution, 28, 29
Self-determination, 66, 177
Self-determination theory, 46
Self-preservation, 130
Self-programming computer, 143
Self-repairing robots, 24
Self, the, 127, 133–136
Sensitive biometric data, 59
Silicon-based AIs, 28
Siri, 129
Sleigh, C., 129
Smith, A., 132, 139
Sneek, 83
Social care, 135
Social construction, 182
Social environment, 176
Socio-material analysis
  vignettes
    critical information management, 96, 97
    identity management, 99, 100
    opinion management, 98, 99
Socio-material methodology, 94, 95
Socio-political environment, 183
Social relations, 181, 183
Social reproduction, 62
Social structure, 181
Sonic, 113, 115, 116, 118, 121, 122
Stiegler, B., 155, 156, 161, 162
Subjective, 72, 73, 79, 82, 84
Superintelligent computers, 144

Surveillance, 3, 11, 12, 76, 80, 83, 84
Surveillance capitalism, 180, 181
System behaviour, 26

T

Taylor, C., 139
Techlash, 78
Technical rationality, 174
Technics, 164, 165
Technogenesis, 169, 171, 173–176, 178, 179, 181, 184
Technological singularity, 9
Technologies, 126–129, 131–133, 135–138
Technology Acceptance Model (TAM), 44
Technomoral virtues, 138
Technostress, 35, 47
Technosystem, 174, 175, 178
Teleology, *telos*, 134
Thatcher, M., 132
Timbre, 118, 121, 122
Tinker identities, 92
Traditional analog practices, 22
Traditions, 128, 130–133, 138, 139
Transcendent conformity
  colonialism, 181–184
  competing schools, 169
  competition, 176–178
  competitive and controlling logics, 169
  critical posthumanism, 169
  dynamic co-evolution, 169
  efficacy, 170
  heuristics, 181–184
  human agency, 169
  human beings, 169
  individual self-determination, 170
  morphological freedom, 171
  posthuman agency, 172–174
  posthuman data, 178, 179
  posthumanism, 170, 171
  profit, 176–178
  surveillance capitalism, 180, 181
  technosystem, 174, 175
  totalitarianism, 181–184
  war, 176–178
Transcendental imagination, 164, 165
Transhumanism, 157, 169–171, 174
Trolley Problem, the, 129, 130
Turing test, 27–29

U

Ultraviolet radiation, 157

Index

V

Vallor, S., 138
Value, 126, 128, 131, 136
Value-neutrality, 175
Virtual interface, 36
Virtual life coach (VLC)
    adolescents for life skills training, 36
    aesthetic appeal, 42–43
    automated process, 38
    case study evaluation, 35, 36
    challenges, 48
    chat-based application, 38
    chatbot, 35
    content, 38
    Covid-19 pandemic, 48
    ease of use and functionality, 43–44
    face-to-face support, 36
    interaction phase, 39
    life coaching, 36
    motivation and external factors, 46
    in non-clinical domain, 36
    pattern of use, 39–40
    performance, 37
    postdigital, 36
    and personalisation, 35
    potential importance and usefulness, 44–45
    private nature, 40
    purpose, 40–41
    qualitative analysis, 40
    recruitment and data collection, 37–38
    virtual interface, 36
Virtue, 128, 133, 138
Viruses, 24
Visible light, 111
Vorstruktur, 164

W

War, 176–178
Whitehead, A.N., 159, 160
Whole brain emulation, 9
Wiener, N., 146, 147
Wittgenstein, L., 147
Women, 129, 136
World-construction, 147

Z

Zero-one computation, 23
Zuboff, S., 180–184